S0-BAQ-958

Consortia
and
Interinstitutional
Cooperation

Edited by
Donn C. Neal

American Council on Education Macmillan Publishing Company
NEW YORK
COLLIER MACMILLAN PUBLISHERS
LONDON

230675

1 0001 000 016 382

378.104
C 755

Copyright © 1988 by American Council on Education and
Macmillan Publishing Company,
A Division of Macmillan, Inc.

The American Council on Education/Macmillan Series on Higher Education

All rights reserved. No part of this book may be reproduced or
transmitted in any form or by any means, electronic or mechanical,
including photocopying, recording, or by any information storage
and retrieval system, without permission in writing from the
Publisher.

Macmillan Publishing Company
866 Third Avenue, New York, N.Y. 10022

Collier Macmillan Canada, Inc.

Library of Congress Catalog Card Number: 87-28256

Printed in the United States of America

printing number
1   2   3   4   5   6   7   8   9   10

Library of Congress Cataloging in Publication Data

Consortia and inter-institutional cooperation.

   (The American Council on Education/Macmillan
series on higher education)
   Bibliography: p.
   1. University cooperation—United States.
I. Neal, Donn C., 1940–   . II. Series.
LB2331.5.C664 1988   378'.104'0973   87-28256
ISBN 0-02-922510-8

Contents

Preface   v

Contributors   vii

Introduction: New Roles for Consortia   *Donn C. Neal*   1

1. The Third-Party Role   *Frederick Baus*   23

2. Academic Programs   *Jackie M. Pritzen*   33

3. Professional Development   *Larry L. Rose*   47

4. Library Services and Information Technologies
   Richard H. Dunfee   61

5. The Purchasing of Goods and Services   *Robert M. Briber*   79

6. Serving Business and Industry   *Garry J. DeRose*   97

7. A Partnership with Business
   John M. Bevan and Ann C. Baker   111

8. School/College Collaboration   *Donn C. Neal*   127

9. Public and Government Relations   *John W. Ryan*   147

10. The Challenge of New Technology   *Diana T. Strange*   163

11. Consortia As Risk-Takers   *Jon W. Fuller*   179

12. The Limits of Cooperation   *Donald A. Johnson*   193

Bibliography   *Mark W. Poland*   201

Index   209

Preface

Today's challenges to colleges and universities bring with them new opportunities for cooperation. If you are a president, other campus administrator, or trustee, no one needs to tell you the kinds of problems that will continue to test higher education during the next decade or so: increasing pressures to improve the quality of instruction, a steady escalation of costs, the demands of meeting new institutional roles, the challenges of incorporating new technologies, and more. Only those colleges and universities that meet these tests creatively and vigorously will thrive—perhaps even survive.

Whether we realize it or not, interdependency has become the hallmark of American higher education, and we must seek to get the most out of interinstitutional cooperation if our colleges and universities are to succeed. The contributors to this book believe that the consortium, by harnessing interinstitutional cooperation, can be a vital management tool for achieving greater institutional effectiveness. The consortium can help you and your college or university to address and to meet the challenges that face higher education. Interinstitutional cooperation, we think, offers one more option for a college or university determined to strengthen itself, and the consortium represents an unparalleled means of stimulating and implementing interinstitutional cooperation. The contributors hope that this volume will excite your interest and increase your willingness to explore the potential offered by interinstitutional cooperation through a consortium.

The chapters in this book include some fresh and provocative thinking about the roles that consortia can play in bringing such cooperation into being. They also emphasize some practical values of that cooperation in a dozen of the areas that are of concern to colleges and universities today. We hope that you and your institution will ask more of interinstitutional cooperation, and of the consortium that serves to translate it from idea into reality, so that all of us can explore these challenges together.

Editing this volume has been truly a labor of love. Consortium leaders are nothing if not helpful and cooperative—it is their profession, after all. I am grateful to the contributors for the time and energy that they lent to me, as well as for their patience and understanding as we put the book together.

In addition, I would like to acknowledge the College Center of the Finger Lakes, the Great Lakes Colleges Association, and the Pittsburgh Council on Higher Education for what they have taught me about interinstitutional cooperation, and about consortia.

Contributors

Ann C. Baker is Executive Director of the Charleston (South Carolina) Higher Education Consortium.

Frederick Baus is President of the Association for Higher Education of North Texas in Dallas, Texas.

John M. Bevan recently retired as Executive Director of the Charleston (South Carolina) Higher Education Consortium.

Robert M. Briber recently retired as Executive Director of the Hudson-Mohawk Association of Colleges and Universities in the Capital Region of New York State.

Garry J. DeRose is Executive Director of the College Center of the Finger Lakes in Corning, New York.

Richard H. Dunfee formerly was President of the Colleges of Mid-America in Sioux Falls, South Dakota, and is now Assistant Vice President for Research at St. Cloud State University in Minnesota.

Jon W. Fuller is President of the Great Lakes Colleges Association in Ann Arbor, Michigan.

Donald A. Johnson formerly was Executive Director of the Quad Cities Graduate Study Center in Rock Island, Illinois, and is now Director of Corporate Relations at Augustana College, also in Rock Island.

Donn C. Neal formerly was Executive Director of the Pittsburgh (Pennsylvania) Council on Higher Education and is now Executive Director of the Society of American Archivists in Chicago, Illinois.

Mark W. Poland recently completed his Ed.D. at the College of William and Mary in Williamsburg, Virginia.

Jackie M. Pritzen is Associate Coordinator for Academic Programs of Five Colleges, Inc., in Amherst, Massachusetts.

Larry L. Rose is President of the Kansas City Regional Council for Higher Education.

Diana T. Strange formerly was Executive Director of the Northeast

Consortium of Colleges and Universities in Massachusetts in Lawrence, Massachusetts, and now is Associate Director of the Alumni Fund at the Massachusetts Institute of Technology in Cambridge, Massachusetts.

John W. Ryan is Executive Director of the Worcester (Massachusetts) Consortium for Higher Education.

Introduction:
New Roles
for Consortia

DONN C. NEAL

With well over 3,000 higher education institutions in the United States, there is, inevitably, a considerable amount of cooperation. After all, many of these colleges and universities are similar in mission, in program emphases, in character, or in sponsorship; in addition, many colleges and universities find themselves neighbors.

Much of this cooperation is informal and develops out of networks of people who know one another and have discovered ways in which they can help each other. The many benefits of this kind of cooperation are evident and beyond measure. Sometimes this cooperation also involves formal linkages between institutions, as when two colleges or universities establish a joint degree or engage in some sort of exchange program. There are, in addition, innumerable entities, ranging from the American Council on Education to the Michigan Intercollegiate Athletic Association, that enable colleges and universities to cooperate in some larger endeavor. Here, too, the advantages of mutual activity are significant and readily apparent.

It is less common for two or more colleges or universities to advance to a further stage of formal cooperation by creating or joining a "consortium": a semi-permanent organization, typically supported largely by financial contributions from its members, that employs a professional staff whose

1

sole responsibility is to encourage and to facilitate cooperative activities between and among the members, and between them collectively and others.

Informal and formal cooperation within higher education undoubtedly has existed for many decades, but most consortia represent a relatively new phenomenon. The first examples are the Claremont Colleges, founded in 1925, and the Atlanta University Center, which originated four years later. The growth of consortia was slow until following World War II, but during the 1960s private and public financial support for the concept of consortia led to a rapid increase in their number. Foundations, and the federal government in particular, helped to foster and underwrite consortia in many parts of the country. This development stemmed partly from an intellectual commitment to the notion that collaboration is a good idea, but it also reflected the realization that if colleges and universities were to meet the new demands being placed upon them they needed to find ways of sharing their energies and resources.

With higher education's "Golden Years" behind them, however, colleges and universities began to view consortia in a different light. Campus leaders and others came to expect more from this cooperative vehicle, and they abandoned the consortium if it did not deliver assistance in helping the institution to meet its needs. A good many consortia fell by the wayside or were reduced to nominal functions. Some, however, embraced the new demands being placed upon them, and each year there has been modest growth in the number of consortia. In 1987 there were over 135 organizations of this type.

There is no typical consortium. Consortia differ from one another because they have different types of members; because they are large or small; because they serve different communities; because they range from local to regional to national in scope; because they are organized in different ways; because they have matured at different rates; and because they have had different histories, leadership, and program emphases. Some consortia are best equipped to concentrate on one or two activities, whereas others are able to address a wide range of areas. Each is a unique response to a set of conditions.

Even if the lifespan of most consortia—indeed, the "consortium movement" as a whole—does not exceed a quarter of a century, this phenomenon has been a positive one. That colleges and universities, traditionally autonomous and often fiercely jealous of their independence, can join together in common purpose is an encouraging sign, for it shows that they recognize their inevitable limitations even while they continue to reach for excellence. When colleges and universities form consortia in order to implement—one might even say institutionalize—their desire to cooperate, they signal that they are serious about building such collaboration over the long haul. (It is also true that most colleges and universities seek to *limit* that collaboration, but the consortium would not exist at all if there were no commitment from its members.)

By cooperating with other similar or dissimilar colleges and universities, an institution can achieve more, do something better, or reduce the cost of an activity. These are the three principal objectives that the consortium can help its members to achieve. Every member institution sees the consortium in somewhat different terms, since each college or university has somewhat different needs. Each, however, expects to get something of value out of the time, energy, and financial resources that it invests in consortium membership and participation.

Much of the early development of the consortium as a vehicle for interinstitutional cooperation focused on the academic potential that these organizations could help to realize. Through cooperation, a college or university seemed to have the best of both worlds: a stronger academic program without any loss in institutional autonomy. Other functions for consortia also excited the imagination, but it was the prospect of an expanded and enhanced academic program through consortial cooperation that captured the attention of most educational leaders.

That this promise was not always kept did not keep consortia from finding roles to play and ways of making themselves valuable—occasionally even indispensable—to their members. Many consortia, either consciously or otherwise, developed their own niches, and retained or built their members' support.

Consortia that have survived into the late 1980s have explored new means of service to their members, sometimes discovering new roles that their founders either never imagined or else disdained. In today's climate for higher education, the potential of interinstitutional cooperation through consortia—how these organizations can help their members—deserves additional scrutiny. As colleges and universities themselves are expected to take on new roles, and to perform their traditional roles better or less expensively, they should find in consortia invaluable tools, allies, and inspiration.

The chapters that follow explore in detail some of the areas where interinstitutional cooperation through the mechanism of a consortium can improve what colleges and universities do. These chapters reflect the experience, thought, and imagination of some of the best consortium leaders in the United States. Their topics encompass the broad range of issues that face colleges and universities today, from continuing education to technology, from faculty renewal to cost containment.

Frederick Baus, president of the Association for Higher Education of North Texas, develops many of these points about the roles of consortia in his chapter, which explores the "third-party" function that they can serve. Baus argues for a new definition of what consortia do, and can do, as organizations that are external to, but also intimately related to, their members.

As consortia "come into their majority," Baus says, they must shed their preoccupation with academic complementarity, cost savings, and other preconceived programmatic roles (where, in fact, they have had little real impact) and must seek to satisfy the imperative needs of colleges and universities. Although there is no "generic role" for consortia, Baus believes that they represent a logical response to certain conditions within higher education today. If consortia do respond to those conditions, then they can be "fundamentally valuable rather than merely opportunistic."

Baus draws upon the model of higher education's efforts to reach out to other groups—businesses and schools, for instance—to show how consortia can be more valuable within higher education. As cooperative relationships between higher education and these other groups mature, a third-party agency becomes useful in sustaining those relationships. The agency can focus on the issues rather than on institutional self-interest; it can provide continuity over the ups and downs of institutional priorities, budgets, and personnel; and it can furnish a professional staff with the skills and perspective to consummate cooperation.

Since these same attributes are required to achieve institution-to-institution cooperation within higher education, Baus declares, the consortium can be vital to this cooperation if it performs a third-party agency function. As a result, academic collaboration and exploiting economies of scale become only examples of a broader vision of how the consortium can be useful to colleges and universities.

As Baus acknowledges, academic cooperation has often been regarded as the core activity and true test of a consortium's success. It is appropriate, then, that the next chapter comes from the associate coordinator for academic programs of what is generally considered the nation's leading example of a consortium that has succeeded in achieving academic cooperation: Five Colleges, Inc.

Jackie M. Pritzen cites the conditions that encouraged colleges and universities during higher education's growth years to search for academic enrichment and economies through cooperation. She then examines in detail the two major forms that this collaboration has taken: "programs that give colleges and universities access to each other's resources through exchange or articulation agreements, and curricular programs that are jointly planned and maintained by the participating institutions." The latter, being more difficult to accomplish, are less widespread.

Cross-registration, which primarily serves individual students, and faculty exchanges, which strengthen the curriculum, are the principal types of exchange programs. Cross-registration enables institutions to draw upon one another's complementary assets; here, though, geography, institutional character, and other factors may limit the opportunity to share. Pritzen describes how colleges and universities can encourage these exchanges. Faculty exchanges often parallel cross-registration; Pritzen illustrates how these can meet immediate problems, avoid needless duplication, and allow imaginative pooling of faculty talents. She also points out that building academic complementarity through existing strengths is a slow process.

Turning to the creation of joint curricular initiatives, Pritzen describes how this form of cooperation calls for considerable commitment from the institutions and a consensus on how to satisfy a common need. Joint faculty appointments and jointly sponsored nondegree programs bring an added dimension to an institution's academic character without too much commitment. Joint degrees and departments, which are more difficult to create, may enable the partners to achieve a level of academic excellence that each cannot attain alone.

Few groups of colleges and universities have ideal conditions for cooperation, and there are many barriers. These include, Pritzen says, competitive urges, tradition, and a concern about autonomy. Inadequate time and resources to plan for cooperation also are factors. What should surprise us, Pritzen says, is that so *much* cooperation exists in the face of such obstacles.

What factors help to overcome these barriers? Among the most critical ones, Pritzen contends, are a sense of commitment on the part of institutional leaders, a strong organization that can mediate and manage the cooperative initiatives, and specific incentives for cooperation. Without a feeling of community among faculty members of the colleges and universities, though, academic cooperation cannot succeed.

The new challenges to higher education are in one way identical to those things that brought many consortia into being: both confront colleges and universities with the problem of achieving quality education with scarce resources. Cooperation today, Pritzen concludes, is less focused on "diversity, flexibility, and experimentation" and more on how to allocate these limited resources better, on how to maintain a high level of quality during tough times, and sometimes on self-preservation. The potential for consortia, she affirms, still exists.

The Kansas City Regional Council on Higher Education (KCRCHE) has long been a leader in consortial professional development activities. Its current president, Larry L. Rose, argues that this is an area where interinstitutional cooperation through a consortium is particularly effective. Individual institutions will not or cannot put adequate emphasis on professional development and will not plan well enough for it, he says. The consortial program can buttress the campus program so that the combination will meet the college or university's needs.

Professional development, Rose continues, is one of the consortial activities that meets all of the tests of effective cooperation: it is feasible, important, and wanted by the members. By putting the consortium directly into contact with important educational issues, professional development may do more good than a large number of peripheral academic initiatives. In addition, professional development in a consortial setting is cost-effective, and shared professional development activities are qualitatively better because they enable institutions to share experiences across campus boundaries.

Rose concedes that there are problems in mounting a consortial professional development effort, but there are also significant advantages. The consortium has a larger "bag of tricks" than any single college or university does: there is more expertise within the group, there are more strategies to employ, and there is a larger pool of money. The consortium forms a community that the institution can turn to for information and consultation; additionally, there is sufficient interest to support a conference when that response is called for.

Rose uses the KCRCHE experience to show the kinds of activities that succeed in a consortial professional development program, some of which only the consortium can undertake. These include grants to assist individuals, consultations by outsiders and by the consortium's staff, and a vast array of conferences. Rose contends that clearly defined topics and target groups make the best combination for effective professional development activities. One of the most valuable contributions a consortium can make is sponsoring an informal, collegial group of counterpart administrators who can share ideas and information. The same model can serve faculty members too by encouraging ongoing relationships and candid discussions about professional problems and challenges.

A consortial professional development program has the added

advantage of being free to experiment—and fail, and so the member institutions can use it to tackle issues like identifying and improving the quality of teaching. Rose concludes his chapter with a call for focusing professional development programs on learning objectives and outcomes. Consortia can play a vital role in making that happen, Rose maintains.

As Richard H. Dunfee observes, library cooperation was one of the earliest (and most successful) forms of interinstitutional cooperation. In today's information society, sharing in this realm takes on renewed importance. Dunfee, until recently president of the Colleges of Mid-America, asserts that many librarians have embraced cooperation, and even interdependence, in order to maintain the quality of their programs and services.

The dramatic increase in information, the decline in library purchasing power, and the advent of new information and communication technologies all are propelling libraries toward greater cooperation. Since over 800 regional, state, national, and even worldwide networks exist to facilitate this cooperation, librarians must choose which of this multitude of networks will enable the individual library to serve its users and to deliver information better in the future.

Dunfee describes the forms of cooperation that exist today and how consortia can help. Interlibrary loan, a traditional form of cooperation, is increasingly employed to share materials, especially on the local level, where members of a consortium can make library resource sharing a major goal. Union lists assist librarians and patrons in knowing who holds what materials, either nationally or within a smaller area. Shared access, often through the exchange of borrowing privileges, also brings libraries closer together, particularly when they are within a consortium. Cooperation in collection development—dividing the responsibility for acquisitions—is also increasing, especially in periodicals and specialized collections.

The growth of automated means for exchanging information has also spawned greater cooperation, and on-line cataloging is now common. A standard format helps to eliminate problems of incompatibility. Now, regional and local consortia have begun to use automated systems, and both large and small libraries have turned to these systems.

Data base access is yet another type of library cooperation, Dunfee says. A large number of these services assist any subscribing library in gaining access to a myriad of specialized information, and some consortia achieve efficiency by coordinating their searches. Finally, many institutions cooperate in order to share the costs of supporting the learning-resource centers that their libraries often host, and soon many consortia may serve as on-line local area networks to exchange information and software alike.

Using a hypothetical group of four institutions, Dunfee illustrates how the typical college or university library today "sits at the center of a complex . . . matrix of consortia, service agencies, and membership organizations." He provides some specific examples of how organized cooperation strengthens the quality of the support that the library can give to its institution's academic programs. His examples include the joint purchasing of equipment and software; cooperative planning to achieve greater compatibility and to reduce duplication; the cooperative training of personnel; and the sharing of resources and expertise. As the role of the college and university library changes, Dunfee concludes, a consortium that sponsors this kind of activity offers a way of coping with new demands.

Cooperation in academic endeavors may be the most dramatic form of consortial activity, but cooperation in functional areas can be a linchpin of the consortium. As Robert M. Briber points out in his chapter on the purchasing of goods and services, cooperation here can save money that the institutions can use better elsewhere. Briber, who recently retired as executive director of the Hudson-Mohawk Association of Colleges and Universities, uses his association's longstanding success in group buying to explain how this process works. Although many academics support cooperation for its own sake, cost containment is a natural goal for a consortium and enables it to accomplish other things as well. As Briber puts it, "The cost savings available through purchasing pay our bills; we engage in the rest of our projects because they are good ideas."

Briber shows how cooperation is one more purchasing route available to a college or university. Many institutions use state buying programs or national cooperatives to secure better prices than they can on their own. In addition, more than 30 consortia engage in cooperative buying: they serve as intermediaries between their members, who exploit an economy of scale, and vendors, who are able to pass along the savings of bulk purchasing.

The consortial buying process is straightforward. Campus purchasing officials, using a consensus approach, identify certain generic items—office supplies and paper products are good examples—that might yield savings. What a group chooses to buy together is unimportant so long as it can reach broad agreement.

The group estimates quantities, invites bids, and makes a decision. A good agreement usually experiences increasing sales; if this does not occur, the vendor may be at fault, or the product may not be ripe for joint purchasing. The bidding procedure should be as open as possible, with formal invitations and advertisements. The decision is frequently obvious, although sometimes the lowest bidder is not the best one. After the agreement is reached, the member institutions buy as usual from the successful vendor—but at reduced prices. The consortium typically merely pools the members' buying power and facilitates the process.

Measuring savings is difficult, according to Briber, because the "list price" is so uncertain. Comparison with what the college or university had been paying can be helpful, but this information becomes obsolete; in addition, many institutions can effect internal savings by buying cooperatively. Each consortium will approach calculating its savings in its own way. In the case of the Hudson-Mohawk Association, Briber reports, the aggregate savings (as measured by the members) have topped $1 million in less than 10 years, with an average savings of about 12% over the prices previously paid.

Sharing faculty members and visiting speakers is also feasible, Briber notes, although it is more difficult to arrange cooperation here, since these services are hardly generic products.

Since success in joint purchasing depends on the development of mutual trust and cooperation, good communication—and, often, geographic proximity—is essential. Campus purchasing officials must possess a sense of ownership of the program. Developing all of this takes time, and an ongoing organization can play a vital role in cultivating the program. A consortium, established to find ways for its members to cooperate, can provide that service.

Before leaving the topic, Briber addresses the possibility that cooperative purchasing violates antitrust laws. In his opinion, voluntary cooperation among colleges and universities is not vulnerable unless the members compel a vendor to sell at a loss or boycott a vendor for some reason.

Colleges and universities have long served a constituency larger than the campus community through continuing education programs, but this area has experienced great change in recent years. Garry J. DeRose, executive director of the College Center of the Finger Lakes, argues that an interinstitutional organization is a particularly effective device for meeting business and industry's growing demand for education and training. The strength of the consortium, he says, is its ability to form ingredients from its members into an innovative new entity that can identify and meet the shifting needs of business and industry.

Companies invest in education in order to become more productive, DeRose points out. An educational provider thus must comprehend the business or industry, its special needs, and the process of learning so that it can respond with education and training services that increase the company's effectiveness. Every aspect of the educational product—

faculty member, content, format, teaching method, and price—must be reevaluated. The provider must take care to insure that the business client receives the quality of instruction that it expects.

DeRose then describes three interinstitutional structures that mount programs especially for business clients: the Southwest Washington Joint Center for Education, the College Center of the Finger Lakes, and the New Hampshire Industrial Consortium. Each serves an audience previously without access to educational services of this type, and each has added new students to the sponsoring institutions' rolls. All three have an exclusive emphasis on serving business and industry, which makes them sensitive to the needs of employed students. In addition, their academic offerings focus on engineering, business administration, management, and technology courses.

All three consortia are controlled by their colleges and universities, which minimizes conflict among them and with neighboring institutions; each, however, also has an advisory council drawn from business and industry, which puts them into touch with their clients' needs. The consortium and its small staff thus connect higher education and businesses, facilitating the delivery of educational services and linking the business clients with one another.

DeRose next explores the advantages that the consortium has over an individual institution. The consortium can be client-centered, since it and the client initiate proposals and take them to the campuses for action. The consortium can draw upon the intellectual resources of several colleges and universities, an option that makes for a good match between company and provider and spreads the demand over the entire higher education community. With the resources to hire experts in education for business and industry, the consortium can furnish an ongoing process for determining client needs, housing the instruction, and supervising quality. The consortial approach is not only more comprehensive but more efficient: there is less duplication of contacts (and of weak programs).

All three of these consortial programs are relatively young, DeRose notes, and they may well develop into more complex entities. He speculates about the kinds of developments that may occur: an "umbrella" or consortial degree and closer ties between the consortium and training and education departments. In addition, the consortium might do more, DeRose says, to assist faculty members to become better teachers and researchers by learning more about business and industry.

If the consortium serves to link higher education and business and industry, providing, in DeRose's words, "educational excellence to an exacting audience," how can it capitalize upon the particular business and research resources of its region in innovative ways? The next chapter, by examining the partnership with business that the Charleston (South Carolina) Higher Education Consortium has forged, continues to look at how consortia enable colleges and universities to work with other institutions in American society.

The authors, John M. Bevan (who recently retired as executive director of the consortium) and Ann C. Baker (his successor), describe the consortium's efforts to bring campuses and companies closer together. They review the different objectives that the two have: the former is concerned primarily with personal development, while the latter focuses mainly on professional competency. Yet, as Bevan and Baker note, it is also crucial for businesses to cultivate "an expansive reach" of the mind if they are to succeed. This need gave rise to a consortium-sponsored executive seminar, modeled after that of the Aspen Institute, that emphasizes the liberal arts. Employing provocative readings and lively discussions, this seminar stimulates and broadens the business leaders who participate in it.

Economic development is another area where the Charleston Consortium has been active. Here colleges and universities can be important resources for attracting and retaining companies and for strengthening economic growth. When the city of Charleston began to work with a major corporation to attack unemployment through small-business development in a depressed neighborhood, the effort required an effective educational component. None of the area's colleges or universities served this neighborhood, the East Side, so the consortium stepped forward to identify needs and to assemble the necessary educational resources. In the end, the innovative, broadly based learning center that the consortium helped to establish has made a significant contribution to the recovery of the East Side. Overcoming the alienation of the residents as well as institutional barriers, the consortium brought about a new form of community interaction.

Bevan and Baker also describe how the consortium has been active in working with the local schools, assisting them in dealing with problems of school management, teacher preparedness, and student performance. In this instance, co-ventures involving higher education, the schools, and the business community have been quite successful. One program, for example, enables principals to acquire better managerial skills and to observe the management styles being practiced in local companies.

Baker and Bevan enumerate the many advantages of the cooperation of business and higher education through a consortium. These co-ventures benefit from the consistent approach of a unified effort, and when colleges and universities collaborate they offer the community an impressive collective resource. There are also financial advantages to working cooperatively, including new funding possibilities for higher education, and consortial intervention increases the possibility of an innovative and experimental response to a problem. When a consortium acts on behalf of its members, moreover, communication is simplified and a broader perspective prevails. Finally, the cooperation that the members display presents a positive model for the community as a whole.

Cooperation between business and higher education is not without its difficulties, though, and Bevan and Baker mention these as well. Higher education must remain true to its values, they say, and these values—indeed, the very ethos of higher education—may confuse the business partners. The consortium can function as a leveling influence as it also keeps the focus of attention on the successful accomplishment of the co-venture.

If the advantages of working through a consortial mechanism outweigh the disadvantages, as Bevan and Baker believe, there is reason to explore how cooperation can help higher education to collaborate with business and industry. The expanded partnerships that result should benefit society as well as both partners.

One of the most promising new areas for cooperative activity today involves higher education and the schools. Here, too, the consortium can make a special contribution by encouraging and facilitating this cooperation. In my own chapter, written while I was executive director of the Pittsburgh Council on Higher Education, I explore this topic.

The chapter begins by addressing why schools and colleges should cooperate. All of us in education have a stake in quality throughout our educational system, and colleges and universities can improve only if the schools excel. Major social and economic changes in American society also make cooperation between schools and colleges essential today. The interests of the two sectors are not only compatible but complementary, I contend, and so collaboration will help both to succeed.

Turning to how schools and colleges can usefully cooperate, I show how a consortium can bring an important added dimension to these areas of mutual interest. These areas include consultations on a wide range of academic issues, the delivery of certain specialized educational services, teacher training, precollegiate counseling, efforts to build greater awareness of the importance of education, and the recognition of excellent teaching. A consortium can place the schools into contact with the fullest possible range of higher education institutions, maintain good communication, and coordinate the cooperative endeavors. Consortium-sponsored programs will often be stronger, more comprehensive, more consistent, more visible, and more credible than those with institutional sponsorship. While colleges and universities work together to bring their impressive collective resources to bear, moreover, they will learn things about one another that might generate greater cooperation on the collegiate level as well.

How colleges and universities in Pittsburgh have used their consortium to undertake initiatives in several of these areas is the next theme of the chapter. Opportunities for classroom instructors to exchange ideas on topics of mutual academic interest, an enrichment seminar for local science and mathematics teachers, exploration of the implications for education of economic change in western Pennsylvania, and strengthening contacts between college presidents and school superintendents—all these activities illustrate how this consortium has sought to bring about increased school/college collaboration in its region.

I enumerate the advantages of working through a consortium to foster school/college collaboration. Since few if any of the members are already deeply involved in this kind of activity, the opportunity to move forward together may be welcome. The consortium is probably proficient at employing collaborative techniques and in brokering connections between higher education and other groups, so an initiative in school/college relations will likely be regarded as consistent with its mission and character.

Consortial decision making is another strength, I argue. Decisions made in an interinstitutional context require thorough deliberation and clearly stated objectives, and thus strong support from the members. The members, by communicating with one another (and comparing themselves with one another), help each other to do their best in cooperating with the schools.

Since the consortium is a neutral and disinterested party, it can serve to limit the risk for its members as they experiment in cooperation with schools; neither schools nor colleges have to make choices from among all the potential partners, since everyone is a partner in a single, consolidated effort. The solidarity that stems from a consortial approach also should attract funders who want to concentrate their impact and should also attract considerable public attention.

I acknowledge the potential shortcomings of consortial sponsorship of school/college collaboration. A consortium may not have the full attention and support of the people on its campuses; it must, therefore, focus its ventures in areas where the institutions' goals and needs can be attained through joint action, and the consortium's staff must look for areas where common interests will produce direct benefits for the members.

For all its attributes, moreover, the consortium is still probably rather undeveloped in its goals and priorities and may be relatively inexperienced in managing cooperative ventures. If the members are tentative about their institutional commitments to the consortium, they may not welcome its initiatives in school/college collaboration. These initiatives can be only as strong as the assistance that its members want to proffer, since the consortium has no independent authority to act. Finally, since the consortium operates in a complex multi-institutional framework, any initiative demands time and patience—which may make some outsiders skeptical about its ability to produce results.

Although these potential disadvantages and limitations should be considered, I observe, the consortium is a proven vehicle for successful cooperative initiatives, including school/college collaboration. As a matter of fact, this kind of cooperation may well provide the consortium with a renewed sense of energy and purpose that will make it more successful in other areas as well.

The chapter closes with a look at strategies that will make school/college collaboration through a consortium work. Strengthening communication between the cooperating groups, acknowledging the self-interest that is motivating each of the partners, and attacking unflattering stereotypes that exist are all important steps. Although administrators on both sides will play a key role in school/college collaboration, for cooperation to succeed classroom counterparts must be able to build strong professional relationships; both groups, then, must be involved in and must endorse the collaborative plan. Expanding school/college cooperation will take the best efforts of persons on both sides, and dynamic and resourceful leadership is likely to make the difference between success and failure.

In implementing these strategies, I conclude, interinstitutional cooperation through a consortium can help to develop lines of communication, to identify factors of self-interest, to build mutual trust, and to deepen commitment. The members of a consortium learn from one another's experiences and can be more ambitious together than alone. Through a consortium, the schools can participate in a well-rounded, consistent, and outstanding program of collaboration. Those who are searching for ways to increase cooperation between the schools and colleges will find in the consortium an immediate and useful vehicle for doing so.

Nowhere are the advantages of speaking with a united voice more apparent than in providing the public and policymakers with information, and in attempting to influence the attitudes of these two groups. John W. Ryan's essay on this topic draws upon his rich experience as executive director of the Worcester (Massachusetts) Consortium for Higher Education. He explains how the consortium can focus and amplify higher education's message for these two similar audiences so that the members of the consortium build a better understanding of and more support for what they do.

Ryan emphasizes sound principles of communication, which apply in an interinstitutional setting as much as they do otherwise, but he acknowledges that some aspects of higher education may diminish collective efforts. These include the pluralistic nature of higher education, status and prestige clashes within the membership of a consortium, and marginal commitment to a common effort from some institutional leaders. Nevertheless, he says, a consortium has many opportunities for blending the information, insights, and voices of its members so that all of them benefit.

"Establishing and maintaining a unified public relations program and approach presents a unique opportunity and challenge," Ryan reports. There is much competition for the public's eye and ear, and the consortium must rely upon the media (with its predilection for "hard" news) to reach a broad audience. Every member of the consortium can furnish something of value to a joint program, although, as Ryan notes, the fact that each is jealous of its own identity may make achieving a common purpose difficult. The consortial public relations effort thus should be reserved for areas where the institutional interests intersect. A good example is a common economic impact document, which can make a more profound impression on community attitudes toward higher education than several institutional studies. Colleges and universities thus have more leverage when they address common issues and concerns together. They can deliver a more comprehensive, more accurate, and thus more persuasive picture of higher education's importance than individual institutions can alone.

Ryan cites several ways a consortium can call a community's attention to its higher education institutions. He observes that a community takes civic pride in the presence of these colleges and universities, and the consortium should strive to show how they are part of the "intellectual, economic, and social fabric of the community." The members of the consortium should also remind the public how they provide the community with services; how colleges and universities work to strengthen neighborhoods, schools, the quality of housing, and the environment; and how higher education serves as a partner with business to enhance economic development. In addition the public may not realize how faculty and staff members and students serve in a wide range of leadership positions throughout the community. The important point to emphasize, Ryan says, is that higher education's collective expertise and resources are one of the community's prime assets. A united approach to telling this story makes sense.

There is, Ryan continues, a similar value in speaking together in legislative arenas. He points out that political leaders welcome useful and informed recommendations, since they are looking for sound solutions. Solid information rather than rhetoric is what they need. Many persons in higher education have a distaste for "lobbying," but it is vital today for colleges and universities to help shape public policy—particularly in light of the importance of government dollars in financing higher education.

Effectiveness in the political arena requires an ability to tell one's story simply and well, good political instincts and interpersonal skills, and a knowledge of how legislative bodies (and especially their committees) work. It also helps to target key legislators (and their staff members) and to identify who—trustees, for instance—can assist in influencing them. It is essential to keep legislators and their assistants informed all of the time and not to call upon them for help only during crises.

Operating in legislative forums also benefits from a collective approach, according to Ryan, especially when sympathetic business and community leaders lend their voices to that of higher education. He advises colleges and universities to develop their common interests and then to communicate their views jointly to political leaders. A joint effort here will be more credible, since a broad range of institutions is involved. Although the compromise solutions that emerge out of the political process are unpredictable, Ryan concludes, colleges and universities can enhance their chances for success when they act together.

"Perhaps no other challenge to higher education is as perplexing to most of us, or as radical, as the challenge of new technology." This is the opening sentence of the chapter by Diana T. Strange, who until recently served as the executive director of the Northeast Consortium of Colleges and Universities in Massachusetts. Strange takes a look at the nature of that challenge, with its implications for higher education as we know it, and then shows how the consortium can help to develop the kinds of innovative solutions that colleges and universities will have to find in order to cope with technological change.

Strange, alluding to the changes that the computer has brought to the campus, identifies six major developments that mean change for higher education. First, there is less and less importance of the written word, so that we now learn differently—more by images and sounds than by reading. In addition, the new technologies have created new capabilities in how information is created, saved, and retrieved; as a result, the nature of research is different. A third change is that retraining has become a fact of life for every worker today, since we all work in an increasingly dynamic environment. Lifetime training for young people is no longer what colleges and universities are all about.

Another change is that we are surrounded by technological phenomena, and more than one-half of us soon will be using computers in our work. A fifth change is that large data bases make enormous quantities of information available to all of us, so the educator's role is to help students to gain access to information, to analyze it, and to use it in solving problems. Finally, the learner is in charge now: using an array of interactive, integrated, portable, and individualized technologies, the learner can control his or her own learning.

Strange asks how colleges and universities will respond to these challenges. Quoting one authority, she contends that they will have different clients, different delivery systems, different content, and different ways of approaching education itself. Students will be older, enrolled part-time, and more interested in retraining (and in personal enrichment). Gone will be neat, compartmentalized classroom-oriented coursework with an emphasis on the memorization of facts. Content and methods both will have to be revised in favor of a problem-solving approach.

Strange suggests that innovation through sharing is one way for colleges and universities to meet these inevitable changes that our society is experiencing. She describes the conditions that foster innovation, emphasizing the need for cooperative mechanisms like the consortium. Strange then describes some ways in which higher education is meeting that challenge through consortia. Given the importance of sound and images, she says, it is significant that some groups of colleges and universities are employing cable television to provide instruction, often to nontraditional learners. Information is now being distributed by local and national networks, including consortia and other cooperative vehicles. Some of this information is the product of jointly created data bases, too. Consortia are also helping their members to furnish the retraining that the rapidly evolving American workplace demands.

The biggest challenge to higher education, Strange says, may be finding a way to cope with a situation in which the learner is in control.

Nevertheless, she is able to point to promising developments here as well, and cooperative solutions (including new consortia) seem likely to bring some revolutionary changes to higher education.

There are barriers to cooperation, of course, especially in an environment as highly segmented and structured as higher education. The consortium may be the only setting where people from different levels within different higher education institutions can come together in order to solve problems. Innovation requires collaboration, Strange asserts. The consortium is uniquely on the edge of higher education yet connected to the key persons within it; if it has sufficient support and resources, Strange concludes, "it can be an effective tool for educators eager to participate in the changes brought by the new technologies."

The ability to take risks is one of the primary attributes of a consortium. So argues Jon W. Fuller, president of the Great Lakes Colleges Association (GLCA). His chapter uses the quarter-century experience of his own quite successful organization to show how cooperation has enabled the 12 small Midwestern colleges of GLCA to innovate successfully.

GLCA was created in large part to permit these colleges to enlarge their educational opportunities while remaining small. The initial impetus, in the 1960s, was to expand teaching about the non-European world and to establish a number of overseas study programs. Pooling and coordinating their already good individual efforts allowed these colleges to exploit institutional strengths and interests in order to build some impressive collective resources. The same reasoning later permitted GLCA to develop some unusual domestic off-campus programs as well.

Whatever the locale, these programs utilized economy of scale to sustain a high level of participation and quality, and sharing in these ventures also enabled GLCA's members to survive the unavoidable setbacks. Because the off-campus programs were often experimental in nature, they benefited from the shared responsibility and greater tolerance accorded a consortium-sponsored program. On the other hand, Fuller notes, consortial sponsorship of a program involves closer scrutiny of quality, another strength.

Another area where GLCA has served is members is faculty development. The members greeted this topic with some skepticism when it arose during the 1970s, even as they recognized the need for greater attention to teaching quality and the growth of individual faculty members. Through the consortium, the members could sample many different aspects of faculty development—some quite traditional and others more controversial—before making institutional commitments to it. A major grant thus helped the GLCA members to experiment together and to measure consortial programs against the institutional programs each was developing, and the GLCA program became a permanent feature of the consortium's services.

Women's studies, which evolved out of GLCA's faculty development program, also established itself as a permanent consortial activity. Here the members were able to explore and test a field that was new and potentially exciting but that was unfamiliar and controversial as well. The members learned from one another, and on each campus a curricular focus on women's studies grew at least in part out of the GLCA initiative. At the same time, the consortium attracted the involvement of a large and enthusiastic group on each campus. A by-product of the women's studies initiative, Fuller says, was added collective attention to the status of women—hiring policies, for instance—on the 12 campuses, which demonstrates how the power of example can operate within a consortium.

The special problems of untenured faculty members has provided another opportunity for GLCA to assist its members in handling a difficult issue that they would have found even more difficult alone. The consortium's staff realized that the colleges were experiencing similar frustrations in this area. The problem was discussed at meetings of GLCA faculty members, who could vent and consider feelings here that they could not express on their own campuses. A consortial initiative studied the problems of untenured faculty members, legitimized discussion of the topic, allowed comparisons of campus policies on evaluation and tenure, and facilitated collegial relationships between senior and junior faculty members on different GLCA campuses. A study of information about career patterns and tenure outcomes within GLCA was also valuable.

This, Fuller points out, was another good illustration of consortial risk taking: many of these issues were potentially explosive ones, but the neutrality of the consortium's setting helped to lower the emotional level. Even though GLCA could hardly solve the basic problems, it enabled the members to reexamine their own policies without confrontation and defensiveness while they retained their autonomy.

A final example of the advantages of cooperative risk taking comes from a recent GLCA partnership with the University of Michigan's area studies centers. In conjunction with the Associated Colleges of the Midwest (a similar consortium that collaborates with GLCA in some of the off-campus programs), GLCA has enabled its faculty members and students to gain access to the special resources of these centers. An existing consortium, Fuller says, could respond promptly and decisively to the university's willingness to cooperate and could absorb the costs of preparing a major funding proposal to support the program.

Fuller mentions several other topics that the consortium has explored but that have not matured into successful initiatives, pointing out how the consortium serves as a useful mechanism for such exploration. By assuming most of the risk, a consortium like GLCA can permit its members to overcome their own inherent traditionalism, and, consequently, to enjoy greater academic benefits than if they were to stand alone.

Donald A. Johnson's chapter reminds us that the consortium is anything but a panacea for all the problems of American higher education. Johnson, who recently left the Quad Cities Graduate Study Center, helps us to close this book on a note of realism and caution—and yet of hope as well.

Johnson emphasizes that there are reasons why interinstitutional cooperation will not succeed; there are also barriers to successful cooperation; and, there are limitations that consortia impose upon themselves. All of this, he warns, should make us careful before we propose an interinstitutional solution to every problem. (As we have seen, the other authors in this volume have also acknowledged the limitations and disadvantages of the consortium.) Yet Johnson, "an eternal optimist," believes—and the chapters in this book prove—that it is possible to shape "educational and institutional diversity into an organization with common goals." He also finds some positive aspects in what are usually regarded as barriers to cooperation.

What are some of the reasons why interinstitutional cooperation is not a universal solution for higher education? First, Johnson says, in our society "competition is condoned, rewarded, and encouraged." Consortia simply "run against the grain of higher education." But, Johnson continues, this pervasive aura of competition compels the consortium to be entrepreneurial and innovative in order to survive, and a successful venture in this kind of environment is a true triumph.

A second barrier, in Johnson's eyes, is the concern over institutional autonomy. Cooperation is not the same thing as consolidation, he points out, but a consortium's members' concern about autonomy may be reflected in limited resources, a decision making process that impedes cooperation, minimal support for programs, and a lack of rewards for those who do participate in consortial activities.

Diverse missions can be another major constraint for a consortium. In extreme cases, some colleges and universities can find too little in common to cooperate usefully, but usually differences actually enable them to complement one another, Johnson says. He also cites numerous other potential barriers to cooperation.

Why has interinstitutional cooperation through consortia not grown as it might have? Too often, Johnson suggests, the consortium is seen as an "outsider" and does not receive acceptance from faculty members and others. When the leadership for a consortium is focused at the presidential level, there can be too little involvement of other key campus figures. In addition, Johnson says, the consortium may lack a clear mission or charge; these, he adds, should be broad and visionary and not narrowly restrictive. The consortium's staff may also impose a limitation unless they have the right qualities and experience.

Johnson closes by describing three "strawmen" that should not serve to restrict interinstitutional cooperation: inertia, tokenism, and "turf claims." He suggests some ways of overcoming these artificial barriers to cooperation; primary among them are the development of mutual trust, the use of small steps toward fuller cooperation, and vigorous leadership on the part of those strongly committed to cooperation. We should not be paralyzed by the potential barriers to cooperation, Johnson advises, but we should navigate around them and "deliver the advantages that a consortium provides."

This is advice that all of the authors of this book would concur with, and we hope that our contributions, both individually and severally, will stimulate you and other decision makers in higher education to take a closer look at how interinstitutional cooperation through a consortium can lead to better-managed and more successful institutions. Even if consortia cannot solve all of higher education's problems, there is little doubt that their full potential has yet to be plumbed and that more creative and productive interinstitutional relationships will make colleges and universities better at what they do.

The volume concludes with a bibliography prepared by Mark W. Poland. Because he recently completed a dissertation (at The College of William and Mary) on consortial cooperation, Poland is unusually well informed about the literature of this field. He has provided brief annotations for many of the works in the bibliography.

—1—

The Third-Party Role

FREDERICK BAUS

It is the thesis of this chapter that the academic consortium in American higher education is in the process of being reinvented as a third-party agency that promotes many valuable forms of collaboration. The higher education legacy of the 1960s and early 1970s includes a strong disappointment that consortia were never able to fulfill their potential as reformers of the academy.

The truth is that higher education has not been fundamentally changed by efforts to improve its efficiency or its academic character through voluntary institutional cooperation—academic consortia. In responding to the challenges of an increasingly information-based society, however, higher education is well-served by third-party agencies that promote collaboration—collaboration that involves flexible mixes of colleges, universities, and other nonprofit and for-profit organizations.

Successfully managing complex relationships among large numbers of disparate institutions calls for a strictly maintained attitude of neutrality, a continuity of effort that rises above the many changes that occur in the constituency, and a high degree of professionalism. It is these attributes of consortia as third-party agencies—not their predetermined roles in

The Association for Higher Education (AHE), incorporated in 1980 after the consolidation of several predecessor organizations, serves 18 colleges and universities and 25 corporations in the 13-county region surrounding Dallas and Fort Worth, Texas. AHE operates a telecommunications network, coordinates resource-sharing services, and supports professional education programs on behalf of its members.

accomplishing certain programmatic ends—that point to the future success
of the form.

What Are Consortia Good For?

In an article in the August 24, 1984, edition of *Science,* Texas A & M
President Frank Vandiver observes:

> Consortiums may be the outline of what universities will become in the next
> century. Intellectually or geographically kindred campuses that are linked by
> agreements might be able to achieve a matrix organization that would provide
> wider research and educational opportunities to students and faculties while
> still preserving separate campus identities and loyalties.

At the heart of Vandiver's vision lies the notion of the academic characters
of sets of universities significantly improved through a cooperative matrix.

If indeed this concept of linked campuses is to be the university of
the twenty-first century, it is an idea whose time has not yet come; and
academic consortia are not yet recognized as having any significant generic
contribution to make in pushing, pulling, or escorting higher education
into a meaningful future. Nevertheless, some significant trends do suggest
that consortia are about to come into their majority—a possibility that may
irritate consortium and institutional leaders equally, and probably for the
same reason that Vandiver's comments are irritating to both.

To understand these irritations, one must look back to the recent
history of higher education consorting. Considered a seminal work by
early students of the consortium movement, Franklin Patterson's 1974
book *Colleges in Consort* laid an ample foundation for many of the myths
about consortia that are prevalent today. In an indictment of consortia
called "Reality and Possibility," Patterson wrote:

> The performance of consortia up to this point [1974] has not measured well
> against the real opportunities and needs that have existed in American higher
> education in the past several decades. The general failure of the movement
> to deliver significant academic complementarity or significant planned coop-
> eration in capital outlay or significant attention to the operating economies
> or any substantial long-range planning of change and development—together
> with the continuing pre-eminence of institutional autonomy regardless of the
> redundancy of results—reflects a major opportunity thus far lost by consortia
> in terms of higher education as it has been.

Although the intended shock value of that indictment moved higher
education not in the least, it left in its wake a set of assumptions about
consortia that have not been effectively challenged in 10 years. The
burden of consortia, that of solving decades-old problems of institutional

autonomy and efficiency, and the lack of meaningful long-range planning, weighs heavily on consortium professionals. The resulting sense of mission that most of them pursue focuses on academic cooperation in the form of joint academic programs and joint faculty appointments—academic complementarity—and a crusading sense that opportunities abound in higher education for near- and long-term economies of scale.

The simple fact of the matter is that academic complementarity is not what the vast majority of consortia in America are about. In a Council for Interinstitutional Leadership (CIL) *Newsletter* in 1984, I challenged the common wisdom that consortia can or do make a major contribution to higher education by promoting academic cooperation. If such cooperation means joint faculty appointments and joint degree programs, then almost all consortia have no real impact on higher education; and, under the rising pressures for competition in the academy, it is unlikely that most consortia ever will have such an impact.

Further, the notion of economies of scale is a difficult reality to achieve and a harder one to demonstrate, as recent efforts show. In a 1979 publication, *Benefits of Collegiate Cooperation,* Lewis Patterson presents case study information about the dollar benefits of various consortial programs and services. The effort is a worthy one, and the consortia represented in the publication are valuable examples of what works for numerous consortia across the country.

The shortcoming of *Benefits of Collegiate Cooperation,* however, is that it fails to document dollar-cost savings that can make other consortia want to emulate the examples. Where some justifiable basis exists for real dollar savings, the indirect costs of staff time, travel, and other expenses are not documented—and perhaps are not documentable.

In many cases, further, the technique is to cite cost avoidance as a measure of cooperative success. The problem with cost avoidance, however realistic the numbers might be, is that avoidance per se is hardly a motivation for cooperative ventures. This approach smacks of the hypothetical: many of the cases are at best tenuous and at worst simply suspect. This effort shows not only the difficulty that cost/benefit analyses present to the consortium movement, but it also shows that consortium professionals are self-conscious about the need to validate the cost of their activities.

What Is the Future of Consortia?

If no clear argument can be made for consortia based on academic or economic agreements, one might well ask what the future of cooperation in higher education is. Here are some principles that may form the basis for an answer to that question:

- Consortia are derivative organizations. Consortia have no independent missions but derive their missions from the individual and collective missions of the colleges and universities that they serve. Consortia are successful to the degree that they either enhance the programs and objectives of their constituent institutions or provide solutions to problems confronted by those institutions.

- Each consortium has a unique character that reflects the organizational mix of institutional constituencies, the historical factors that created and sustain member institutions, and the styles of leadership and motivations for cooperation that are operating in member institutions at a particular time.

- The basis for consortium activity is consensus formation. Although the immediate motivation for institutions to cooperate may be related to cost savings, program development objectives, or political factors, the essential ingredient in effective consortium activity is the establishment of a consensus among institutional leaders.

- Consensus is reached in a consortium as an expression of institutional will. Cooperative activity, even within mandated co-operatives, is voluntary: regardless of the legal, economic, or political pressures to cooperate, real cooperation will not happen if the institutional partners do not want it to happen.

- The primary motivation for institutional cooperation is enlightened self-interest. Cooperation for the sake of cooperating provides insufficient justification for a consortium to be created or sustained. Cooperation must be developed out of a sense of strength and gain on the part of collaborating institutions.

- The existence and effectiveness of any consortium is dependent on two conditions: each institution in the consortium must know and accept its limitations as an institution, and each must recognize the value of exceeding those limits by entering into a consensus-forming process with other institutions. If the possibility exists, real or perceived, that an institution acting alone can exceed or expand its limits to seize an opportunity or to resolve a problem, then the consortium alternative is not a "live" option.

What Types of Needs Do Consortia Meet?

It is not possible to be prescriptive about the role of a consortium. Many of the factors upon which successful consortium activity depend are particular to the character of the consortium and the timing of the question, What should this consortium do? There is no generic role that consortia play across time, geography, and institutional types.

Nor is it particularly fruitful to investigate the idiosyncratic roles of consortia. These roles are too varied and too complex to provide useful information outside of the individual consortium context. However, one should not dismiss consortium activity as defying analysis. There are conditional roles for consortia that tend toward the generic and the prescriptive, and away from the idiosyncratic.

The conditional roles of consortia are those activities that a consortium ought to attempt because there are conditions higher education faces that logically call for institutional cooperation as a response. These conditions may be transient, but they do exist and can be defined—and, therefore, systematically studied. One example of a condition calling for cooperative response has to do with the mobility of students in higher education. In dense population areas with high concentrations of higher education institutions (a major precondition for consortium formation), students tend to move to and from higher education institutions; therefore, the set of student services that governs and facilitates that movement lends itself to formal institutional cooperation, both to control costs and to improve the integrity of the process. Time or circumstances may change this need for cooperation; but, under conditions such as those that obtain in many parts of this country today, consorting to assist mobile student populations is a clear need.

Three other areas of need that lend themselves to consortium activity are

1. information processing (data base access, library services, telecommunications services)

2. professional development services (for both faculty members and administrators)

3. joint purchasing services (quality control and cost reduction)

As these needs increase in significance, the conditions predisposing institutions to enter into formal, cooperative responses will increase in influence. To the extent that these needs are real, consortia based on responses to these needs will be fundamentally valuable to higher education rather than merely opportunistic. To the extent that certain conditions affecting higher education continue to be significant, the future value of consortia will tend to be predictable while the specific form of consortium response will remain case-specific.

What Must Consortia Do?

There is growing evidence that what constitutes a particular higher education institution—a mix of philosophy, mission, and ambience—can be sustained in the future only if that entity is able to reach out to capture resources and to provide linkages to other similar (and dissimilar) organizations. In an evolving higher education environment, consortia can provide the networks of resources and influence that help to sustain such higher education institutions.

Consortia need a clearer sense of what they are (and are not) as institutional forms, and of how they relate to higher education. There must be a clearer sense of consortial dependency on the evolving mission of higher education nationally and a bolder articulation of how consortia serve the purposes of higher education. These clarifications can come only through careful examination of the issues and conditions affecting the future of higher education and the type of response and responsibility consortia are uniquely able to provide.

By implication, therefore, consortia must stimulate a better dialogue with and among the leaders of higher education institutions. In one sense, it would be more appropriate if higher education leadership could take the initiative in pursuing that dialogue, but consortium leaders have a special responsibility to understand this need and to begin the process of dialogue.

As the first step in that process, consortium leaders must develop better channels of communication among themselves. "Better" means more frequent and higher quality discussions about issues that have meaning to, and responses that are "live options" for, higher education. Consortium leaders have foundered long enough on the rocks of institutional autonomy and consortium uniqueness. It is time for consortium leaders to accept these conditions of their existence as just that, conditions—but not as central issues or solvable problems. Consortium leadership must be more sophisticated in understanding itself and its institutions; it must be more political and creative in exercising its role in the future of higher education.

Who Must Respond to These Needs?

Consortium leadership ultimately must defer to higher education leadership to make the decisions that will make cooperation work. The first step is for consortium leaders to understand what higher education's needs are and where consortia fit in. The second step is for consortium leadership to engage the interest of higher education leadership in examining the values of the network relationships that consortia provide. Much attention is being given today to the need for consortium-type structures to assist in developing and managing the outreach relationships between higher education and the private sector, and between higher education and the school systems. In principle, the requirements of such outreach activities apply equally well to relationships among higher education institutions themselves. Approaching the issue from the outreach rather than from the interinstitutional perspective can help us to avoid some of the baggage of past assumptions about consortia.

As information moves from the sheltered domain of the clerisy and the academy into the marketplace, as a commodity, colleges and universities find themselves in an unaccustomed role—that of being competitors in a highly competitive field. Academic institutions inevitably are drawn into the information infrastructure not simply because the institution itself is both a supplier and a consumer of information. The institution's students, its immediate clientele, are also consumers of information, not all of which can possibly be supplied by even the most sophisticated university. Further, various types of institutions outside the academy are taking on more and more of the educational-cum-training roles traditionally reserved for the academy and also are assuming competitive postures vis-à-vis the academy.

In this context of changing roles, outreach to school systems and to public- and private-sector institutions is an inevitable result. At first these network relationships help to bolster academic institutions financially, but inevitably they also create new perspectives for both parties as the informational and economic ties grow more complex and as involvements at arm's length become interdependencies with intermediate or long-term implications.

Increasingly, the agencies that conduct these relationships take on a life of their own in that the time and resources necessary to build and sustain effective relationships cannot simply be additive functions to the workloads of already overtaxed internal staffs and budgets. Therefore, partly to spread the costs and partly to empower a neutral agency to handle the subtleties of relating the needs and resources of dissimilar institutions, a role for a third party develops. What are the contributions and the requirements of this third-party agency to develop and sustain effective network relationships?

First, a middle-ground perspective is important. The interfacing of dissimilar institutions requires that a focus be sustained on issues, instead of merely on the vested interests of any one institution. The issue of orientation is critical because it gives each institutional partner a position against which to test its interests without engaging in a confrontational process. The third-party approach is invaluable in finding accommodation between institutions, while at the same time buffering the institutions from the sometimes counterproductive effects of direct communication.

Second, the continuity of organization-to-organization relationships is difficult to maintain as institutional priorities rise and fall, as institutional budgets rise and fall, and as people come and go. Yet, if interfaces are to be sustained and interdependencies relied upon, some form of continuity is important. The third-party entity can provide not only a perspective but a concrete reality to bolster the relationship through periods of change. The downside risk of sustaining such relationships beyond the end of their useful life is met by another contribution of third-party agencies—the provision of a professional staff.

The expertise and professionalism of the third-party role are vital to the integrity of the relationship. Professional attitudes not only assist in sustaining valid relationships, but they also provide a safety valve for the termination of useless relationships, as well as a source of continuous attention to new and fruitful ways for both parties to benefit. The most significant contribution the third-party agency makes is the development of a sense of trust that all parties' interests are being protected. The quality of the professional staff is, therefore, without question the most critical element in these relationships. The professional staff is successful only to the degree that it keeps the missions of its respective constituencies and the validity of interdependencies uppermost in its considerations—even relegating the form or existence of the third-party agency itself to a lesser priority.

Having dealt with these relationships in the context of outreach to the public and private sectors, it is a short leap to apply the same third-party role requirements to the institution-to-institution relationships that are traditionally associated with consortia. The same sense of perspective, continuity of effort, and high degree of professionalism that are required of outreach relationships are required of institutional cooperation.

Put in this context, it is moot whether academic cooperation or economies of scale per se have anything to do with consortia. This is a judgment that institutional and consortium leadership must make on a case-by-case, year-by-year basis. Academic cooperation and cost savings are, therefore, hardly prerequisites to successful consortia; they are, rather, two examples among numerous ways that higher education might benefit from the services of a third-party agency.

—2—

Academic Programs

JACKIE M. PRITZEN

During the 1960s and early 1970s, when hundreds of colleges and universities in the United States became involved in consortial arrangements, it was the general belief and expectation that the most fruitful area for developing interinstitutional cooperation was in academic programs. There were both social and economic forces at work to support this view. In the wake of World War II, colleges and universities found themselves faced with a knowledge explosion in the sciences, a revolution in geographical consciousness—especially as it related to the third world of Asia, Africa, and Latin America, and a new national concern for the rights and privileges of minority populations.

The pressures on higher education created by the confluence of these revolutionary changes became even more acute when colleges and universities were confronted by a restless generation of students who had been born under the threat of nuclear war and who were inclined to measure the value of education by its relevance to their own lives. At the same time, rapidly rising costs in an inflationary economy made it increasingly difficult for postsecondary institutions to respond to new demands on their educational programs.

There is no need to recapitulate the curricular acrobatics that characterized much of higher education's response to this challenge,

Five Colleges, Inc., administers cooperative programs for its members, all located in Western Massachusetts. These programs include two joint departments, several joint degree and certificate programs, and a wide variety of cooperative arrangements that benefit students, faculty, and staff of the five institutions. A fare-free bus system links the campuses.

especially at the undergraduate level. It is sufficient to note here that large numbers of institutions, both graduate and undergraduate, began to look at their neighbors in a new light—as potential partners in solving problems or meeting challenges that they were not easily able to handle by themselves.

The academic area seemed the logical place for many institutions to start because it was the area of most pressing need and the one they were most anxious to protect. Given the large share of operating budgets normally devoted to instructional costs, it also seemed to be a promising area for achieving significant economies in their effort to offer quality education in a rapidly changing educational scene.

There were two notable models of academic cooperation at the time: the Claremont Colleges, a deliberately planned group of complementary institutions sharing resources, and the Atlanta University Center, a cluster of predominately black colleges that had been sharing resources and developing joint programs since 1929. There was foundation interest in the idea of cooperation and, after 1965, Title III funding by the federal government to support institutional development through cooperation.

In search of academic enrichment, on the one hand, and substantial cost savings, on the other, more and more institutions began to explore ways to pool their academic resources and to develop joint curricular programs. Some of them met with early success in specific programs, but most institutions soon discovered that academic sharing does not come easily to colleges and universities, and that it is more difficult to measure cost savings from academic programs than it is from other forms of cooperation.

After an initial period of frustration, some consortia have concentrated their efforts on academic support services, such as library cooperation and faculty development, or in nonacademic areas, such as student services and joint purchasing. Others, after taking a more realistic look at the potential for meaningful academic sharing among their members, have made slow but steady progress in building a wide variety of academic programs.

The kinds of collaborative programs that have developed over the past two decades are as various as the needs that generated them and the kinds of opportunities that have been found to address those needs, but most forms of academic sharing fall into two broad categories: programs that give colleges and universities access to each other's resources through exchange or articulation agreements, and curricular programs that are jointly planned and maintained by the participating institutions. In general, the former type is less difficult to institute and, consequently, more widespread.

Exchange Agreements

One of the earliest and still most prevalent forms of academic sharing is cross-registration, which allows students to enroll in courses at the consortium's other member institutions without paying additional tuition. Cross-registration gives students access to a richer, more diverse curriculum than any one institution can easily make available, and it provides the opportunity for each institution to resist pressures for curricular expansion in fields that are already available within the consortium. This flexibility allows the member institutions to develop complementary offerings in new or emerging fields, or in specialized areas of traditional disciplines when and if resources become available.

The degree to which cooperating institutions are able and willing to take advantage of the opportunities offered by cross-registration agreements will determine how greatly they will benefit from them. Colleges and universities that are geographically close enough to each other to allow for routine movement of students from campus to campus can benefit more extensively than those at greater distances, although proximity alone does not necessarily generate such movement. Neighboring institutions with widely diverse academic missions and curricular needs may find themselves with little to share. A theological seminary and a technical college may live in amicable proximity, yet have little to offer each other academically.

Even institutions with similar missions and curricular objectives may find it difficult to take the fullest advantage of student interchange programs because the climate of institutional relationships is not generally conducive to academic sharing. Traditional rivalries, different educational styles, different academic calendars, and internal concern for protecting "the integrity of the degree" are only a few of the barriers that can slow down student movement among member institutions.

A cross-registration program can be a marginal fringe benefit involving a trickle of students among consortium institutions, or it can be the cornerstone of a system of academic resource sharing that the member institutions may build upon. In order to take full advantage of the opportunities available, colleges and universities must actively encourage student interchange by making cross-registration as convenient as possible. Furnishing information on course offerings at the other member institutions to both students and faculty advisers is essential. Devising simple, clear, and convenient cross-registration procedures and informing students about the rules, regulations, and operational practices of other institutions will help to make the program less formidable.

Providing transportation among the member campuses, if that is needed, will give more students access to courses off the home campus and will help them to fit such courses into their academic schedules. Offering dining privileges at host institutions will provide even more options for students who wish to enroll at another campus. If colleges and universities are unable, or unwilling, to invest administrative time and institutional funds to provide the services that are needed to make cross-registration a convenient option, they cannot count on the complementary strengths of the consortium members significantly to expand educational opportunities for their students.

Most consortia that maintain cross-registration programs also support some form of faculty exchange among their members. Faculty exchange agreements serve much the same purpose as student interchange in that they enrich the curriculum without expanding the size of the faculty; however, the impact on the home institution differs slightly. Cross-registration is geared to serving the needs of individual students, whereas faculty exchanges are meant to strengthen the curriculum offered on the home campus.

The forms of exchange vary. Faculty members may be borrowed from a member institution to teach a course on an overtime basis for an agreed stipend. In other cases, the member institutions may agree to trade courses: two departments of English, for instance, might exchange a course in linguistics and literature for one in modern critical theory, and no money need change hands. A third type of exchange releases part of a professor's time at one institution to provide a course on another campus. Such arrangements are relatively rare and usually involve faculty specialties that no one institution needs full time but that both wish to offer on the home campus. Colleges and universities that make exchanges over greater distances usually make full-time arrangements for a semester or more, or else utilize communications networks to bring faculty members and courses to other campuses through live televised classrooms or taped telecourses.

Faculty exchanges and cross-registration help consortia to capitalize on the educational diversity of their members, but they are also useful in areas where the members are similar. When faculty members go on leave or resign unexpectedly, or when enrollments are unexpectedly high in a given field, students may find equivalent courses on other campuses; or, a faculty member may be borrowed to teach the course on the home campus, thus providing continuity of curriculum.

Successful faculty exchange programs depend upon the willingness of professors to teach off campus (or be televised), and the willingness of the other institutions to use them. These programs work best between departments whose members know each other, or in consortia where there is a broad sense of intellectual community that crosses institutional lines. Once begun, exchanges can actually help to build such community, as more professors experience the rewards of interacting with faculty members and students in another institutional setting. Developing such relationships can be a slow process, but the long-term educational and financial benefits to consortium members are significant.

Colleges and universities that have successfully developed mechanisms for routinely sharing each other's resources are in a position to maximize their complementarity for the greatest mutual benefit through planning and consultation. A history department looking for an Asianist may search for a specialist in Japanese history if Chinese history is available elsewhere in the consortium. Or, two history departments looking for Third World specialists might agree to search in different geographic areas.

Through such agreements, consortia can both avoid unnecessary duplication in disciplinary offerings and make possible interdisciplinary concentrations in a wide variety of fields—area studies, period studies, urban or communication studies—that no one institution could equal acting alone. The result can be an impressive gain in curricular options for students and the opportunity for them to choose among a wide variety of concentrations in developing their educational programs.

Developing academic complementarity, except where it happens fortuitously, can be difficult, however. Since the seat of curricular planning in most colleges and universities is the academic departments, their cooperation in building complementarity is crucial. If departments resist such agreements—whether out of concern for departmental autonomy, inertia, or lack of interest, the opportunities for achieving complementarity will be commensurately fewer.

Joint Curricular Programs

When colleges and universities are already committed to sharing academic resources through various kinds of exchange agreements, it is only a short step, logically, to the joint development of new programs that are deliberately planned in order to meet joint needs. For many institutions, though, this can be a major step in terms of institutional commitment. Exchange agreements, once in place, leave it up to students and faculty members (or departments) to take advantage of resources at member institutions and to piece together curricular programs that suit their own needs. These agreements can function effectively without much attention from the central administrations, and the costs—except perhaps for transportation—are minimal.

Joint programs, on the other hand, articulate for students a program or course of study that is jointly planned and sponsored by the member institutions, and to which they are jointly committed. These programs usually involve extensive planning and may require faculty legislation and even trustee approval. Some, though not all, involve a substantial commitment of institutional (or outside) funds, and most require an interinstitutional governance structure to oversee them. Such programs include joint degree programs, joint departments, joint faculty appointments, and a wide assortment of nondegree programs.

The targets of opportunity for such programs will vary from one group of institutions to another, but they all reflect consensus on the desirability of developing specific curricular programs and the advantages (financial, educational, or both) of maintaining them cooperatively. It is not easy for institutions to arrive at such a consensus very often; hence, joint programs tend to be less common than other forms of academic cooperation. When they succeed, however, they have a kind of multiplier effect, bringing a new measure of distinction to member institutions through a single shared program.

Joint faculty appointments, though not programs in themselves, can be key factors in building and sustaining joint programs. They may fill a crucial gap in an area where no one college or university is willing to make a commitment to a full-time faculty member but when all want access to the specialty for their students. A joint program in East Asian studies, for example, may be weak in Chinese language offerings. A joint appointment is a cost-effective way to strengthen the program without committing any one institution to the whole financial burden of adding another member to its faculty.

The most popular joint ventures are nondegree programs that add a special dimension to the education of students—on campus or away—that would not ordinarily be available. Such programs often become desirable and feasible on a joint basis in cases where no one institution has either a sufficient student pool or the resources to mount nondegree programs alone. Although neighboring colleges and universities are likely to have the widest range of opportunities for developing joint programs, proximity is not essential. Consortial groups of geographically distant colleges and universities with fewer opportunities for exchange have been able to enhance their off-campus programs with a variety of jointly managed programs that provide opportunities for specialized studies not available on the home campuses.

Two pioneers in this area, the Associated Colleges of the Midwest and the Great Lakes Colleges Association, which between them represent 25 liberal arts colleges spread over 8 Midwestern states, offer students opportunities for overseas and area studies in 14 foreign countries on 4 continents as well as advanced study in the arts and sciences at various locations in the United States. Other consortia maintain a variety of similar programs, including summer language institutes, government internships, field research in earth and marine sciences, and advanced study in the humanities and arts.

These programs add a significant dimension to the curricula of the member institutions, helping them to attract and retain superior students who might seek such opportunities elsewhere and providing an added attraction in recruiting faculty members, especially in undergraduate institutions where opportunities for combining teaching and research or field experience tend to be fewer. Campus-based nondegree programs, though usually less exotic, may serve some of the same purposes through undergraduate interdisciplinary centers, special concentrations within the disciplines (early music, volcanology, or children's theater, for example), or career-oriented studies through affiliations with professional schools or agencies.

Most consortial nondegree programs are additions to the basic academic programs of each institution—valuable supplements that enhance and expand the curriculum but do not alter the core. New joint degrees or departments, on the other hand, imply a basic modification or expansion of the academic program offered by each institution. They represent the most advanced level of integration that cooperating colleges and universities are likely to achieve (short of outright merger) in that they become an integral part of the degree-granting structure of each institution. As a result, protecting "the integrity of the degree" becomes a mutual obligation in which all participating institutions have a stake.

Joint degrees or departments may be difficult to negotiate initially, but in some cases they may be the best means for achieving academic excellence in a discipline that all members wish to offer but that has no apparent chance for adequate development at any of the institutions. This was the rationale that led to the creation of a joint astronomy department by Five Colleges in 1962, and to the formation in 1980 of the Westchester Social Work Education Consortium, the only cooperative program maintained by a group of five colleges in southeastern New York.

Joint departments and degree programs are anomalous structures with a paradoxical mode of existence, living both inside and outside each institution. As consortial programs, they serve the needs of the individual members; but as *academic* programs, they are ultimately accountable for the quality of the joint enterprise, to which each institution contributes only a part. Because of this twofold obligation, joint departments and degree programs walk a thin line between institutional autonomy and institutional interdependence.

Since these programs are usually composed of faculty members drawn from different institutions, and since they serve students spread over several campuses, it is in the interest of the member institutions to encourage a mode of operation as close as possible to that of their counterparts within the institutions—that is, as single faculty units maintaining one curriculum serving the needs of one student constituency under a single operating budget. Such a structure allows the faculty to integrate the needs of each participating institution into the planning process for maintaining the integrity of the program as a whole and thus decreases the likelihood of conflicts of interest. It also helps if they operate under a single governance system with an equally complex set of responsibilities.

A certain amount of separate negotiation with the individual institutions is essential, of course; personnel actions and curricular offerings will require institutional approval through the usual channels. Principal oversight of the department, however, should rest with a central (interinstitutional) administrative body that represents not only the individual institutions but also their common responsibility for the quality of the program as a whole. Programs that are able to function as unified bodies under a joint governance system have a better chance to attract the best faculty members to their ranks and thus achieve the distinction that motivated their creation.

There is, then, an enormous range in the degree of institutional involvement and interdependence that colleges and universities have developed to date in cooperative academic programs. If the benefits from academic cooperation have fallen short of the high expectations of some institutions, it is perhaps because they expected too much too soon. Some of the programs cited here as examples presuppose a kind of ideal setting for academic cooperation: institutions that are close enough geographically to allow for routine movement of students and faculty members from campus to campus; colleges or universities with enough commonality in their missions and curricular objectives to permit sharing of faculty members and courses; and a climate of interinstitutional relationships that is receptive to the idea of cooperative ventures as a viable option for meeting curricular needs.

Needless to say, there are very few academic settings in which all of these conditions prevail. For most institutions, something less than the full spectrum of cooperative opportunities is available, and barriers of one kind or another may discourage initiatives that attempt to take advantage of those opportunities that do exist. Not surprisingly, some of the most formidable barriers to cooperation come from within the institutions themselves.

If progress toward meaningful academic sharing has been slow in American higher education, even among institutions that have found ways to cooperate effectively in other areas, many of the reasons are easy to find. Academic cooperation challenges traditional institutional attitudes and practices and requires new forms of institutional behavior. There is nothing sanctified about a purchasing contract (unless it is one with an alumnus), but a grading system is a sacred icon.

Traditionally, the climate of interinstitutional relationships has been competitive rather than cooperative. At the heart of the competition is the institution's claim to academic excellence, resting mainly on the quality of its faculty and its academic program. Institutions have tended to compare themselves to those with whom they compete (or would like to compete) for students, faculty members, outside funds, and prestige; those outside the competitive circle can be politely ignored. For those who think in this vein, collaboration with one's rivals is faintly treasonous and with one's "inferiors" demeaning. Either course promises to compromise one's status as a competitor.

This traditional psychological impasse is reinforced by the tendency of academic institutions to resist any change in their internal structure and routine operations. Highly articulated organizations, each is intricately and complexly structured to pursue academic excellence, and to protect the integrity of its degree, in its own way. And most institutions are indeed set in their ways. Accommodation to interinstitutional programs raises fears about loss of institutional autonomy, the lowering of academic standards, and the invasion of "turf" heretofore protected by the internal structure of the institution. To those who regard cooperation as a threat to the institution or, in some instances, to their personal status, the sea of cooperative opportunities may seem like shark-infested waters.

These barriers to cooperation, which Frank E. Vandiver, president of Texas A & M University, summarized in *Science* (August 24, 1984) as "habit, history, and hubris," can make slow work of getting together academically. On the other hand, their relative absence does not necessarily make cooperation easy. Even when faculty members and administrators are favorably disposed toward the idea in principle, other factors may limit the institutions' opportunities for academic sharing.

Limited time and scarce financial resources are two chronic deterrents to cooperative initiatives. Planning, developing, and sustaining cooperative academic programs takes time and energy, not to mention tact and patience. Many faculty members, jealous of their time and typically resentful of committee obligations—or meetings of any kind—may feel that cooperating is simply more trouble than it is worth. Busy administrators, their hands already full, may resist the claims that cooperation would make on their time and attention.

A similar problem arises in the allocation of financial resources. Most cooperative academic programs cost money. To be sure, a few of them actually make money, and some break even, but most of them require at least a modest investment of institutional funds. However cost-effective they may prove to be in the long range—stretching institutional dollars through sharing costs—they still must compete with internal programs. When funds are scarce and the internal competition for resources is intense, new cooperative initiatives may be given lower priority, or even be ruled out.

Given the many factors that can discourage cooperative initiatives, it is scarcely surprising that more institutions have not voluntarily committed themselves to academic sharing, nor that efforts to legislate regional coordination have had uneven success. What should surprise us, perhaps, is that so many institutions have found ways to cooperate effectively in spite of themselves.

Some of the considerations that enter into the process of helping things along have been adumbrated earlier, but there is no set formula for guaranteeing success, since every consortium is in a real sense unique, with its own combination of problems and opportunities. Nevertheless, some broad generalizations are possible about ways in which institutions can actively develop the conditions under which cooperation is most likely to thrive.

Providing Leadership through Institutional Commitment

In academic programs, as in other major areas of cooperation, the first and most fundamental desideratum is commitment among the leadership of the consortium to the cooperative enterprise. Institutional leaders—presidents, chancellors, deans, and the like—must encourage and support academic cooperation and commit their institutions to a financial and academic policy of continuing support. To be sure, a certain number of ad hoc cooperative arrangements or projects for special purposes can develop within any institution without much attention from the central administration, thriving on benign neglect so long as they do not strain institutional resources or rock the institutional boat. But such enterprises will be very limited in kind and number unless cooperation is widely perceived as a priority concern of the leadership.

The degree of institutional commitment, and therefore the likelihood of cooperative success, might be roughly measured by how many of the following questions would be answered "yes":

- Are the member institutions willing and able to define common needs and common goals?

- Is each member clear about what it hopes to gain through the cooperative program, and is there a reasonable expectation that these gains can be realized?

- Are the members prepared to provide adequate financial resources and administrative support to make the program work? Are they willing to furnish some "hard money" support?

- Is each institution willing to bend itself a little to adjust or revise some of its regulations, procedures, or policies in order to accommodate cooperative activity?

- Is each institution prepared to publicize its commitment to the cooperative program to its own constituencies—faculty, staff, students, and alumni?

Developing a Central Organization

A strong central organization gives form and voice to institutional commitment. It provides a mechanism and structure for institutions to define common needs and to pursue common goals, as well as a staff to help plan, implement, and monitor specific programs that achieve these goals.

The roles of the central staff in supporting academic cooperation are multiple and complex. First, the staff functions as both intermediary and advocate—intermediary among faculty members from different institutions (and, at times, from different disciplines), and advocate on behalf of faculty needs and objectives as their representative to the central governing structure of the cooperative enterprise. In order to perform the dual function of intermediary and advocate, the staff must have access to institutions at every administrative level of their governance structure.

Without such open lines of communication, it is extremely difficult for those responsible for cooperative programs to follow up on decisions and to monitor their implementation.

The second major role of the staff is to provide substantial administrative assistance to faculty members who are engaged in cooperative projects. In a specific sense, the staff may be called upon to coordinate meeting times, to record deliberations, to facilitate discussion, to arbitrate disagreements, and, over time, to precipitate consensus. This type of staff support helps to overcome inertia in the planning process and minimizes the time and effort that faculty members must give to the consortial enterprise.

Building a Consortial Community

The commitment of leadership and the formation of a central organization, though essential, are not in themselves enough to provide the climate in which academic cooperation will flourish. Any academic program, even a modest one such as occasional teacher interchange, requires the good will of faculty members and the approval of departments. More elaborate programs involve faculty members in time-consuming deliberations and planning with their counterparts from other institutions. Since strangers make poor bedfellows, it is in the interest of the institutions to find as many ways as possible to encourage faculty interaction across institutional lines.

Faculty members who have previously met congenially as colleagues discussing subjects of mutual professional interest will usually be more willing to work together than those who have only their institutional biases to bring to the planning table. Of course, there will be a number of existing personal and professional friendships among members of neighboring faculties, and these can be the starting point for developing more organized modes of interaction.

Jointly sponsored conferences, lecture series, or symposia, with attendant opportunities for social mingling, will encourage a sense of intellectual community that can provide the basis for further activity. Such groups are especially useful for establishing new professional communities across disciplines. Faculty members with kindred interests, if given a little assistance and funding, might establish seminar groups, meeting at regular intervals during the semester or year, for the purpose of sharing works in progress, discussing current issues in the field, and hosting guest speakers. Latin Americanists, medievalists, neuroscientists, or others who have relatively few colleagues at home will welcome the expanded opportunities for professional interaction that the consortium offers. If familiarity sometimes breeds contempt, it can also breed enthusiasm—for guest lectures in the classroom, for team teaching, and for collaboration in research.

The most fruitful outcome of faculty seminars or other developmental activity may well be the creation of new curricular offerings or even joint cooperative programs. Moreover, participants in consortium-sponsored professional activities will be more likely to become advocates of the cooperative enterprise, thus helping to alleviate the fears and to overcome the recalcitrance of their less-adventurous colleagues at home.

Creating Incentives

To help counterbalance institutional constraints and reward systems that retard cooperative development, it is important to offer consortial rewards and other forms of support that encourage this development. To be sure, cooperation that produces such direct and visible effects as the opportunity to devise new courses or to establish new directions in research will be evident in the professional achievements of the faculty members concerned. Thus, it will carry its own reward, and faculty members are likely to embrace it.

Specific incentives, though, are often necessary to support and to promote additional forms of academic cooperation. Establishing a central pool of resources to finance new activities growing out of faculty planning efforts will encourage joint planning and will provide the incentive to build new programs through resource sharing—programs for curricular development, cooperative research, joint faculty appointments, interdisciplinary seminars, and many more.

It may be difficult for institutions to find or to raise funds for such projects, but without this or some other incentive, many faculty members will feel that they have nothing to gain—instead, something to lose—from cooperating.

Conclusion

Many of the challenges facing higher education in the 1980s are different from those that prompted institutions to look for cooperative solutions 20 or more years ago. An expanding (and inflationary) economy has stabilized, but the costs of education continue to generate pressure on college and university curricula, while public support for higher education is diminishing. Colleges reacting to a dwindling pool of "traditional" students, plentiful 20 years ago, are scrambling to adjust their programs to attract "adult learners."

In short, while the new challenges, like the old, boil down to the perennial problem of allocating limited resources to provide quality education in a rapidly changing society, for many colleges and universities the challenges are more acute now than then, as the problem of maintaining quality shades into the question of survival.

The purpose of cooperation in the 1980s is, as it was in the 1960s, to enhance the educational offerings of the individual institutional members. However, financial constraints and competitive pressures, requiring that institutions focus and rationalize their efforts, have modified some of the immediate objectives of cooperation. Whereas institutions originally viewed cooperative arrangements as convenient mechanisms for providing diversity, flexibility, and experimentation, in the 1980s they are increasingly viewing them as mechanisms for better allocating limited resources, for maintaining the quality image of the institution through times of financial strain, and, in extreme cases, for ensuring the survival of the institution itself. Cooperative programs and agreements were the vehicles of growth and expansion during the 1960s; today, they may be becoming the vehicles for consolidation, focus, and self-preservation.

—3—

Professional Development

LARRY L. ROSE

My purpose is to encourage readers to strengthen professional development activities in the consortia with which they are affiliated or, conceivably, to create consortia for that purpose. The argument is that professional development is one of the areas in which interinstitutional cooperation is most effective and, for practical and educational reasons, it ought to be developed as a consortial activity as fully as possible. The practical reason is that academic consortia need to grasp their opportunities and to pursue them vigorously. The educational reason is that professional development is too important to be left entirely to the colleges and universities.

Left to their own devices, college and university administrators, like most other professionals, will not place sufficient emphasis on the importance of professional development and, as a result, will not plan for it carefully and systematically. The voluntary academic consortium can make an important, substantive contribution to its member institutions by doing for them what, bluntly put, they will not do for themselves: by helping them cooperate to institute a carefully and systematically arranged, substantive and purposeful, program of professional development for faculty members and for administrators.

The Kansas City Regional Council on Higher Education (KCRCHE) was founded in 1962. KCRCHE manages cooperative purchasing, professional development, and promotion for 19 colleges and universities in the Kansas City area.

47

It is necessary to qualify that bald assertion. Given the thinness of the program budgets of most consortia, it is unlikely that there are sufficient funds to mount a comprehensive program. Equally, centralized programs cannot attend to idiosyncratic institutional needs and will not reach large numbers of faculty members and middle managers. For these reasons, an effective professional development program will combine institutional and centralized programs. Ideally, many of the former will also be shared activities, open to participation by staff members at other consortium institutions.

Why Cooperate?

There are additional reasons why it is appropriate for a consortium of colleges and universities to cooperate on faculty and staff development. For one thing, it is one of the activities that meets all of the tests for effective cooperation. In our consortium we ask: Is it feasible? Is it important? Do the members want it? Not many programs pass all three tests. Cooperative professional development does.

It is by now a truism that collegiate cooperation is more effective in administrative than in academic areas. This has to do, apparently, with the academic integrity and felt autonomy of institutions, as well as with issues of feasibility. The result is that many consortia, including my own in Kansas City, become preoccupied with administrative support services and wind up with a kind of "nuts and bolts" approach to cooperation and few significant academic accomplishments. Professional development thrusts the consortium directly into issues of educational importance. The result is a greater contribution and, for the consortium, greater respectability.

There has been much gnashing of teeth among consortium directors about the difficulty of achieving academic cooperation—meaning arrangements for shared curricula. I contend that, those issues notwithstanding, effective professional development for faculty members and for administrators is a significant and telling instance of academic cooperation. In fact, there is more good to be done by this means than by most largely marginal programs of curricular cooperation.

Beyond that, it is cost-effective for a group of institutions to manage staff development cooperatively. This point is so obvious that it does not need elaboration. Suffice to say: If I can hire one consultant on an issue of common concern for 15 colleges and universities, those institutions have achieved an important cost benefit (defined in this case as cost avoidance).

Cooperative professional development puts the consortium on the academic map. It provides an intelligent and thoroughgoing approach to a problem that colleges and universities are otherwise likely to neglect. And it is a superb instance of cost-effective college administration. There is more.

Some professionals will go off campus for training but will shun more visible campus events. Intercollegiate events make possible active sharing of information across institutional boundaries—and there is no substitute for hearing how other practitioners are doing things. Some consultants are more easily attracted to an event at which a group of colleges and universities will be present, preferring to use their time for wider institutional impact. And, off campus, it is easier to ask difficult questions and, sometimes, easier to admit ignorance. My experience is that those who learn most from an in-service training event are those who find it easiest to ask questions and, in that process, to say what they do not know.

Some Problems

There is no such thing as an unadulterated good. That is why each of us surely must plan to write a book some day on the ambiguities of life. Cooperative professional development presents problems as well as attractive advantages.

It is difficult to tell what the real needs are. Formal needs assessments are notoriously flawed. To the extent to which the consortium office is viewed as an outside agency, it will be even more difficult to get helpful responses from the member institutions and their personnel. The consortium staff must use a skillful blend of research, personal contacts, educational experience, and common sense in order to put together a program that is genuinely helpful.

Sometimes you win; sometimes you do not. My advice is that your best ally in this battle is your own educational experience, and that you should trust your judgment about what people need to know, especially on broad issues in higher education. Often the consortium director has a better view of the entire educational process than any of his or her campus colleagues, by virtue of having to be regularly involved with the work of most of them.

Another problem is that running conferences is a difficult business. For every conference that is successful, there is one with marginal results.

There are many reasons for this, most commonsensical. One is that there are too many variables for any person or agency to control. Worse, some of those variables are entirely outside our control—for example, what the consultant will, with the best of coaching, finally say.

Presenting conferences is a little like professional gambling. It is in the final analysis a matter of chance. The challenge is managing the risk effectively and, in the process, arranging the odds in your favor. One useful strategy is controlling the conference agenda yourself, making yourself the moderator—even to the point of giving the consultant tactful but firm direction during the course of the day.

Perhaps the most significant problem with cooperative approaches to staff development is the "class effect." Even though we may agree with President James Garfield that the ideal college is Mark Hopkins on one end of a log and the student on the other, we meet students in groups (classes) because it is economically effective to do so. The result is that instruction often proceeds less effectively than it might, because the students represent widely varying stages of growth in their understanding of the subject matter.

When, in our consortium, we have the opportunity to do so, we assign a person with a problem a consultant, for just this reason. Far more often, however, the issue in question is one being faced by a large number of people, and we decide to mount a conference. The challenge, then, is to minimize the "class effect" and, in doing so, to maximize the likelihood of success of the conference. Notice that this is far more likely to be a problem when working with a group of institutions than it would be in the normal campus setting—for all the obvious reasons.

There are some remedies:

- Concentrate your conferences in areas in which most institutions have, as yet, little experience. This is a good incentive for staying on the cutting edge of issues in higher education.

- Vary that approach by offering certain meetings with broad, perennial themes. Time management (to select a commonplace example) is an organizational problem that does not entail cumulative knowledge.

- Give target audiences as much information as possible about the program, so that individuals will be able to self-select based on their interests and previous experience.

- Always encourage conference participants to be active questionners. Student-centeredness and active participation are useful antidotes to differential preparation.

Strategies for Successful Cooperation

One of the virtues of a consortial approach to professional development is that the consortium has a bigger bag of tricks than a single institution has, both quantitatively and qualitatively. There is substantial expertise, already assembled in the consortial group, to call on; and there are more strategies available to the consortium director than to the campus coordinator of faculty or staff development activities.

Campuses can give grants (sometimes large ones, called sabbaticals), or they can convene conferences (or send their personnel away to attend these). Consortia can do the same things. In addition, consortia can offer consultation and information to individuals. Often, neither a grant nor a conference is relevant to the learning that a staff member or a faculty member needs. That person may need to get some information and get it quickly—and the information clearinghouse capabilities of a consortium are a very significant supplement to the resources available on the campus or through other professional connections. I can put current personnel policies in the hands of a needy dean in 24 hours, a turnaround time that that dean simply cannot get anywhere else, and information that he or she has no other means of getting.

Sometimes the need goes beyond information to consultation. In that case, the consortium is equally well equipped to help. It is rare that a campus can afford to hire a consultant to train a single individual, but it is common to make that kind of arrangement within the network of colleges and universities that constitute the consortium. I can find the person who has already worked through the problem and arrange for a consultation at an early date and at no cost. That service is understood in the member institutions to be a collegial matter that will be returned in kind, in due course. The important point here is that the consortium is peculiarly well suited, by its very nature as an association of colleges and universities, to serve professional development needs.

A parallel point that bears further comment is that "professional development" is a marshmallow phrase, and we ought to be clearer than we are about what we mean by it. The trick is to look at the problem, to look at the options, and to develop a solution that fits. It is not appropriate, on the campus or in the consortium, to create a professional development "program." Typically, we make such arrangements in nearly complete isolation from any tangible sense of what we are trying to accomplish thereby. There is no effective professional development apart from specific problems that need to be solved. And, just as the problems differ, so do the styles and the content of the potential solutions.

The appropriate strategy is to identify a training or educational need and then decide which of the battery of developmental tools at our disposal is the one that is most likely to be effective in that case. If a counselor wants to know more about the Myer-Briggs Type Indicator, that may be

- a reference question, in which case office material is mailed;

- a referral question, which leads to a telephone conversation with a counselor at another institution;

- a modest research question, in which case we administer a survey or otherwise locate the information;

- a larger research question, for which a small staff development grant is appropriate;

- a consultation question, for which we locate an expert within the consortium who will visit the campus and offer assistance; or

- a conference question, in which case others with the same problem come together in order to share information, to hear a consortium consultant or, as a last resort, to hear from an outside expert.

It is useful to point out that the standard approach to staff development—hire a consultant and schedule a conference—is the last and, often, least likely of the range of options available to the consortium director. That all these options should be examined is a lesson about managing professional development. That all of them are available only in a consortium setting is a lesson about locating professional development.

Financing the Program

Consortial professional development programs will be paid for mostly out of the collected annual dues of the members or from the most recent foundation grant. Sometimes some of the costs can be defrayed by selling the service to nonmember institutions and individuals. When campus programs are opened up to participation by persons from other member institutions, financial considerations do not ordinarily obtain. In general it is appropriate to bargain with outside consultants, pleading poverty. And, as I have stressed in the comments just above, the beauty of consortial professional development is that the consultative resources of many institutions are put at the service of the needs of any one of them, for little or no cost.

One of the most critical unresolved problems of financing cooperative staff development is that of substituting local for national programs. Consortium directors should weep at the funds their members spend to send personnel away for conferences. If even a fraction of those funds could be spent on local programs, the return on investment would multiply at an incredible rate. Consider that institution X spends $50,000 per year on conference-related staff travel. Consider that the colleague institutions of the consortium (10 of them, for example) average the same amount. And consider, further, that half of that expenditure is for access to conference topics and experts that would be of interest to persons in other institutions with similar problems.

If, under those circumstances, that same money could be spent to bring the consultants to the area, for conference programs in which many college and university staff members could participate, a quarter of a million dollars worth of professional development services would have been discovered; each institution's professional development budget would, effectively, have become $300,000; and, over and over again, not one person but 20 would have been trained. On this subject there is work to be done.

Our Experience in Kansas City

In the Kansas City Regional Council for Higher Education (KCRCHE), we have been at work on staff development for about 10 years. We have tried a lot of different things, since one of the nice aspects of consortium work is that you can experiment without being burdened by failure. The result is that there have been, in our 10-year experience, more than 20 different programs and projects in professional development.

A standard and popular approach is grants. Before we ever conceived of a consortial program in staff development, we were administering Title III funds for faculty development. Those grants were sizable, and they were research-oriented. Later, we ran a small-grants program under the auspices of the W. K. Kellogg Foundation. That program was flexible in funding whatever the staff member thought would be useful for career advancement, and the grants were made as part of a larger program of personal consultation and career planning. More recently we have focused our grant activity on the improvement of teaching and have made that a criterion for the awards.

My conclusions are as follows:

- Consortium activity in the grants area is highly desirable, providing as it does one more place for staff members to look for support and one more set of "carrots" to get them to think about change.

- Foundations and corporations look favorably on consortium administration of such programs and, often, there is money there for the taking.

- Small grants are adequate as an incentive for change.

- Bureaucratic arrangements should be kept to a minimum, and extensive reporting on results is not necessary.

- Participating colleges and universities should contribute some matching funds.

- Except for certain very broad eligibility criteria (e.g., teaching effectiveness), you will do well to allow the applicants as much latitude as possible; in general, they are better judges of what they need than we are.

Consultation is another approach to staff development that is peculiarly well suited to the consortial setting. We have had some grants that included "pass-through" monies for campus consultation, with the college or university responsible for arranging for its own consultants. We are now exploring a new cooperative consultation program that would bring nationally known consultants to the city, several times over the course of a year, for conversations with groups of campus administrators.

On this latter point, it seems to me that we have vastly overstated the degree to which college and university programs and problems are different. Colleges are colleges are colleges. Improved money management, for example, requires the same introductory reviews and lessons at one institution as at another. It seems likely that arrangements for one consultant to meet with several financial managers, in a series of group sessions, would be a cost-effective approach to staff development and institutional change. Time between sessions could be spent on institutional adaptations. Additional consultation time, to deal with idiosyncrasies, could of course be scheduled. This approach could be used with a variety of problems and administrative positions, so "group consultation" may be one area for consortial development that has important potential. It is importantly different from conferences, in that institutional problems are put first and the style is one of problem solving, not theorizing.

Our experience in KCRCHE is that consultation by the consortium staff is, mostly, not accepted—however generously offered. Consultation by colleagues from other institutions is more effective, and we will soon be making even more systematic use of campus people for this purpose. Our experience is also very pointed on the subject of local versus national consultants. Unlike the conference setting, where the distinctions are much less telling, there is simply no substitute for using someone with extensive national experience (when you can afford it).

Conferences are of course the mainstay of a consortium professional development program. I estimate that KCRCHE has held some 750 of them during the last 10 years. Our current conference programs include a teaching effectiveness series, a management effectiveness series, a special conference series, an exemplary programs series, administrator conferences, and discipline-group conferences.

For these conferences we have used a very large number of nationally known educators, both academic and administrative. As a group they are good consultants, but they are depressingly poor as conference presenters. Since we know that expert knowledge does not guarantee good classroom teaching, we should not be surprised that that is true of conference presenters as well. In my estimation, nationally known presenters are usually not worth the money.

Our least effective conference sessions are those with very broad topics. The most effective conferences involve clearly defined topics and carefully targeted groups. Most of our meetings are half-day sessions. Our experience is that there are few topics that need a full day.

The most difficult meetings are those for faculty members. Since faculty members are primarily interested in their subject matter, the most desirable model is the professional meeting. But the groups are usually not large enough to justify a number of concurrent sessions; and, failing that, some are sure to say, "The papers are not in my area of interest." We have not found a good formula for faculty discipline groups.

The most successful meetings are those for colleague administrators. We routinely bring together groups of administrators for the sharing of ideas and information. The agenda is informal, constructed on the spot from those issues people are currently concerned about. Such a meeting, for academic deans for example, offers a professional development opportunity, with regional peers, that cannot be duplicated anywhere. A program of administrator conferences is one of the most effective things that a consortium can do and is, by itself, sufficient reason for its being.

Such a program does more for the professional development of campus administrators than anything else they do, at home or away.

In addition to conferences and consultation and grants, our consortium has offered a student-centered instructional improvement program, using a train-the-trainers methodology; a series of policy-issues conferences, focusing on key issues in higher education; educational ideas symposia, focusing on important intellectual issues; personal growth groups, for career counseling and development; full-semester, credit-bearing seminars in teaching and in management, under the auspices of a grant from the Fund for the Improvement of Post-Secondary Education; a program of "excellence in teaching" awards; a faculty development newsletter; and a higher education issues newsletter.

We also provide what we call a "telephone reference service," in which staff members are invited to call the consortium office for assistance on job or professional development problems. We handle well over a hundred requests a year, many of which become "paper-and-pencil surveys" of colleague institution information.

The Challenge to Consortia

The general argument of this chapter is that the consortium setting is an excellent place to do professional development. The assumptions are that a group of colleges and universities can devise a better program by working together and that they can operate that program cost-effectively. I also assume that a good professional development program will include on-campus work as well, which, when combined with national meetings, results in a three-part professional development program for the consortium's members.

It is important for consortium staff members to remind themselves that their purpose is to help their member institutions do together those things that they cannot do individually. Hence, an evaluation of proper professional development activities in a consortium setting should always examine whether that objective is being met.

Most administrators have substantial professional opportunities through regional and national conferences and, usually, adequate travel budgets to take advantage of those opportunities. For them, the key consortial advantages are collegiality and informality. Only the local or regional consortium can provide an opportunity for meetings with peers with whom one will have an ongoing relationship and with whom one feels sufficiently comfortable to talk openly about professional problems and challenges.

The style of most regional and national professional meetings mitigates against real candor in sharing information. Acquaintance developed in the consortium setting, combined with a deliberately open style, makes possible a level of sharing that cannot be accomplished anywhere else. I am a very strong advocate of informal conferences for colleague groups: I believe that there is more learned there than in any other professional development setting. The voluntary, academic consortium is the perfect place to make that happen. This is our central professional development contribution to campus administrators.

The situation with faculty members is much more problematic. As I have indicated above, it is difficult to duplicate in the consortium setting the kind of professional meeting most disciplinary faculty members seem to prefer. Alternatives, including discussions of teaching and of curriculum, are useful but will appeal to a limited number of people. Yet unlike administrators those campus faculty members, especially those teaching at small colleges, do not have the travel budgets to allow them to take advantage of regional and national opportunities for professional development.

This means that the consortium must continue to provide opportunities for faculty development. We must continue to experiment with alternative methods for interesting and attracting faculty members. And, in general, the informal, collegial model that I have advocated for administrators strikes me as the best one for faculty members as well. It is more difficult because faculty members have more "hang-ups" about status and because they are, as a result, less likely to share their teaching and research problems with one another. But that is a problem to be overcome, not a reason for inaction.

In our consortium we are reinstituting our series of disciplinary meetings. Based on past experience, we will be pleased to reach 20% of the eligible participants. In doing so we will have accomplished something that could not have been done otherwise. Only the local or regional consortium can provide an opportunity for meetings with peers with whom one will have an ongoing relationship and with whom one feels sufficiently comfortable to talk openly about professional problems and challenges.

The Bottom Line

One of the reasons for doing professional development in the consortium setting is that it is "safe." The member colleges and universities can do things through the consortium that they cannot do at home. There is room for experimentation and for failure. You can ask the difficult questions and mount radical programs, and you can get away with it. Academic consortia are, at their best, powerful agents for change.

In the case of faculty development, the academic consortium has an opportunity and a responsibility to press hard for teaching improvement. We can take risks that no campus academic officer can take. And the risk in this case is calling direct attention to ineffective teaching and proposing to do something about it.

As important, I suggest that what we have tried to do about improving teaching during the last 15 years of the faculty development movement has, for the most part, missed the mark. That is so because the main problem with teaching is not a problem of process, but one of content; not a problem of technique, but one of aims; not a problem of style, but one of outcomes.

The challenge of good teaching in the undergraduate program is to clarify the objectives of the course and to develop a coherent plan for achieving those objectives. Most of our faculty development programs, however, have concentrated on teaching techniques, not on the aims of teaching. In the process, we have missed a great opportunity.

The problem with undergraduate education is that, often, we are not clear about its objectives; and, even when we are, we do not have any way of determining whether or not we achieved those objectives. If that is true of the curriculum as a whole, it is even more painfully true of individual courses in that curriculum. The problem is not "covering the content"; nor is it, as most faculty development programs have rephrased it, "improving the presentation of the content." The problem is, What do we want these students to learn, how will we see that they do it, and how will we know if they did?

Faculty development programs in the 1980s and 1990s should be about the learning objectives of courses and of the curriculum. Having assured ourselves that we know the subject matter, and having reviewed our capabilities for presenting and displaying that subject matter, we now must give direct attention to *why* we are teaching that subject matter and what is to happen as a result of teaching it. In sum, faculty development programs must become "outcomes-oriented."

Faculty members, as a group, do not understand this issue. To understand it and to deal with it will take deliberate training and retraining. To help faculty members understand the issue of "college outcomes" or results; to help them understand ways of effectively measuring the achievement of college outcomes; to help them work together in order to institute comprehensive college-outcomes systems at their institutions; and to help them adapt those same techniques to their own coursework—those are the challenges for faculty development. To the extent to which the purpose of good administration is to provide the environment in which the aims of the institutions can be realized, they are the challenges for administrator development as well.

The major item on the agenda for consortial staff development, then, is clarity about college outcomes and systems for securing those outcomes. If consortia pursue that issue effectively, many students will get a better education than they otherwise would have gotten. That would be an accomplishment worth savoring.

—4—

Library Services and Information Technologies

RICHARD H. DUNFEE

Libraries serve a number of vital functions on the American college campus. It is in this institutional unit that responsibility rests for the collection, storage, and dissemination of information. Also, libraries function as the major support mechanism for new academic offerings and the basis of the continuing strength of existing programs.

Because of the importance of this mission, decisions about library services today pose serious challenges for higher education administrators. Budgets are declining in terms of "real" dollar purchasing power. Resource acquisition options multiply as tough decisions are made about what can be eliminated from the local holdings. The costs of necessary library technologies escalate as user demand for these services increases. In response to this crisis, librarians have chosen increasing levels of cooperation and interdependence as a means for maintaining the integrity of library programs.

The Colleges of Mid-America (CMA), established in 1968, includes eight private, liberal-arts colleges in South Dakota and Iowa. The primary mission of CMA's cooperative activity involves strengthening both the academic and the student-life programs on the individual campuses.

61

It could be asserted that no aspect of interinstitutional cooperation dates further back than library resource sharing. Since the founding of higher education in this country, libraries have cooperated through formal and informal systems of interlibrary loan. Today it is impossible for libraries to operate in isolation. Each depends on a sophisticated and complicated system of regional, state, national, and international networks.

In the environment of the 1980s, the difficult decision related to library and information management in higher education is not whether to engage in cooperative activity; instead, college and university administrators are required to choose among a multitude of associations that offer a variety of services to the individual institution. The quality of user service and information resource delivery in the future hinges on these decisions about interinstitutional cooperation.

The expansion and growth of library cooperation is chronicled in *The Report on Library Cooperation 1984.* Since 1976, the number of organized cooperative associations has grown from 515 to 806—a 57% increase during this eight-year period. Until the 1960s, many institutions sought to hold in their collections all the information needed by the college or university and the geographic community they served. Although this goal was always seen as difficult to attain, the "information explosion" has made it virtually an impossibility. In the words of Douglas Bryant, former director of the Harvard University Library:

> This doctrine of self-sufficiency is finally coming to be realized for what it is: a will-o'-the-wisp. We are seeing at last the gradual abandonment of this creed, even for the very largest of libraries. That any library could provide all the resources for research required by its readers is now generally recognized by scholars and librarian, albeit reluctantly, as an unattainable aspiration.
>
> Accordingly, a sharing of holdings among libraries is increasingly accepted as an ineluctable necessity and as the only realistic means of providing the full range of resources needed for scholarly research. ("The Changing Research Library," *Library Science,* 4, p. 2.)

Thus, the doctrine of self-sufficiency has been abandoned, and the need to engage in the extensive sharing of resources now and in the future has been established.

Why Cooperate?

There are essentially four environmental and institutional factors that have compelled librarians to choose cooperative means for solving campus information problems. First, an individual library can no longer cope with the dramatic increase in the number of books and periodicals being published. It is now estimated that the amount of information in all of its forms doubles every 10 to 15 years. The number of books published worldwide has increased to over 500,000 per year, and the production levels continue to grow. In the face of this flood of information, it becomes impossible to maintain adequate holdings at even the largest libraries.

Second, as information acquisition needs have increased, college and university budget allocations for libraries have declined in "real" dollars. Although the average share of institutional budgets committed to the acquisition of information resources has declined only slightly—from 4% in 1976 to 3.6% in 1980, inflation in the publication industry has served to make the buying-power loss significant. Colleges and universities have therefore found it increasingly difficult to acquire the books, periodicals, and other resources required for scholarship.

Third, information technologies have increased the abilities of higher education institutions to communicate with one another. At the same time, advances in equipment have also created new learning-information storage media. This has prompted many institutions to commit significant proportions of their budgets to library equipment acquisition. In order to offset the increased costs and to utilize equipment capabilities fully, librarians have been encouraged to explore resource-sharing strategies.

Finally, technological development has also afforded opportunities for simplifying some traditional library-management tasks. For example, ordering and cataloging functions can be handled through technological systems, resulting in less duplication of effort in each library. Librarians are encouraged to take advantage of these cooperative systems in order to reduce personnel and overhead expenses.

Forms of Cooperation

Cooperation between and among institutions comes in many forms. Various organizational structures serve to support educational decision makers as they seek to solve the serious problems facing libraries in the 1980s.

INTERLIBRARY LOAN

A standard feature of virtually all library programs is interlibrary loan. Whether an individual library engages in formal or informal resource sharing, interlibrary loan has become an ever-increasing means of delivering resource materials needed by students and faculty members. Almost all libraries employ standard forms for interlibrary transactions and follow rules based on those established in the American Library Association Interlibrary Loan Code.

Loan service has become so common in recent years that many libraries use multiple access or tiered approaches to searching the holdings of other libraries. First, the resources of libraries within the immediate geographic area are examined. Loan policies tend to be most liberal on this local level, and many formal cooperative services agreements exist. Next, the search is expanded to the state and, if necessary, to the region and nation. Finally, it is possible to engage in international interlibrary loan activity, although this is not common and is often unsuccessful because of the inability of some libraries to share material across national borders.

Problems in interlibrary loan have arisen as the number of transactions have increased. Many large research libraries have been flooded with requests for materials, whereas they have little need to borrow from those libraries making the greatest loan demands from them. It has recently become more common, therefore, to have loan requests rejected or ignored when formal agreements do not exist. It has also become standard practice for some libraries to charge a fee for loan services to help defray the costs associated with this activity.

In order to overcome the problems connected with interlibrary loan, many existing consortia have added library cooperation programs to their lists of activities or have undertaken new cooperation initiatives that have library resource sharing as their primary goal. Additionally, most states have implemented interlibrary loan systems in order to meet the demands of their library patrons.

Because of the need for prompt delivery of library loan materials, the bulk of the resource sharing is taking place today on the local level. Urban library organizations like the Cooperative Libraries in Consortium (Saint Paul, Minnesota) and the Chicago Academic Library Council have established formal procedures for sharing library resources. The activities of these local consortia often include a courier service to speed document delivery.

In more rural settings, colleges and universities have found it advantageous to associate with institutions within their region, and it is not uncommon to find multitype library cooperatives that include public, college and university, and school libraries. MINITEX in Minnesota was founded for this purpose in the early 1970s, and the Wisconsin Library Consortium (WLC) was begun in order to encourage the sharing of resources among academic libraries in that state.

The emphasis today is on more formal interlibrary loan arrangements. This movement minimizes the problems associated with disproportionate reliance on large research libraries and inconsistent fee assessments. When the intercampus transport of materials is also a part of the cooperative activity, the speed of access and delivery is enhanced.

UNION LISTS

Union catalogs and union lists of serials have developed rapidly since the 1940s. The growth of these services has been prompted by the desire of librarians to maintain records of who holds what specific book or periodical. Better information on holdings, in turn, has aided in the growth of interlibrary loan and resource sharing.

Every section of the country and most state library systems cooperate in the publication of union lists that serve to provide regional information on library holdings. On the national level, the *National Union Catalog,* the *Union List of Serials,* and *New Serial Titles* serve as the vehicles for coordination of regional services and provide information on compiled holdings throughout the country.

As regional and local library cooperation has become more formalized, the compilation of union catalogs reflecting the holdings of participating institutions has become more common. A few examples of cooperative arrangements that engage in the collection and distribution of this type of information include MINITEX, whose Minnesota Union List of Serials (MULS) includes the holdings of libraries in three states, and the Pennsylvania Area Library Network (PALINET), which includes catalog listings from over 130 libraries of Pennsylvania, Maryland, Delaware, and New Jersey.

The development of a union catalog means that patrons can obtain information on the holdings of local libraries by visiting only one of the catalog sites. In these cases, the bibliographic information will include a notation of the participating or consortium library at which the book or periodical is held.

SHARED ACCESS

As a natural extension of union lists, many library consortia have developed common checkout procedures and have made arrangements to honor library cards from all participating institutions. For example, in South Dakota, students enrolled at Augustana College can use the library facilities at Sioux Falls College, another member of the North Central University

Center, and can check out materials on their Augustana cards. The introduction of these shared patron-access systems requires that libraries consult and plan with regard to the development of circulation systems, as well as communicate effectively in order to retain control of their holdings.

ACQUISITION COOPERATION

Cooperative collection-development programs serve to divide responsibility for acquisitions among libraries. In most cases, arrangements of this nature have not been strict or rigid in their approach. Instead, most local consortia have focused on nonduplication of periodical subscriptions and have achieved this through informal communications and general agreement among librarians.

Acquisition cooperation is seen as one means of coping with inflation and information-resource proliferation. This is particularly true in the small library, where resource sharing is becoming a critical supplement to collection development. Cooperative collection-development can also be useful in planning for the creation and sharing of specialized or rare-book collections. Such a program exists at the University of North Carolina at Chapel Hill, the University of North Carolina at Greensboro, and Duke University.

In a few cases, cooperative acquisition of specialized holdings has also led to centralized or joint storage activities. Several central storage facilities were developed during the 1940s and 1950s in order to encourage resource sharing. The New England Deposit Library, the Hampshire Interlibrary Center, and the Midwest Interlibrary Center are facilities that were developed to speed interlibrary access to certain of the holdings of the member institutions' libraries.

AUTOMATION

Against the background of significant increases in interlibrary loan and resource sharing among higher education institutions of all types and sizes, librarians are attempting to utilize new technologies in order to speed information exchange. The first communication technology to be adopted for library use was the teletype, or TWX (Teletypewriter Exchange Service). The number of libraries using teletype services grew slowly at first after they were introduced in the early 1950s. This early expansion of technological use was attributable to a few states (led by Indiana) and special-interest library networks (such as the National Library of Medicine), which adopted teletype networking systems.

Growth of the teletype systems was further encouraged by the passage in 1966 of Title III of the Library Services Construction Act. This legislation called for ". . . the establishment and operation of systems or networks of libraries, including state, school, college and university, public, and special libraries, and special information centers. . . ." Following the passage of this legislation, most states created teletype networks, and the number of individual libraries making use of this technology dramatically increased.

Although teletype communication markedly enhanced the speed with which one library could communicate with another, the introduction of computers into library use was the basis for an even greater revolution in information sharing and interlibrary loan activity. During the mid-1960s, early work in introducing the computer as a tool in library work focused on the compilation of union lists. Experiments were undertaken—in New York, in Minnesota, and in North Carolina, to name a few areas—to place in machine-readable form all new acquisitions. Some retrospective conversion was begun at this point, but problems arose due largely to inconsistent data-storage formats and the incompatibility of machine operating languages.

By the mid-1970s, OCLC (originally the Ohio College Library Center) had established itself as the most broadly based union catalog. OCLC introduced on-line cataloging service in 1971 and has grown through the 1980s to become the major source of holdings information for libraries of varying sizes and types. Other library networks that developed and that continue to serve a national clientele are the Library Computer Systems (LCS) in Illinois, the Washington (State) Library Network (WLN), and Research Libraries Information Network (RLIN), which is housed at Stanford University.

In addition to the efforts to automate on college and university campuses, many states have introduced on-line cataloging services during the last 10 years. This movement has been led by Minnesota, New York, Kentucky, and Indiana, among others.

Aside from the fact that OCLC serves today as a national on-line union catalog, one of the greatest contributions of this system has been the prompting of widespread acceptance and use of the MARC format for automated record keeping. Originally developed by the Library of Congress, MARC has become a national standard for machine-readable storage of bibliographical information. Its adoption has served to eliminate some of the problems associated with the incompatibility of holdings records at libraries in various parts of the country.

Since 1980, a great number of regional and local library consortia have begun implementation of automated systems. Initially these computer-based networks were founded on the use of a central (mainframe) computer facility that served various library locations through on-line terminal access. The introduction of these automated systems was prompted by developments on large university campuses with distributed library networks. Ohio State University was one of the first academic libraries to introduce on-line catalog service to its patrons at 26 on-campus library sites. Examples of other cooperative automated systems include the Minnesota State University System Project for Automated Library System (MSUS/PALS), the Southeastern Library Network (SOLINET), and the University of California Statewide System.

The last five years also have seen the development of library software by service vendors and large state and private university libraries. Programs developed at Northwestern University and Virginia Polytechnic Institute and State University, to give examples, are available for purchase. Commercially written software tends to encourage intercampus system compatibility and to increase levels of automated communications possibilities. In fact, it is estimated that 65% of the operating large-scale commercial "turnkey" systems are today being used in more than one library.

As machine-based information storage has proliferated, the capabilities of the computer-based systems have also expanded to the point where automated on-line public access catalogs (OPACs) are replacing the traditional card catalog. Services that are now available through automated systems include:

- cataloging existing holdings and new acquisitions

- maintaining authority files and authority controls

- generating catalog cards, labels, and lists

- handling interlibrary loan communications and maintaining records

- ordering and claiming acquisitions

- recording circulation information and maintaining serials controls

- searching holdings on the basis of author, title, and subject

- performing record-keeping, budgeting, and other administrative functions.

The development of increased computer-storage capability has also had an impact on automated library system development. Powerful microcomputers and networking capabilities, recently introduced, can serve the automation needs of smaller libraries. The Western Pennsylvania Buhl Network (WEBNET) is based on a system of microcomputers linked to a minicomputer at the University of Pittsburgh; and the University of Toronto Library Automated System is now marketing INFOQUEST, a microcomputer-based OPAC software package. OCLC has introduced the LS/2000 software system, which can serve to automate a library system of fewer than 100,000 volumes.

As more libraries introduce automated systems based on the use of the microcomputer, the emphasis on resource sharing is being placed on cooperative planning for hardware and software acquisition, the compatibility of local systems with regional and state networks, and the combination of multiple service options into a single automated system.

DATA BASE ACCESS

Access to remotely stored data bases available from government and commercial operation is one automated service many academic libraries offer today. For the cost of a compatible terminal and printer and the payment of line charges and membership or access fees, library patrons can make use of an increasing number of bibliographic and informational sources. In an environment in which it would be impossible for any but the largest libraries to hold all the specialized indexes to periodicals, reports, and research documents that are currently being produced, access to an automated data base is the best means for providing adequate retrieval systems for information.

The number of service agencies and data bases has grown rapidly during the 1970s and 1980s. The *Directory on On-line Data Bases,* published by CUADRA Associates, lists in its 1983 edition more than 1,800 on-line data bases and 277 service agencies. Utilizing these various information services, an individual library can access information sources as diverse as ERIC (Educational Resources Information Center), *Chemical Abstracts,* United Press International, *Commerce Business Daily,* and the yellow pages (from 5,000 United States cities).

Some of the larger on-line search service companies and agencies are the National Library of Medicine, DIALOG Information Retrieval Service, Bibliographical Retrieval Service (BRS), and SDC Information Service. Through these on-line search services, it is possible to obtain citation lists and entry abstracts.

Cooperative approaches to on-line search services have been useful to individual libraries for three reasons:

- Automated literature searches are more thorough and much less time consuming than manual reference work.

- Access to these data bases requires knowledge of the specific system protocols and key words. Staff members who are well trained and who use the data base searching facilities often are better able to find a desired entry quickly, to target a specific research topic, and to limit the number of reported titles.

- The cost of many of these services is high, particularly for those specialized indexes that may have limited use.

Some local or regional consortia have, therefore, coordinated data base searching activities through one location. The Tri-State College Library Cooperative (28 institutions in Pennsylvania, Delaware, and New Jersey) is an example of a small-college consortium that successfully cooperates in data base access. This strategy reduces the number of trained personnel required to conduct the searches, contains equipment costs (because only one link is needed), and reduces line and service charges (because all activity can take place during low-use time periods). Line charges can be reduced further when facilities exist to prepare the search off-line.

LEARNING RESOURCES SHARING

New technologies have produced change in the typical college or university library that goes beyond systems to handle the library holdings. Many institutions have implemented sophisticated and machine-based learning-resource centers that are typically housed in the library and that are integrated into the ongoing library program. In order to cope with the rapidly expanding software and support materials market, libraries are working cooperatively to purchase machinery, to acquire and experiment with software, and to develop systems to expand usage and access. The media on which these learning resources are stored include laser discs, video tapes, audio tapes, and computer courseware.

Although it is not yet common for libraries to adopt on-line access capabilities between and among campuses, the planning groundwork is being laid for local networks to serve this need. Concerns about machine compatibility, acquisition planning, and methods for resource sharing have interested many consortia over the last several years. As technologies are refined, the possibility exists that on-line links for the transmission of this type of information among and between libraries will be established. As long as copyright regulations are respected, libraries of the future could well utilize existing and emerging fiber-optic, microwave, and satellite capabilities in order to share resources.

Complex Relationships

The foregoing analysis demonstrates that the typical college and university library sits at the center of a complex (and sometimes confusing) matrix of consortia, service agencies, and membership organizations. These relationships can occur at several levels, as illustrated in Figure 4.1.

On the local level, institution A (which is hypothetical but will not be atypical by 1990) is a member of an urban library consortium. The three colleges and one university in this group established a formal relationship in order to develop a shared on-line public access catalog (OPAC). This automated system provides full user services, including the capability to perform subject, title, and author searches. A student or faculty member at any one of the library sites can access the holdings of all four institutions.

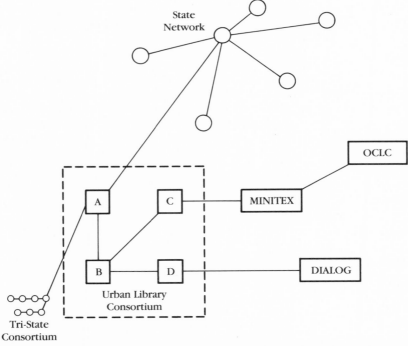

Figure 4.1. Cooperative Relationships Involving the Library System.

Since circulation is also a part of the system, the library user can determine the status of the title—whether it is on reserve, checked out, etc.—and can also request that the book or periodical be held in the user's name for up to 12 hours. All of this information can be obtained and requests generated through the use of the automated system.

The card catalogs at the four institutions have been abolished. In their place, 8 to 15 terminals at each site provide access to the 1.5 million titles held by the four libraries. The large minicomputer that serves the system is housed at institution B. On-line terminal links serve as the basis of the communications network from the three remote sites to the central processing unit.

Librarians and other college administrators at the four institutions have engaged in a great deal of planning with regard to the compatibility of circulation systems, holdings control, and holdings development. Attempts have been made to minimize duplications in acquisitions, and plans are currently under way to have each of the libraries focus its future collection activity on specific and complementary academic areas.

It is at this local level that the greatest amount of interlibrary loan occurs. A shuttle service makes the rounds to the library locations twice each day, delivering requested materials and returning books to their permanent collection sites.

In addition to the local library consortium affiliation, institutions A and B are also members of a tristate, multipurpose college consortium. The activities of this regional consortium include a variety of faculty, curriculum, and administrative development programs. Each of the college libraries in the regional association has developed a single-campus automated system based on the use of either a minicomputer or networked microcomputers. These campus systems were planned to be compatible with the hardware and software of the urban library group. Dial-up links that are in use permit communications with the urban consortium's computer system from these regional locations within the consortium. When a search at institution A does not yield the desired information within the urban consortium, the holdings of the regional consortium can also be accessed.

The members of the regional group also share learning-resource materials and courseware, and librarians on the six campuses participate in numerous cooperative professional development activities.

Another interlibrary loan regional backup for institution A is the state's automated system. Again, equipment and software compatibility exists between the urban and state systems. On a dial-up basis, the holdings of libraries throughout the state can be searched and requests made to have the title mailed to institution A.

On a national level, the library consortium institutions share access facilities to both DIALOG (data bases) and OCLC. Institution C serves as the access point for communications with OCLC. This automated service is handled through MINITEX—a regional service broker for access to the OCLC system.

Institution D maintains on-line access to all of the data bases available through the DIALOG service. Students and faculty members who desire to search a data base contact the librarian at institution D and receive assistance in designing and conducting a search.

There are actually two kinds of cooperative relationships represented in Figure 4.1. First, there are those associations in which libraries cooperate in order to purchase a service or to receive support. Examples of this include MINITEX, OCLC, and DIALOG. The urban library association, the multistate consortium, and, to a lesser degree, the state association are membership organizations or consortia in which the relationship is symbiotic. It is assumed that all the libraries make equal contributions to and receive reciprocal benefits from participation in the programs.

The Benefits of Cooperation

Higher education institutions can profit from cooperative activities. In a library facing the serious problems of acquisition development and budget control, resource sharing can markedly affect the quality of educational support services.

Technological development offers benefits in two ways. First, national and international communication networks are now available that make it possible to collect information for the library user literally from anywhere in the world; second, the capabilities of micro- and minicomputers have advanced to the point where fully integrated, locally controlled systems are now available for every type and size of library. It is now possible to develop on any campus a total information-resources program that respects both the value of decentralization and the necessity of interdependence.

Through a commitment to cooperation, library programs can be designed so that they effectively and efficiently meet the needs of the clients of the academic library—students and faculty members.

JOINT PURCHASING

Equipment and software cost savings can be significant when purchases are cooperative. Some vendors offer as much as a 40% discount when volume orders are placed, and most suppliers have developed joint purchasing agreements through which consortia can acquire equipment at substantially lower prices. IBM's Education Affiliate Program is one example of this kind of arrangement. It should be noted that several of these major vendors, including IBM, will not enter into formal agreements with college and university associations formed for the exclusive purpose of purchasing computer equipment. Instead, these companies recognize only consortia that are multipurpose and that have a rich and varied history of cooperation.

SHARING OF RESOURCES

Even with the striking increase in the amount of information generated during the last ten years, the majority of college and university libraries have not been able to increase their subscription or acquisition budgets; in fact, many of them have had to make decisions about what to cut. Resource sharing in this environment represents the best hope for maintaining the quality and integrity of library holdings. Establishing general policies governing cooperative acquisitions and interlibrary loan, communicating library needs, and engaging in cooperative library systems development are the bases for reasonable library operation in the future.

The issue here is not budget savings. Instead, maintaining quality learning resources and containing budget increases are the incentives in this area of cooperative library operation in the future.

Institutions can realize budget reductions, however, by participating in cooperative access to OCLC and data base search facilities. Shared access can result in reduced line charges, minimal equipment demands, and better professional service support. Sharing access to OCLC also yields benefits for a consortium staff by reducing unnecessary duplication of acquisition information and by encouraging greater levels of communication among libraries.

Local consortium networks can also realize significant savings by investing in software and hardware that allows for off-line search development and the down-loading of information. Both capabilities can save considerable on-line time as long as legal (piracy) issues are considered.

ACQUISITION PLANNING

Another logical step is to establish formal agreements covering what books and periodicals each institution in a cooperative arrangement will acquire. Reducing the amount of duplication within a local or regional consortium has the potential to be an effective means for containing costs. However, implementation—and even agreement on the specifics of these cooperative acquisition systems—holds many problems.

A formal acquisition agreement would establish guidelines for each library (1) to acquire certain periodicals not duplicated elsewhere in the consortium; (2) to agree regularly on books and reference text acquisitions (again eliminating or reducing duplication); and (3) to require increasing levels of interdependence in serving the needs of library users. Stated "tongue in cheek," library A would buy the red books, library B the yellow, and library C the blue. But what happens when library B withdraws from the consortium? And what about a situation of financial exigency, when college A is forced to cut its acquisitions budget or to close its doors entirely? No more red books!

The potential savings, however, compel librarians to find ways to overcome the barriers to resource sharing. It was recently estimated that the seven members of the Colorado Alliance of Research Libraries could save in excess of $1 million a year in journal costs alone if they were to develop a careful acquisitions plan. Resource sharing becomes enormously attractive to decision makers under these circumstances.

COOPERATIVE TRAINING

It is no simple task for the typical librarian to maintain currency in the multitude of technical areas having an impact on library program development. It is therefore useful to engage in cooperative staff training on topics about which information needs exist. The benefits of this activity include (1) involving greater numbers of staff members in professional development; (2) sharing the cost of information presentation among the participating institutions; and (3) developing common and consistent understanding of library automation issues among consortium professionals. The benefits of cooperative professional development can also be realized through personnel exchanges and the development of library staff trained in specialized areas of information access.

COOPERATIVE PLANNING

A natural extension of common training is cooperative planning for library program development. Considering the level of interdependence that is portrayed throughout this chapter, librarians must communicate effectively if cooperative systems are to be installed. Manual circulation systems must be compatible if interlibrary loan and cooperative access are to function. The establishment of automated systems demands agreement on compatible software and hardware. Cooperative acquisition activities require planning and coordination at a sophisticated level.

Savings can be realized most prominently in planning for automation. The introduction of an on-line catalog requires much technical support and often consumes a vast amount of the time of institutional staff. Sharing this work load can reduce costs for the consortium participants in both of these areas.

EXPERTISE DEVELOPMENT

Sharing expertise among library professionals within the consortium can result in significant personnel savings. For example, accessing data bases requires a thorough knowledge of search procedures. It is difficult for the typical librarian to remain current with this information for even the most commonly used data bases, let alone those for which utilization is infrequent. Designating just a few individuals to handle search requests for all consortium members saves time for the institutions and improves the quality of the searches.

Expertise assignments can also be utilized as a tool for keeping the librarians within the consortium current on other topics of interest. For example, one librarian could be given the task of gathering information on equipment; another might develop expertise related to software capabilities; and a third becomes an expert on videodisc applications. Each could then contribute to the knowledge of the consortium decision makers as key library development plans are formed.

Conclusion

The role of the college and university library is changing. Increasingly, libraries are more than repositories for books; they have become the focal points for access to knowledge in our emerging information society.

The definition of librarianship is also experiencing rather dramatic change. It is true that the tasks of acquisition and organization continue to consume a significant proportion of the professional librarian's time. The introduction of information technologies and the exponential growth in publications, however, require increasing attention to resource interpretation and user service.

Cooperative activity provides the means to cope with the changing information service environment. Thoughtfully applied and developed, library networks have the potential to solve many of the problems facing libraries today and to carry institutions far beyond what any of them can provide independently.

—5—

The Purchasing of Goods and Services

ROBERT M. BRIBER

Ask why cooperation among colleges and universities is a good idea; often the answer comes back, "To save money." Cooperation among higher education institutions can, of course, save money. This chapter describes one of the most effective ways of doing so: the cooperative purchase of goods and services commonly used by colleges and universities working together in groups. I will discuss cooperative purchasing as it is practiced in the Hudson-Mohawk Association of Colleges and Universities, explain how this process fits into the purchasing operation on the individual campuses, and compare HMACU's methods with those used by others.

A Rationale for Cooperative Purchasing

I will compare our way of purchasing cooperatively with practices elsewhere. Although such comparison is instructive, examples from elsewhere are not as common as they ought to be. Colleges and

The Hudson-Mohawk Association of Colleges and Universities (HMACU), which was founded in 1969, is a general-purpose consortium of the public and private, two-year, four-year, and graduate higher education institutions of Albany, Rensselaer, Saratoga, and Schenectady Counties—the "Capital District" of New York State.

79

universities are slow in accepting cooperative purchasing—slower, for example, than hospitals have been.

It is not clear why this apparent sluggishness exists. Perhaps the process and its benefits are not well understood; if that is so, this chapter will help. Perhaps the complexity of the process is not understood. Some may perceive the act of agreeing to purchase cooperatively as the same as doing so. The agreement is an essential part of the process, but, as I shall indicate, much more is required from many individuals.

Perhaps, though, this sluggishness stems from the fact that some academics will *not* answer "To save money" in response to the question about the value of cooperation. Some say that we ought to cooperate for cooperation's sake. Cooperation should be second nature to us. We should not have to justify it, or even work very hard to have it happen. Some particularly resent the intrusion of costs (and cost containment) into the "natural" act of cooperation. Involving money, for them, somehow sullies the act.

These people may not appreciate the fact that finding ways for groupings of higher education institutions to work together is a formidable intellectual and social challenge. Cooperation across institutional lines is not an automatic act; it needs to be learned and encouraged. Colleges and universities in America have grown and prospered here and there, willy-nilly, and for years they have learned to operate independently of one another. Traditionally they pride themselves on that independence; getting them to work cooperatively is more difficult than it may seem to the uninitiated.

Herein lies a reason to involve money in this work. Cooperation, like competition on the athletic field, needs a goal. There has to be an end in mind worth the effort. Winning the game is the obvious goal in sport; cost containment is a goal for cooperation among educational institutions. Presidents of the member colleges and universities recognized the importance of such a goal and charged the staff with pursuing it in order to justify our association. The goal was clear: to save money to save the consortium.

Many men and women on our campuses are very concerned with costs; offer them a way to save money and you have given them both a reason and a vehicle for cooperation. Most college and university presidents (and most other people, for that matter) recognize the benefits that come when people work together. They profit from affiliation with their peers, learn many things, and engage in projects of value to their institutions. The first goal, though, should be to save money.

We have felt in our association that the cost savings available through cooperative purchasing pays our bills; we engage in the rest of our projects because they are good ideas. We earn the right to cooperate because we can prove, first, that cooperation will save money and, second, that we can manage well enough financially to justify our cooperation.

Cost containment can even play an important role in activities that are more academic than the purchase of fuel oil or photocopier paper. We have shared the cost of bringing poets and acting companies to our campuses, and the cost of specialized faculty members. These activities did not involve purchasing agents, but they did—in our case, at least—use the consensus-building techniques that this chapter describes. Cooperation among colleges and universities can enable them to do many things, as it also saves them money, along the way.

Our society and our world both badly need successful examples of cooperation among established institutions and nations. It is perhaps too much to hope that our educational institutions could lead society in learning this important skill, but at least we should recognize that learning it is a worthy challenge. Cost containment can help us to meet that challenge.

The Routes to a Purchase by a College or University

Alert college and university purchasing officials usually have several routes to the purchase of goods and services. They can buy as a single institution, through a state contracting system, or through cooperatives. A few words about each of these will place cooperative purchasing in the campus purchasing framework.

Historically the most common, and still the most popular, route is to "go it alone," through a purchasing procedure that can be as simple as placing a telephone order or as complex as purchasing can be, with paperwork that bristles with legal footnotes and conditions. The busy purchasing agent works to get the best price available for the requested product, often dealing personally with the vendor, and then goes on to the next purchase on his or her list.

As a second choice, he or she often can purchase through a state contracting system. New York State, for instance, has an excellent set of contracts available, both to the public and to the independent institutions. The "State Contract Price" is the byword for the lowest available price for thousands of products. The campuses of the State University of New

York system—though not the community colleges—are required to use a state contract if an appropriate one exists. The independent colleges and universities, and the community colleges, can use the state contracts or not, as one more route to the best buy for their campus. Other states have developed their contracting systems differently, but often this is an excellent way to buy.

A purchasing agent who is able to choose will compare the state contract with the costs and other advantages of buying as a single institution, pick the route that appears better, and, again, go on to the next task.

The final route is through the cooperative. It can offer an important third choice. The largest, oldest, and best known of the college and university purchasing cooperatives is the Educational and Institutional Cooperative Service, Inc., of Woodbury, New York (commonly known as "E & I"). Although E & I operates differently than do most consortium purchasing efforts, it offers member institutions an important route to the purchase of certain products. Originated in 1934 as a cooperative venture of three college purchasing agents, the E & I Cooperative has grown into a nationally significant nonprofit purchasing organization with many hundreds of colleges, universities, preparatory schools, and hospitals among its members.

For a product to make the E & I roster, it must be suitable and usually nationally distributed. It must also have broad appeal, high quality, an advantageous price, and a reliable vendor. E & I staff members commonly negotiate their contracts with the vendor. The Cooperative is supported by a small service charge added to the cost of an item. All funds left over from E & I's operating expenses are returned to the members in proportion to their purchases through the system.

The remaining college and university cooperatives are the subject of this chapter. Perhaps 30 groups of higher education institutions, with some 300 members in total, engage in cooperative purchasing. In the *1983 Consortium Directory,* published by the Council for Interinstitutional Leadership (CIL), 26 consortia (out of 134 listed) describe themselves as being involved in some aspect of cooperative purchasing. Jake E. Bishop, Director of Procurement at the University of Massachusetts, contacted 18 consortia and found 5 others, not included in the CIL directory, that described their cooperative purchasing procedures to him by letter.

The number of institutions participating in a consortium purchasing arrangement can range from as few as 2, as in a College of New Rochelle/Iona College cooperative, to 53, in Bishop's active statewide program. Membership typically ranges from 5 to 15 institutions. These groupings of colleges and universities, usually organized on regional lines—and thus smaller and more localized than the E & I cooperative—provide the final alternative route for many purchasing decisions.

Hospitals seem to be ahead of colleges and universities in this area. Our association's work in purchasing was preceded locally by the Iroquois Hospital Consortium, a vigorous cooperative of hospitals in a somewhat larger geographic area than ours. In two cases, we have included hospitals as well as colleges in order to increase the number of cooperating institutions on the contract, and thus lowered costs even further. Others working to set up cooperative college and university arrangements have found that local hospital purchasing groups are already well established.

Cooperative purchasing is more common among hospitals than it is among educational institutions. As Dean S. Ammer points out, in *Purchasing and Material Management for Health Care Institutions* (1975), "Hospital group purchasing arrangements have existed for 50 years. In the past 25 years they have come to account for a significant part of hospital purchases. There are now purchasing groups in almost every part of the United States and most hospitals belong to them." There is still ample opportunity for groups of colleges and universities to explore this route. It works, and yet only about 30 of them use it.

The Mechanism

If leaders at a group of colleges and universities want to purchase cooperatively, and a logical grouping of institutions exists (I examine what is "logical" below), the way into the process is simple and straightforward. Certain commonly used products or services are identified; quantities to be purchased are established; vendors are notified and invited to bid; a decision is made; and vendor/college relationships are inaugurated, because all billing for and movement of goods takes place between vendor and campus. Ultimately, too, the savings realized are estimated so that the results of the effort can be evaluated.

The process is more precisely "joint pricing," rather than cooperative purchasing. The association does not take title to the product, store it, or pay for it; all of these relationships take place between the college or university and the vendor. The members agree to buy an estimated quantity of the product from the vendor, to take delivery directly as specified in the bid letter or as negotiated, and to pay the vendor directly. The cost advantage is realized because they have pooled their requirements into a single large purchase quantity, which makes an attractive contract for a vendor.

There is a practical reason why the vendor will often lower its prices in order to obtain a cooperative contract. The consortium is providing a service for the vendor that would cost money to replace. We are offering a market for a stated and, often, large quantity of product. The vendor's sales expenses are substantially reduced; he or she need not devote the sales time that would otherwise be necessary to obtain equivalent sales. We identify the men and women the vendor must contact on each campus and so spare the vendor that administrative expense. We enable vendors to schedule their own purchases economically, and to contract with their own suppliers for a specified quantity to be delivered over a predictable time. These acts by the association can produce important cost savings for the vendor that *should* be passed on to us.

I will describe each of the steps in cooperative purchasing, touch on some of the problems and issues that have arisen, and then discuss what constitutes a logical grouping of institutions. Each of these steps is well understood by an experienced purchasing agent.

A word, first, about why we got into purchasing, and a tribute. In early 1977, at a meeting of presidents of members of our association, Dr. George Low, late president of Rensselaer Polytechnic Institute (RPI), said that he would put the purchasing power of his institution behind an effort to save money through cooperation. He said he believed that the association had to prove cost-effectiveness, and that savings were possible. The director of the association agreed, arguing that purchasing would save participating members at least the equivalent of their dues payments annually. The chief executive officers of Hudson Valley Community College and the Albany Medical College agreed, committing their institutions to the effort. Thus the three institutions in the association with the greatest available purchasing power were embarked by their presidents on an experiment that would in time save them hundreds of thousands of dollars.

The importance of such a presidential commitment cannot be overestimated. A convincing demonstration of cost benefits was necessary for them to continue supporting our organization. Such an agreement was a powerful motivator for staff, as one might surmise. It also made possible the concerted cooperative effort of purchasing agents and others who were not yet acquainted with one another.

The description that follows should be read with our purposes in mind. We were stimulated into cooperative purchasing by that group of presidents, and by the immediate need to prove that cooperation among our institutions could work. Time and again I have seen this phenomenon at work in cooperation: if the presidents want it, it gets done. Now let us turn to how the joint purchasing process works in practice, at least in our association.

IDENTIFY THE PRODUCTS OR SERVICES

The Hudson-Mohawk purchasing group quickly began its efforts with three members agreeing to buy fuel oil. We then moved on to other products, even before the first results of our effort in fuel oil were apparent. Miscellaneous office supplies, mimeograph and photocopier paper, and typewriter maintenance followed quickly. These are all "generic" items and, except for fuel oil, are purchased routinely on every campus in our association and elsewhere.

Each of these contracts had features that made a cooperative purchase attractive. In miscellaneous office supplies, for example, RPI had already demonstrated to itself that these products could be lumped together and bought by contract. Paper clips, typewriter ribbons, manila folders, and lined yellow pads—and hundreds of other items—could be bought from an office supply house on a contract that provided a set discount from list price for all items. By doing so, purchasing agents could minimize the time spent dealing with vendors on an item-by-item basis. The benefits described by the RPI people were immediately grasped by the other purchasing agents, and a cooperative miscellaneous office supplies bid was launched.

As another example, transportation costs for paper products could be minimized because the purchasers were in a limited geographic area. Products could be brought to the region in bulk and redistributed here. To compete effectively in service contracts, another successful category of contract (e.g., typewriter maintenance), vendors had to be local firms with service staffs available economically to colleges and universities in a limited geographic area. The cost to bring service people here from a distance usually disqualified out-of-region vendors.

In general, our purchasing group has always looked for product or service areas where the cooperative offered particular advantages. Since we always had the state contracting system for comparison, we sought products that were sensible to buy through the cooperative rather than through state contract. (It made no sense to buy an item cooperatively if it could be bought less expensively and also satisfactorily from the state contract. We stayed away from light bulbs for years because, as several people said, "You cannot beat the state contract.")

Price was often a factor in a successful association contract; we were frequently able to get a lower price than the state contract because of transportation or other economies our group could realize. Convenience was sometimes a factor; to be able to buy any of hundreds of items at a substantial discount offered administrative advantages over finding items one by one from the relevant state contracts. Whatever advantage we felt we had, we tried to be objective about each item we considered.

The group identified items by consensus. Our staff felt, and still feels, that whatever the item or service was, its identity was less important than that the purchasing agents agreed to buy it. They had to deal with the vendors, pay the bills, and explain on campus why they bought from one vendor rather than from another whom someone else preferred. They were entitled, therefore, to choose the items toward the purchase of which they had assumed such responsibility.

Because we had a number of such decisions to make, the group quickly became an effective decision making body. Our staff conducted the surveys, identified the vendors, and prepared the contracts, but the group of purchasing agents decided which products to buy. They reached consensus rapidly and established the association's purchasing effort as an effective alternative route for college and university purchases.

Apparently subjective considerations occasionally entered the discussion when products were being chosen. One college reported that a local vendor of a contract being considered was a well-heeled and generous member of the college's board of trustees. It was reported that he gave the college more money than it could possibly realize from cost savings on his product. None of us is unrealistic or doctrinaire about purchasing. The college stayed off that contract at the beginning and is still off it years later. Colleges and universities in such an association are free to join or not to join in a particular contract or purchase as they see fit, for their own reasons.

We have not in our efforts spent much time seeking "standardization," a commonly raised spectre. "Our colleges will never agree to buy the identical product," goes the refrain. We have not found that to be a problem. We just stay away from the products that require precise agreement from campus to campus. Most of our products are generic and are pretty well standardized by the vendors. Plastic bag liners come in a widely accepted range of sizes and weights, for example, and we have surveyed usage on the basis of those sizes and weights. Fuel oil comes in only a handful of different grades, which are widely understood and can be bid for without argument.

We did, for two years, have a contract for coarse paper (handtowels and toilet tissue) and found that individual colleges and universities were buying such different products that there was little benefit from the cooperative purchase. Other products could serve as well as the several we chose to get cooperative purchasing underway. Other consortia would, no doubt, choose other products. The important issue, in my opinion, is that they be products on which people from different institutions can agree.

ESTIMATE QUANTITIES

A common question about cooperative purchasing is, "Do we have to tell the vendors how much we will buy? We just do not know exactly."

In almost 10 years of cooperative purchasing, our estimates of the quantity to be purchased have been seriously inaccurate only once. As a result, that vendor raised her prices when the contract was rebid and wrote a letter indicating that this was the reason for doing so. She had not realized the dollar volume in sales we had indicated she should realize.

We are very careful to indicate that our estimated quantities to be purchased are just that: estimates. Quantities to be purchased, we say, will be modestly higher or lower than the indicated quantity. We also tell the vendor that other institutions in the association may choose to buy on a contract after it begins. That latter provision has never caused a problem. Vendors always seem glad to get the extra business.

An interesting phenomenon has been at work in the estimating of a quantity to be purchased: If the contract is a good one, the quantities actually purchased exceed the quantities we estimated, often by a substantial amount. Our miscellaneous office supplies contract, for example, has grown from about $75,000 in its first year to about half a million dollars annually, and the discounts available have increased substantially. A successful cooperative contract seems to bring out good vendors who recognize that it offers them a legitimate means of increasing their business with the members, and people on the campuses recognize good service and prices. A good contract grows.

If the quantities we estimated are not realized, something usually is wrong with the contract. Perhaps the vendor is not supplying as we had expected, and we have to find another vendor. A lower-than-expected volume may reflect our misunderstanding of the business. We found, for example, that the provision of temporary services is an intensely competitive business, with a lot of marginally effective vendors at work. Price cutting is common; competitive practices can be cutthroat. In an environment like that, it is difficult for a relatively cumbersome process such as ours to be very successful. Since prices are already cut almost to the bone, the individual colleges and universities can do nearly as well as the cooperative can. Here again, comparison against estimates of the quantities purchased on the contract is a measure of success. In this case, quantities have not grown; the contract is not very successful.

NOTIFY VENDORS AND INVITE THEIR BIDS

Our own notification process was worked out by our purchasing agents, building on the public bidding procedures that were in use at Hudson Valley Community College. These include

- Distribution by mail of a formal letter, our "bid letter," inviting vendors to bid

- Public announcement of the bid in the newspapers five working days before the bid opening

- The receipt and holding of sealed bids from vendors until the bid opening, to which all vendors are welcome

- Sworn statements from vendors that they are not in collusion

- Preparation and distribution of a "bid results summary" for the vendors who respond

We choose our vendors by asking each participating college or university to list the vendors they have dealt with in the past. We compare the list with the telephone company's yellow pages and occasionally add one or two more names.

MAKE A DECISION

Usually the decision making process follows automatically from discussion of the bid results summary that we distribute to the purchasing group. The lowest cost is obvious, the bidder is qualified, and the contract looks practical.

Several times, however, we have not chosen the lowest bidder. We do not feel obligated to do so, so long as we agree on our reasons. This decision, too, is an integral part of the group's prerogatives and helps to insure that they are committed to the results. We may feel that the vendor is not equipped to deal with the volume we offered. Our first typewriter maintenance bid, for example, produced responses from vendors who could not possibly service the number of machines for which we bid. They were hoping to get some part of the contract, but we intended to reward a single vendor with our business so we could work with one firm and watch its behavior.

We have since split awards on one or two occasions, but it is not our preferred result. Occasionally we have invited competing vendors to discuss their services with our group before we made the decision; in several cases, we visited the vendor's facility. Whatever the decision, it is reached openly and only after thoughtful discussion.

Such careful procedures as we have described in selecting and choosing among vendors are not required of the independent colleges and universities in the association, but "sunshine" provisions by and large make good sense in a process such as this that requires mutual trust and consensus.

INAUGURATE VENDOR–COLLEGE RELATIONSHIPS

Once the winning vendor is chosen, we notify him or her. The vendor then contacts each institution and begins to provide the needed products or services. The association has opened the door to the vendor, introduced the vendor in the most positive context imaginable, and indicated that this customer is prepared to buy.

ESTIMATE SAVINGS

The calculation of savings realized through group action is an interesting and sometimes controversial subject. The savings stem fundamentally from the economies of scale, which are an accepted element in our economic system. "Ten cents each, 3 for a quarter" is a classic pricing scheme familiar to us all.

Estimating the savings available from quantity purchases is usually much more difficult than this familiar phrase would indicate. In this instance the saving from a quantity purchase would, of course, be 5 cents. The original, or "list," price would be 30 cents for 3; we paid 25 cents and so saved a nickel. Would that it were always so simple.

We can usually tell exactly how much we actually paid. The problem arises in determining original, or "list," price:

1. Is it the published list price, which no one, probably, would have paid anyway? In computer software, to pick just one example, list

price is meaningless. It is the price from which discounts are taken, whoever is purchasing.

2. Is it the price the college or university paid before it entered into a cooperative contract? This has the advantage of being a real price, calculated after any discounts are included. There are last year's invoices, or perhaps the invoices from several years previously. After years of buying through the cooperative, however, such a price may not be realistic, depending on inflation, product changes, etc. It can work when a consortium is just beginning to purchase, but it loses its value with time.

3. Is it some other, calculated price? If, for example, the cooperative contract allows the campus to make personnel changes that save money, does the original, or list, price include the higher personnel costs or not?

All of these are examples of methods for determining original prices that we have used and from which quantity savings have been determined. Little wonder that it is a complicated calculation, subject to different approaches.

Each consortium will estimate its savings in its own way. Jake E. Bishop, in Massachusetts, uses "list price value." The following comes from his *Annual Report of Contract Activity for the Period July 1, 1984–June 30, 1985* (1985):

> Member purchases for 1985 reached $28,027,525 up $5,248,000 over 1984. Conservatively figured, the difference between the list price value of the goods and services purchased and what the members paid for those goods and services was $11,787,891 or a "cost avoidance" figure of 29.6%. This total of almost $12,000,000 is up from the $8,200,000 figure for 1984. The volume of business increased for 33 schools in 1985 over 1984. One hundred vendors increased their volume in 1985, 54 declined and 31 were new to the Consortium.
>
> I cannot emphasize too strongly that our numbers are so significant that we do not inflate them for impact. If anything, average discounts are conservatively reported on the low side. Many, many contracts are reported as "net," although we know the prices we enjoy are lower than those paid by many other users.

Our method of determining savings at Hudson-Mohawk Association flows from the consensus-building model we have used to support our efforts. We first ask vendors to indicate the volume of their sales to the colleges and universities during the contract year. Each purchasing official then justifies the savings according to that information and his or her own procedures. They need report only savings they can justify to their own top management. We use their figures and ask that they do in fact report them to top management.

Hudson-Mohawk Association has been purchasing since 1977; in seven years, reported savings have exceeded a million dollars. The volume purchased on our current list of 20 contracts has grown to $2.25 million per year. Savings over the years have averaged 12% of sales, according to campus purchasing officials.

How much does it cost to obtain these savings? We estimate that association staff spends about 19% of our time on purchasing matters, most of which is related to the contracts we manage. Multiplied by our total budget, that amounts to approximately $24,000, or perhaps 10% of the savings realized. Other groups distribute the work among the cooperating institutions and so do not use the services of a central staff at all. Although costs in such a mechanism may be more difficult to estimate than in ours, they too will certainly remain modest.

Before we describe one or two problems that have arisen, it is interesting to quote a summary of the cooperative purchasing process. This one is taken from the Illinois Educational Consortium, which described its process, in a model of brevity, in the *1983 Consortium Directory:*

> . . . a major contribution by IEC to statewide cooperation is the collective purchasing program. Each of the IEC members has joined in a collective purchasing program where specific items are declared "generic." Collective requirements of such generic items are competitively bid. Once the price and supplier are established, each university purchases its needs for the generic item from the vendor with the lowest bid price. IEC currently lists 51 generic commodities.

Some Potential Problems and Issues

A number of problems common to purchasing have arisen in our efforts, as they do on any individual campus. We have had unsatisfactory vendors; even worse, we have had vendors who pleased some purchasing agents and dissatisfied others. We have had price increases and embittered vendors. Nothing in cooperative purchasing insulates us from these normal purchasing problems.

The basis for dealing with these problems lies in free cooperation. Our group has had arguments but has resolved them all. Occasionally a disagreement will drag on for some months, but ultimately it is dealt with professionally, and none has interfered with the free exchange of information and decision making.

Other issues related to cooperative purchasing, although not classifiable as "problems," are frequently raised. Does the employment of a faculty member by two or more institutions count as cooperative purchasing? Further, what does it mean if a logical grouping of institutions exists to do cooperative purchasing? Finally, are there antitrust implications in this work? I will discuss each of these questions in order.

PURCHASING ACADEMIC SERVICES: SHARED FACULTY AND "BLOCK BOOKING"

We have used association staff and skills to buy the professional services of performing arts groups, administrators, poets, and other things more academic than fuel oil. Our colleges and universities have shared faculty members. These purchases are often, both in the association and elsewhere, more difficult to consummate than is the purchase of products. An analysis of the purchasing process as it applies to such professional services, performing arts groups, and the like gives insight into complications that arise.

We brought the West Coast poet Gary Snyder to the Capital Region in 1985 for a very successful week of seminars, discussions, and lectures. Two of our institutions and two affiliated groups shared the cost of his travel and honorarium. Earlier, two of our colleges shared the services of a Boston-based acting company for two weeks of performances. On a number of occasions, we have brought speakers to various groups in the region. Our institutions often share the same faculty, either on a "moonlighting" basis arranged by the individual or more calculatedly as the conscious sharing of a person's time by the institutions involved. (The latter, incidentally, is arranged between different pairs of two institutions, small subsets of the 15 that maintain membership in this association.)

Five Colleges, Inc., a consortium in western Massachusetts with a long and enviable record of successful cooperation, has a number of shared faculty appointments. To quote from its *Five College Newsletter:*

> Five Colleges, Inc., will host a reception on September 12 for the largest number of Five College Joint Faculty appointees to be supported by the program in a single year since its inception in 1974. Sixteen faculty members will this year fulfill shared teaching responsibilities in fields that have been designated as priorities for cooperative development.
>
> Joint faculty appointees are those whose specializations strengthen some aspect of the curriculum in designated fields, or whose recognized work as artists or scholars makes their presence an invaluable source of enrichment for students and faculty alike.

As indicated above, the cooperative purchasing decision as practiced in buying products involves the identification of "generic" items. The institutions agree that, by and large, photocopier paper is photocopier paper. A poet such as Gary Snyder is hardly generic; he is a recognized, well-known, and highly creative individual. Although one college may wish to bring a figure such as Gary Snyder to speak to a poetry class, another may prefer the less well known graduate of a local college who has just published her first book of poetry. Thus the selection of the professional service to be purchased can become a much more formidable task. Some degree of consensus—about the kind of professional service being sought—must exist before the choice can be made. This often happens only when people at different institutions know each other well, and when their institutions have enough common characteristics to prefer similar professional services.

The choice of an individual is only the first step. All the other elements of a cooperative purchase must still be completed. The quantity of service—how long the individual is wanted—must be established. For institutions on different academic calendars, it is often not easy to establish the best schedule. Both colleges must want the service at about the same time, not only *during* a given year, but also *in* the same year. (How often we have heard the refrain, "You should have asked us last year.") A price for the individual's services must be reached. Finally, he or she must be incorporated into the institutional framework, with fringe benefits and working conditions established. Although purchasing agents have completed all these tasks for the products they buy cooperatively, they are often unfamiliar tasks for academic officials to undertake cooperatively.

The calculation of the savings realized brings up yet another issue: Did both cooperating colleges really need those services, or were they needed at one college and discretionary at the other? Fuel oil is usually not a discretionary purchase; both colleges need it and would have bought it singly if they did not buy it collectively. That may not be true for the services of a West Coast poet or a professor of Chinese. How much does an institution save when it gets a service it wants but does not truly need, even at a lowered price? Perhaps it makes the poet available where he would not have been available at all, or perhaps it prompts the institution to use him rather than a local poet. This makes the determination of savings, if it is used to justify and to support the value of the cooperative process, a little fuzzier than it already is.

DEFINING THE LOGICAL GROUPING OF INSTITUTIONS

Definition of what is a "logical" grouping of institutions follows from these characteristics of the process of cooperation. Cooperation proceeds best when people know each other and are able to communicate easily.

They must talk to each other. Often that means they are close together geographically. If they are geographically too far apart, something stronger than acquaintance—such as the observation that, "We are all in the same state system" or, perhaps, "Only five institutions anywhere now buy this specialized item"—has to be at work for cooperative purchasing to be very successful.

The use of the word "logical," then, implies a grouping within which communication is relatively easy. In the normal case that means colleges and universities close enough together so that people can come together conveniently and periodically.

Another definition of a logical grouping comes from shared interest in the product. Hudson-Mohawk Association does not require all institutions to agree to buy a product together. One of our contracts involves just two members; several contracts involve a dozen or more. (One school, for example, has little need for a chemical waste disposal contract; "Our only waste product," the school's purchasing official has said, "is hot air. That we have lots of.") Other members have contracts in force with a particular vendor; they do not want to change vendors and so do not join in our cooperative effort. We ask at the beginning which colleges and universities are interested in a particular purchase, for whatever reason, and we work with that group.

For Bishop, in the Massachusetts Higher Education Consortium, 55 institutions throughout the Commonwealth are currently members. This includes universities, state colleges, community colleges, and the members of several regional consortia, including the founder, Five Colleges, Inc. The conditions for the purchase of goods and services by colleges and universities are different in Massachusetts than they are in New York, and Bishop's consortium has grown accordingly.

A key element for us is the high level of ownership of the process by the purchasing officials and, by extension, by the institution each represents. Our consortium was established to find ways neighboring institutions could cooperate; for us, the logical grouping was established by considerations of the geographic location of a group of colleges and universities. Other higher education institutions and even local industries benefit from the prices we realize on our contracts, but we do not attempt to get them to join the association. We have included the members of the regional hospital consortium in contracts in order to increase our impact, but we have not discussed joining forces any more formally than that.

ANTITRUST CONSIDERATIONS

A purchasing cooperative is established when different institutions agree to pool their purchases in order to realize some economic benefit, such as lowered prices from vendors. This seems to be in violation of the antitrust laws, which were established in order to insure competition; in fact, cooperative purchasing among colleges and universities does have antitrust overtones.

Carl J. Hevener, an attorney with the Bureau of Competition of the Federal Trade Commission, has spent many years involved in antitrust issues. He spoke to this issue at a 1982 meeting of the National Association of Educational Buyers. His prepared speech—which, he emphasized, contained what were his own opinions rather than those of the FTC—included the following statements:

> The first thing I have to do—even if it is the *only* thing I accomplish—is to disabuse you of any notion that you are not subject to the anti-trust laws simply because you are tax exempt. There is no direct relationship between a tax exemption and anti-trust immunity. If you are outside the anti-trust laws, it has to be for a reason other than that the IRS has granted you exempt tax status. . . .
>
> The kinds of activities in which you engage that might be subject to anti-trust enforcement involve purchasing which—regardless how you do it—is unlikely to produce the substantial anti-competitive effects at which anti-trust enforcement is appropriately directed.
>
> One area in which you could be vulnerable is in connection with joint purchasing. I understand that a number of your institutions participate in some kind of buying group or cooperative.
>
> A group of governmental or non-profit institutions which contains no profit-making entities is an unlikely target for an anti-trust attack. One conceivable charge might be a combination or conspiracy in restraint of trade if the group accumulates and exercises sufficient market power to act as a monopsonist—a buyer with the power to control prices and restrict supply.
>
> Perhaps a more likely scenario is one where an exempt institution engages in joint buying with a non-exempt one. Generally speaking, an otherwise exempt organization may lose its protection when it conspires in restraint of trade with a non-exempt organization. If you are in a buyer consortium, you should consider this possibility, since such a combination or conspiracy is more likely to attract anti-trust attention.

Two specific kinds of behavior need attention. If a group of colleges and universities forces a vendor to sell below costs (i.e., to lose money in order to obtain or to maintain a contract), it is vulnerable to attack for being in violation of the antitrust laws. Second, if a group agrees among itself to refuse to do business with a vendor—to boycott a vendor in order to punish or to force concessions, or for any other reason—it would be acting improperly. Nothing in college or university status as tax-exempt, nonprofit, or educational would protect the group from attack in such cases.

To my knowledge, no instance of cooperative purchasing among higher education institutions has been the target of legal action. It may someday happen—lightning does strike—and we can look to the experiences of that day for more definitive information on these issues.

In our group, we have discussed our program with legal counsel and have informed ourselves about boycotts and other antitrust issues. And we have then proceeded with our programs.

Summary

There are not many absolutes in cooperative purchasing beyond the first one, that money can be saved through cooperation. The economies of scale do work, and they can be put to work for our benefit. They can pay the way for substantial interrelationships among colleges and universities.

Beyond that, it is clear that an organization of colleges and universities must exist or be created in order to support the cooperative contracts. The presidents of the cooperating institutions must encourage the process. Authority must be given to the purchasing people involved, and they must have an administrative mechanism (a person, or at least an agreement to share the work) to manage the contracts. For the health of the process, purchasing officials should summarize the savings realized annually. Savings will vary from group to group, depending on how they are calculated, but they will be real. Costs will be lowered through cooperative purchasing.

The purchasing people involved will benefit substantially from the other attributes of cooperation. The group will include men and women with wide variation in experience and knowledge. Interchange and conversation in such a group can be extremely stimulating—and often worth more to the participants than the cost savings.

—6—

Serving Business and Industry

GARRY J. DEROSE

One of the most significant developments in the educational environment has been the growth in the business demand for education and training. Although the data is at best unreliable, the National Center for Education Statistics estimates that employers paid for twelve million course enrollments in 1981. More than 3,000 corporations currently offer management development training—up from a single program in the 1940s. Fourteen corporations actually offer degrees. Estimates of the total business expenditures on education go as high as $40 billion.

This already immense market may have just begun to expand. Recent developments in the business environment and human-resource management promise an even greater emphasis on education and training. When coupled with changes in the situation of colleges and universities, they make an alliance seem inevitable. Actually, cooperation has occurred only with great difficulty. Although colleges, universities, and businesses alike see the benefits of cooperation, they have encountered many obstacles. An inability to communicate is a recurring theme in any analysis of their interaction.

The College Center of the Finger Lakes (CCFL), founded in 1961, is a nonprofit organization located in Corning, New York. Its primary purpose is to provide working adults with career-related education. CCFL is maintained by regional colleges and universities, businesses, health-care facilities, and other agencies.

The basic argument of this chapter is that an interinstitutional organization of colleges and universities is a highly effective means for meeting the educational needs of business and industry. Consortia have time and again demonstrated their ability to innovate. Made up of educational institutions, yet a step away from the college campus, they operate outside traditional rules and boundaries. A consortium can gather elements from its members and form them into a new entity designed to meet the needs of a changing environment.

Premises

The rationale for a consortium approach rests on four premises:

- The demand for education and training is greater now than it has been for decades.
- Colleges and universities must respond to this demand through systems that are sensitive to the client and cost-effective.
- The response must be energetic and aggressive.
- The response must provide quality education.

The failure to meet the business and industry need will stimulate the development of alternative sources of education and will lead to the eventual isolation of the college or university from a key element of its environment.

Each of these premises points to the strength and effectiveness of delivering education to business through a consortium. The very reason for the existence of this organization should be its ability to define needs, to design programs, and to deliver these programs effectively—in general, to be client centered and efficient in its use of resources.

The Need for Education and Training

The rationale for the interinstitutional approach rests, first of all, on the current need for education and training. Pushed by a competitive environment and pulled by an emphasis on human-resource development, businesses have begun to make education a central part of their operations. Although education and training are not new to the corporation, never before have they been so important.

National and international competition have forced businesses either to excel or to be destroyed. In either case, education has an important role. In businesses striving for success, education supports the drive for effective management, committed workers, and efficient technology. In businesses destroyed or restructured, education provides a way to redeploy human assets and opens career opportunities in jobs outside of the company.

Change, then, has created a vast appetite for education. It is part of the drive to increase productivity, to use technology, to involve workers in decision making, and to make managers more effective. Shifts in demand, industrial restructuring, unemployment, and sharp competition have created large groups that see education as a way to save their jobs or to help them find new ones.

There are a variety of means of meeting this educational need. Most training is, of course, done by the employer. Other educational offerings are given by training agencies, consultants, corporations, and institutions of higher education. Colleges and universities are involved in providing in-house education and external courses. These may be for credit or noncredit and may include workshops, seminars, courses, degrees, and certificates.

Delivery Systems for Education and Training

The unit of the college or university working with business must:

- understand and explain education in terms of its benefits to the client—it should be able to relate instructional methods and course content to the objectives of participants

- have the time and expertise to work closely with the customer—in the case of most businesses, the education and training officer, the managers, and the learner

- have the time and expertise to consult with college and university faculty members on content and on instructional methodologies

- have the time and expertise to administer and evaluate programs

A business invests in education because it aims to increase corporate and individual effectiveness. Often it expects both long- and short-term benefits. A responsive educational unit must therefore explain and design education in relationship to its desired impact on the business and its employees. This requires an understanding of learning in its broadest sense. How do education and training change people and organizations? Are they linked to productivity and quality? Do they produce more effective decision makers?

The answers to these questions cannot be vague generalizations. They must be tied to the specifics of program design. The educator needs to link overall benefits to specific impact. He should be able to suggest instructional techniques and formats that will produce the desired outcomes. Are case studies, lectures, or discussions most appropriate? Should multiple sessions or a marathon workshop be scheduled?

The educational provider must understand learning in its broadest sense in order to see the strategic points at which education can be effective. He must understand education in a specific sense in order to design offerings that achieve a goal. Explaining particular educational units in terms of traditional degrees, credits, or contact hours is only marginally useful. In the business setting, obtaining a degree or a certain number of credits is only meaningful if it makes the recipient a more useful member of the organization. Often, however, colleges and universities can describe their activities only in these terms. This difference in perspective is the single greatest blockage to cooperation between business and higher education.

Effective cooperation with a business requires ongoing interaction. Contact with the Education and Training Department is only the first step. It is vitally important to work with as many divisions and functional areas as possible. The goal of this contact is information on which to base programs.

Formal and informal discussions with corporate personnel constitute exploratory research, brainstorming, marketing, and evaluation. This process most often begins in the personnel department and then works outward to people with ideas throughout the company. At each point, company information and program possibilities can be gathered. Discussions may develop an enthusiasm for education that was not present before. They may create a network of managers who are willing to encourage and to support education.

Other means to probe the company include reading annual reports and other documents and sifting through newspaper and journal articles. An intimate knowledge of the business—its strengths and weaknesses, and its plans and prospects—is essential to providing program suggestions. In addition, program support and attendance can grow from using company information in designing and publicizing educational units. Being close to the business client means developing an ongoing relationship that goes beyond sales visits. It means becoming as much a part of the company as it is possible for an external agency to be.

A company contracting for an education expects instructors and content suitable for the program. The setting, student, and teaching can be quite different from that of the traditional campus situation. The content must be related to jobs and performance, and instructional methods should develop skills and knowledge. Although some faculty members have a natural ability to instruct in the business setting, others need coaching and a few should never be allowed near a business audience. It is the job of the administrator to make sure that suitable faculty members and content are used. At the same time, he may not usurp the primacy of the faculty member in determining classroom activity. Preparing faculty members to work with business and industry is a crucial task for the educational agency.

Another task is to handle the process of contracting, monitoring, and evaluating the educational programs. Each represents a specialized function. Financial negotiations should rest on a strategy already mapped out by the college or university. This strategy should define reasonable profit and cost guidelines. It should not be based on erasing deficits in other parts of the college or university, and neither should it be based on an embarrassment about charging for the real costs of designing and delivering a quality product. In the long run, businesses will accept a clearly explained and rational costing system. Either overcharging or undercharging will eventually lead to a breakdown in cooperation.

A client will expect close monitoring of the educational program. The responsible administrator should attend sessions, interview students, and contact supervisors during the course of the program. He or she should not just assure the presence of chalk and coffee but also observe student response and instructor performance. The administrator should have a strategy for making midcourse corrections if they are necessary.

Finally, the administrator is responsible for evaluation. Evaluation is essential for justifying the program, for identifying measures to improve the program, for maintaining supervisor and student contact, and for developing new program ideas. Evaluation, which is often an afterthought on campus, is a core activity when working with a business audience. It is the basic element of being accountable to the contracting business. It is also a basic component of quality.

In the business and industry context, quality does not necessarily mean complex, sophisticated programs taught by Ph.D.s. It does mean that the educational program delivers what is promised and has a positive effect on behavior, attitudes, and performance. Quality has a great importance in being accountable to the contractor, but in the present economic context it has taken on even greater importance.

It was noted above that the demand for education and training is caused by social and individual change. Businesses are growing, declining, and restructuring. If education is offered as a means to make these changes more positive, the programs had better work. If they do not, a disillusionment with colleges and universities will isolate them from a whole area of society—an area that is essential to their survival.

Case Studies in Cooperation

There are a variety of structures through which colleges and universities deliver education to business and industry. One frequently chosen by community colleges, for example, is a special office to handle business contacts. An interinstitutional project is another alternative. It is an especially effective means because its structure encourages the characteristics crucial to a strong program for business clients.

To illustrate, three examples will be used: the Southwest Washington Joint Center for Education, located in Vancouver, a town in a rural corner of the state of Washington; the College Center of the Finger Lakes, based in upstate New York (in Corning); and the New Hampshire Industrial Consortium, which has its headquarters in Plymouth, New Hampshire.

THE SOUTHWEST WASHINGTON JOINT CENTER FOR EDUCATION

The legislature of the state of Washington founded the Southwest Washington Joint Center for Education (SWJCE) on July 1, 1983. This action culminated a campaign involving industries, educational institutions, and economic development agencies. This campaign began in 1979 when two industries, Tektronics and Hewlett-Packard, announced major plant expansions. Subsequently, several other industries decided to locate facilities in southwest Washington. This influx of business held the promise of 35,000 jobs by the year 2000. The real and projected increases created a demand for education.

The surrounding area possessed two institutions of higher education: Clark College, a two-year institution, and an Evergreen State College extension center. The expanding companies needed advanced training for their engineers, skills training for production workers, and business education for their managers. For the population of Clark County to benefit from the new jobs, people had to have access to the education that would qualify them for employment.

The most economical means of providing this education was to develop a center that would draw courses from several institutions. The coalition of forces that convinced the state legislature to provide funding included Clark College, Washington State University, and Evergreen State College. With state support, these institutions established a center and began to offer courses aimed specifically at the needs of business and industry.

Current program offerings include graduate engineering from Washington State University; a variety of mathematics, science, and technology courses from Clark College; and applied liberal arts from Evergreen State College. A full program of noncredit workshops is sponsored through the center. The distant Washington State University teaches its program through the use of television and adjunct faculty members.

The Joint Center is governed by an administrative council appointed by the institutions that teach at the center. Program proposals come from an advisory committee that includes representatives from the community, from the state legislature, and from business. The Joint Center has three full-time staff members and two part-time coordinators who are based on the campuses of the member institutions.

THE COLLEGE CENTER OF THE FINGER LAKES

In contrast to this recently formed consortium, the College Center of the Finger Lakes (CCFL) began its continuing education program as an auxiliary function in 1965. At that time, the major local industry, Corning Glass Works, requested an MBA program. At the request of the company, a second program was added about 10 years later, but continuing education courses remained an unimportant part of the consortium's total program.

In 1981, continuing education changed from a peripheral function to the main purpose of CCFL. Six additional graduate and undergraduate programs have been brought to the center. Each is taught by a regional college or university. Participating institutions vary according to the programs that are required. Currently working at the center are Syracuse University, Cornell University, Alfred University, Rochester Institute of Technology, and Corning Community College. Programs include the Master of Business Administration; engineering, personnel, and management degrees; and a variety of certificates, noncredit courses, and workshops.

The College Center of the Finger Lakes is governed by a board of local college and university representatives and community members. The program is monitored by an advisory committee made up of business and student representatives. Office staff consists of three positions: a director in charge of program development, an operations coordinator, and a business manager/secretary.

THE NEW HAMPSHIRE INDUSTRIAL CONSORTIUM

There are many similarities between the SWJCE and CCFL, but the third example shows a contrasting approach to interinstitutional cooperation. The New Hampshire Industrial Consortium was founded through a grant from the Fund for the Improvement of Post-Secondary Education (FIPSE). Whereas both of the other illustrations involve large companies unserved by a four-year college or university, in the New Hampshire case the project focuses on small companies. These companies were also unserved— not, in this instance, because they were isolated, but because their size prevented them from contracting for cost-effective education and training.

The FIPSE project formed these companies into geographic subgroups, which then jointly determine their training needs. The next step is to request bids from the colleges and universities in the state; this process is facilitated by the fact that the institutions are members of the New Hampshire College and University Council, a consortium. Each member of the consortium is contacted with the bid request, and the businesses choose from the proposals that are submitted.

This process is monitored by a policy committee that includes representatives from the colleges and universities in the state. The major impetus for activity, however, comes from the regional business committees. The consortium has two staff members.

Why Are These Cooperative Ventures Successful?

According to almost every measurement, these three projects are successful: enrollments and financial resources are growing, college and university participation is increasing, and the number of businesses being served is expanding. A comparison of their structures, their target audiences, their educational programs, and their cooperative base provides some indication of the reasons for this success.

Each consortium serves an audience that previously was without access to appropriate educational services. The Southwest Center is located in an area that had no four-year institution within commuting distance. Although CCFL is surrounded by colleges and universities, either they do not have upper-division technology programs or they have chosen not to serve the part-time student. The New Hampshire project serves a new audience, in this case one based not on geography but on company size. The small companies that make up its industrial consortium could not use college programs in the past because the companies had too few employees.

Targeting an unserved audience is not only good marketing—it is also good politics. It is noteworthy that none of the consortium programs replaced an already operating connection between a college or university and an industrial client. Each consortium created programs that added new students to the rolls of cooperating institutions, and so "turf" arguments and anxieties have been minimal.

In terms of organizational structure, each consortium has business and industry as its sole academic focus. SWJCE was created expressly for this purpose, and CCFL is a nonprofit corporation that has this service as its mission. The New Hampshire project was grafted onto a working consortium, but this aspect of its activity has a distinct organization, with its own mission, goals, and financial structure.

As part of their exclusive emphasis, both the Southwest Center and the College Center of the Finger Lakes have a physical plant that is dedicated to teaching adults. Each is a self-contained instructional unit with classrooms, a library, computer centers, and a business office/registration room. SWJCE is part of an elaborate telecommunications system and shares laboratory facilities with the local community college. The New Hampshire group holds classes in centrally located industrial facilities as a means of overcoming the geographic dispersion of its clients.

The scheduling of classes in these buildings is done to facilitate attendance by employed students. In most cases, classes meet once a week for an extended period, which minimizes both time away from work and missed classes due to travel assignments. Semesters are shortened to a trimester or quarter schedule. This permits rapid progress and allows stopping out during peak work periods.

All three consortia also have sharply focused academic offerings. The Southwest Center and CCFL sponsor both credit and noncredit courses, while the New Hampshire group offers only noncredit workshops. The emphasis for all three is on engineering, business administration, management, and technology courses. Although an occasional liberal arts course may be offered, this is the exception. In the case of CCFL, students in need of liberal arts are referred to one of the local colleges and universities. This "hands off" policy exists because business clients are, in general, less interested in the liberal arts and because it avoids competition with local institutions.

Despite the intense concentration on business, the governance of all three consortia rests almost exclusively with college and university officials. What is perhaps even more surprising is that these people may be chosen from regional institutions not actively teaching through the consortium. Such is the case with the College Center of the Finger Lakes and in New Hampshire. Only at SWJCE are the active institutions alone represented.

The seeming anomaly of boards that are both nonbusiness and nonteaching is explained by their practical function. They have as their primary purpose the avoidance of conflict among and between the participating institutions and their neighbors. They indicate a healthy respect for the tendency of any organization to protect its own territory. These boards are, therefore, relatively passive and perform a watchdog function; they are more likely to prohibit an action than to initiate a project.

The advisory councils represent, in each case, the source for innovation and experimentation. They are made up almost exclusively of client representatives. It is here that the real program development function takes place.

All three consortia described here have small professional staffs whose time is divided among administrative tasks, politics, and program development.

None of the organizations has established cooperation in the instruction of courses and programs. None sponsors a degree in which students join courses from a variety of colleges and universities into a single degree. In all of the programs, in fact, there is minimal interchange of courses and of students between and among institutions.

The reason for this seems, first of all, the desire of the participating colleges and universities to retain control of their programs. In addition, however, both students and companies want a degree or program that fits a traditional view of advanced university training. Finally, there is an implicit or explicit concern that the cooperative organization is not as stable as its institutional members.

The consortium programs form a comprehensive whole in offering needed education to clients, but the parts can also stand by themselves. The programs are clearly identified with their campus sources. Indeed, in all three illustrations there is more cooperation among the business clients than there is among the colleges and universities that provide the instruction.

The consortium office thus connects two independent groups: higher education and business and industry. The consortium provides academic support for the delivery of educational programs and a forum for linking businesses with each other. To some extent, the consortium actually serves to keep business and college from coming together except through the medium of the consortium office.

These three consortia have some common characteristics: their sharp focus on serving the business client, their small staffs, a governance structure that reduces conflict, their role as a forum that permits clients to develop programs, and their emphasis on cooperation without consolidation.

An Interinstitutional Approach

The initial reason for forming a continuing-education consortium may stem from a practical necessity: delivering education to a geographically remote area. Whether or not intended by the founders, however, in most cases the consortium turns out to provide more effective services than a single institution could provide.

The prime positive attribute of the consortium is its capacity to be client centered. In this multi-institution setting, business clients and the central office will initiate most projects; the office works as an independent agency with the client; the restraints and limitations of on-campus policies and procedures are relaxed; and a physical plant designed to serve the client may even exist.

The consortium is free from the control of any single member or client. The campuses place broad boundaries around their activity but do not have a specific program agenda. Program development and innovation come from the consortium office and from the clients. They are the ones who design programs, based on need. Proposals, in complete form, go to the college and university members, where modification and negotiation take place—but within the context of the request. If one institution objects to the elements of a client request, the odds are good that another institution will offer to meet them.

This leads to the second argument for a cooperative approach: the ability to draw from the resources of several colleges and universities. This has two benefits. First, as stated above, it makes programs client centered. Second, it allows the consortium to offer a comprehensive program.

It is extremely difficult for a single college or university, no matter how large, to offer all the programs that a coalition of businesses and industries requires. Even if these programs were present at a single institution, they would be in high-demand areas like computer science and electrical engineering, where the campus already has great difficulty staffing for its own needs. Through a cooperative approach, these programs can be drawn from a variety of sources, and the strain can be reduced.

The cooperative approach provides adequate support services for the programs. Traditional extension centers rent a building for the time of the class and then require students to deal with the main campus between class sessions. No matter how hard the administration may try, these classes have a kind of "orphan" status in the total college or university program.

In contrast, cooperation, such as that in the three illustrations, provides a real base from which to teach. Administrative attention comes from the consortium office. In addition, in two of the three cases there are classrooms and libraries—in short, a complete facility dedicated to the needs of the learner. Problems are taken care of immediately. Companies deal with the consortium the same way they deal with any other valued vendor, without the delays of being part of an organization whose main purpose is to serve another kind of client.

The cooperative approach allows the employment and training of real experts in education for business and industry. Whereas a single campus may not be able to afford this service, a group of institutions can support a staff—albeit a small staff—that spends its time working with its clients.

A cooperative approach also enables institutions to avoid redundancy in programs and contacts. It is plainly ridiculous to have two weak programs, each barely above the break-even point, when one strong program could be operating. In addition, one of the most negative experiences an industrial client can have is multiple contacts from colleges and universities, each asking the same thing in terms of needs assessments and program support. A single contact point reduces frustration and increases the chances of building quality programs.

The creation of a consortium as a separate entity also permits a reward system that is based on performance. There is no reason for the office staff to be part of the traditional salary structure, based on longevity. A system that rewards quality performance with bonuses and benefits can reinforce the client-centered nature of the organization.

In short, the interinstitutional structure centers on the business client. It uses campus and business resources efficiently and provides adequate administrative support. It avoids duplication of effort. The consortium office and its personnel system can be structured to reward service to the customer.

An Agenda for the Future

Although none of the organizations cited as illustrations—the Southwest Washington Joint Center for Education, the College Center of the

Finger Lakes, and the New Hampshire Industrial Consortium—has served business and industry for more than a few years, each is stable and workable as it stands. The future, however, clearly offers the possibility that such centers can provide even greater services to both industrial clients and college and university members. The time may come when consortia like these take on an academic life of their own, above and beyond the individual programs that are offered through them by the participating institutions.

One member institution might offer an "umbrella" degree into which credits from other participating colleges and universities may be freely transferred. This is advantageous because it allows companies and students to design degrees based on technical application. In engineering, for example, a great need exists for knowledge drawn from many of the previously distinct engineering disciplines.

The consortium forms a convenient means for a student to join industrial, mechanical, and electrical engineering courses around a core of basic knowledge. A degree awarded by one college or university circumvents many of the problems of developing a joint degree. All that is asked is a flexible transfer policy and some freedom in design. In case cooperation breaks down at some point, a core institution still provides support to students.

The next step to consider in developing services for the business client is the distinct consortium degree. This approach has its strengths and weaknesses. The strengths of this step rest in the even higher level of flexibility possible in this kind of project. Part of the degree could be drawn from cooperating business-training workshops, taught either in-house or externally; parts could be drawn from colleges and universities; still other parts could be drawn from the student's work experience. The latter could involve credit for life experience, special work projects, or even internships that expose the student to different work responsibilities and environments.

A consortium degree may raise suspicions about its academic integrity and fears that it is an assault on college and university programs. In point of fact, this kind of approach is already growing up—but without the participation of higher education. It would be one way for colleges and universities to become involved in this movement, adding their academic strengths to what seems to be an irrepressible development.

Another possibility for additional service is to make the consortium almost a part of a company's training department. College personnel, for example, could actually work on a retainer basis in order to supplement internal efforts. The company benefits because it can save dollars and have the flexibility of reinforcing its training effort in times of need without having to retain this cost in times when the training need may lessen.

A second line of future consortium development lies in offering additional services to colleges and universities. These services would assist faculty members in learning more about business and industry—not for outplacement but rather as a means of making them more effective teachers and researchers.

One option here would be to supply faculty members with information about their potential clients. This information could include briefings on company developments, on industrial applications of research, and on crucial economic situations. A second option for faculty service could include specific assistance in learning from the business setting. This might involve such teaching techniques as developing case studies or using discussion groups. It also might include internships and other direct exposures to the company setting. This preparation would be focused on transferring knowledge back to the campus.

Similar offerings could, of course, be useful to the industrial client: briefings on research and loaned-executive programs to bring corporate expertise to the campus. Since programs of this kind are already in place, however, the consortium would need to look at the specific situation and to see if further activity was appropriate.

The development of additional functions will require venture capital. One extremely important function of the consortium is educational experimentation. It is, therefore, important that development funds are available to hire faculty members and instructional-design consultants. The consortium must be recognized as a separate fund-raising entity.

Conclusion

The consortium structure efficiently connects college and university resources with the business and industry demand for education. Through it, educational programs are translated into a form that can be used by business. Organizationally, the consortium encourages, supports, and stimulates staff concern and expertise in dealing with the business client.

The consortium exists to provide educational excellence to an exacting audience. The service possibilities of the interinstitutional setting have just begun to be explored.

—7—

A Partnership
with Business

JOHN M. BEVAN AND ANN C. BAKER

As part of its reorganization effort, the Charleston Higher Education Consortium employed in 1982 an associate director, whose responsibility it is to assist the six member institutions in realizing the potential of the area's postsecondary institutions in order to capitalize on the unique business and research resources of South Carolina's low-country region. This person, in pursuance of these ends, visited many of the large industrial plants where research and development play a major role in the company's operation. The purposes of these initial visits included acquainting herself with plant managers and research directors, undertaking the process of building cooperative relationships, discovering the general nature of the research being conducted at these sites, and identifying the major pieces of equipment being used.

Beyond these ends were numerous other objectives: to take what information was gained and make it available to faculty colleagues who might be interested in gaining controlled access to this equipment for their own research; to enable these faculty members to share with fellow specialists information of a theoretical nature and to participate in

The Charleston Higher Education Consortium provides a coordinated working relationship among its six member institutions, facilitates diverse kinds of interinstitutional activities, and maintains and develops projects involving the members. One major program focus of the consortium, which was founded in 1969, is working closely with the public school districts in its three-county region.

111

joint studies; to explore the opportunities for securing summer research appointments for themselves and for their students; to work on projects where faculty expertise contributed to the research resource of the company; and to establish a base for joint publication.

Follow-up developments included: (1) an inventory of all major equipment at each plant, excluding those pieces so highly specialized as to disclose proprietary information; (2) the designation of a research contact person at the plant and a counterpart on each campus; (3) a meeting of campus and industrial liaison persons, so they might better know each other; (4) occasional special programs to exchange knowledge and to provide general reinforcement of professional interests; (5) the strengthening of other interinstitutional programs that either cannot be accomplished by an individual institution or can be done more economically and/or effectively through cooperative efforts; and (6) the maintaining and enhancing of professional development of academic and business staffs through productive exchange of ideas and facilities.

Although the many visits in initiating this program took time, on more than one occasion the comment was made by a plant manager that he was very pleased because this single arrangement covered all six member institutions and relieved him of the necessity of duplicating everything several times. Cooperation of this kind can serve as an effective modus operandi not only for the growth and development of persons and products, but also for relationships. In every contact made, the enthusiasm for cooperation was noticeable, and interest in the consortium extended beyond the matter at hand. Now, months later, a key question remains to be answered: How many of our faculty colleagues will take advantage of this new opportunity?

Thus, this relatively straightforward example of a cooperative project begins to illustrate the underlying complexity of motivation, operating styles, and divergent priorities that naturally emerge and that characterize potential partnerships between business and higher education. It is no coincidence that the sums of money currently being spent on in-house training and education programs by employers are staggering. An estimate is about $25 billion annually, close to the amount spent annually for all of higher education in the 50 states. Is it any wonder that many corporate schools rival public and private schools of higher education?

Cultivating the "Expansive Reach of the Mind"

Of course, there are differences in mission between these two enterprises, and this fact should be recognized from the outset when cooperation between them is considered. The corporation supports the development and renewal of employee skills so as to produce tangible returns; the college or university has as its objective the long-range enhancement of the person. This distinction is not as clearly drawn as it appears, however. Today, perhaps more than ever before, the corporation supports an increasing concern about quality of worklife and personal fulfillment as they contribute to productivity (i.e., better-fulfilled employees contribute to more tangible corporate returns).

Yet, the primary focus of the corporation is on professional competencies and only secondarily on personal development, whereas the primary focus of the college or university is on personal development and only secondarily on professional competencies.

This seems to serve as a clear and sufficient distinction until one hears a less-than-faint echo from the past reminding us that "*the tasks executives have begun to face today and will inescapably confront tomorrow, arising out of the economic and social roles of corporations in American life, are of a magnitude that cannot even be properly grasped, let alone dealt with, except by men with big minds*" (emphasis added). These are the words of C. Scott Fletcher, President of the Fund for Adult Education, which he wrote in 1959 in an introduction to a book entitled *Toward the Liberally Educated Executive.* How formidable a prediction or warning this is now, 25 years later, as one reflects on the corporate challenges that shape the duties and responsibilities of present-day chief executive officers. Thus, the Charleston Higher Education Consortium began to turn to approaches designed to cultivate an "expansive reach" of the mind.

Three of the member institutions of the consortium had been offering, at irregular intervals, a variety of professionally focused business seminars. These had limited success because of competitive seminars being presented by each other, by other colleges and universities from inside and outside of the state, by the chamber of commerce, by the American Management Association, and by other organizations. In these instances, young entrepreneurs organized the classes and recruited the students. As might be expected when the Office of Continuing Education or the Department of Business became involved in such an effort, little in the way of interinstitutional cooperation emerged.

The proliferation of these seminars, sparsely attended because of frequency and repetition, was a clear indication that consortial intrusion with more of the same would meet with resistance and would add to the competition. More importantly, the orientation toward development of professional competencies once again missed the mark of meeting the essential challenge.

Those three consortium colleges (the Baptist College at Charleston,

The Citadel, and the College of Charleston) are in the tradition of liberal studies, the best approach to cultivating an expansive reach of the mind. So it was decided that for executive seminars we would pursue the stated mission of the liberal studies institutions, which avoids what Alfred North Whitehead identified in *The Aims of Education* (1928) as "producing minds in a groove . . . with imperfect categories of thought derived from progressing in one profession only, and where we are left with no expansion of wisdom and with greater need of it."

This approach implied more than an expanded reach or breadth of knowledge alone; it projected the ability to move more confidently in the presence of increasing uncertainty, moving more surely from policy to action because refining humanistic skills provides the added benefit of pulling things together. It would mean reading well-chosen selections by great authors or leaders, selections that grasp your imagination for a moment then give you back yourself enriched, and from which you come away a better person somewhat enlarged and extended. Not only do such readings elicit a clearer perspective of ourselves and our world, but these authors and their thoughts often act as islands of serenity in a turbulent sea—providing the ground and setting for pulling things together.

The next step was to examine the variety of programs based on liberal studies that had been or were being conducted in the training of executives. We explored those of Dartmouth College, Pomona College, Southwestern at Memphis (now Rhodes College), the University of Pennsylvania, and the Aspen Institute—always speaking to persons who had participated in them. Then we spoke with corporate executives and academic colleagues who we thought might be interested in attending this style of seminar. The response was overwhelmingly supportive, particularly when the Aspen seminar format was discussed.

A dialogue with the Aspen Institute was initiated and continued over several months as the consortium and Aspen learned about each other and explored the potential mutual benefits that might be realized through their collaboration. After the associate director participated in a six-day Aspen Executive Seminar, a sample two-day seminar, conducted by Aspen's leading moderator, was held for a select group in South Carolina. These two experiences provided the consortium with opportunities to evaluate the appropriateness of the approach as a means of cultivating an expansive reach of the mind and the viability of the approach in the region.

The individuals invited to the two-day sample seminar were chosen because they represented the upper-level executives and professionals from the Southeast and because they were considered decision makers of high influence and substantial intellect. Most of the attendees were from the private sector. Several who were skeptics were intentionally included, along with a few key persons from the administrations and the faculties of the member institutions.

Prior to attending an Aspen/Charleston seminar, participants are sent a notebook of readings composed of classic works of literature, supplemented by contemporary documents of exceptional merit. The moderator uses these readings to prime or spark the interaction between participants in a group. Although these readings are very important in defining themes and issues, the single most critical component of the seminar sessions is the moderator, who pursues every participant, guides the exchanges, injects humor when needed, keeps the pace of each session lively, and makes the discussion always timely. On the other hand, the participants strive through the Socratic approach to perceive more closely the meaning of the problems, issues, and options. They seek to feel their way more confidently in the face of mounting uncertainty, using the classic readings as guideposts to knowing where they are as they move deeper into dialectic and didactic discourse.

At the end of the sample seminar, participants were asked to evaluate the experience. Without exception, they urged the consortium to develop the concept on an ongoing basis. A small but essential core of promoters had been created.

The staff learned very quickly, however, that personal contact is the only viable means of promoting a program whose very nature is to appeal to the cultivation of the mind and spirit of the person rather than to the acquisition of skills. Through face-to-face conversations, insightful leaders understand that, as important as proficiency in skills is to all of us in an increasingly technological society, the need to broaden ourselves as persons who are adaptable and resourceful enough to maintain and enhance our humanistic heritage in a rapidly changing environment is even more critical. Moreover, the conceptualizing and the bringing into being of a program of such broad dimensions can emerge more naturally out of a consortium, with its greater resources, than from most individual institutions—particularly small institutions.

Opportunities in Economic Development

Another area of involvement and leadership for higher education consortia is in those situations where economic development programs are being vigorously pursued: i.e., where cities and states are trying to attract new companies and industries are trying to expand, and where area colleges and universities are seen, and see themselves, as critical resources for the kinds of training and research necessary to maintain or enhance the economic growth of the locale. This is another instance (maybe the best) in which the community benefits, in which the institutions of higher education benefit, and in which the learners benefit. One such example, in the low-country of South Carolina, involved the city of Charleston, a major corporation, and this consortium.

Charleston is certainly not different from most metropolitan areas in having a large urban neighborhood, such as its East Side, that is dominated by high unemployment, that has a majority of heads of households who are female, that has an alarming school-dropout rate and crime rate, and that has a minority population of 99%. The past several decades have seen vast sums of money and energy spent on trying to revitalize such communities.

These efforts have unequivocally demonstrated that one-dimensional programs, no matter how well done, are not adequate to revitalize neighborhoods so blighted by poverty, illiteracy, and frustration. Effective solutions must be collaborative, creating within the neighborhood the elements that become self-sustaining in their regenerative efforts. When a large private corporation, Control Data, joined hands with the city of Charleston to convert an old factory on the East Side into an "incubator" for small-business development, the project received much attention largely because it introduced a holistic approach and because it had the full force of a city government behind it.

Obviously, having an effective educational/learning component was one essential element if the neighborhood residents were to be given any fair chance of receiving the jobs being created or of being able to benefit generally from the renewed sense of hope being generated throughout the neighborhood. Yet, those residents who most needed to take advantage of the learning program had usually experienced little success in traditional learning settings; thus, an innovative, self-paced approach was needed. In addition, the learning program itself had to focus on much more than cognitive needs.

At the outset of the program, none of the higher education institutions in the area had a physical presence or had attained credibility on the East Side. Although the public school district had an adult-education program, it was serving a small number of people and was attempting only to meet the basic skills needs of the residents. In fact, there was no educational institution or existing training program unencumbered enough to respond quickly and directly to the unusual opportunities on the East Side.

The consortium saw the opportunity and began the informal process of identifying needs and seeking resources that might be available. The process that evolved, although both frustrating and exciting, had access through the consortium to many diverse resources, thus facilitating a flexible and dynamic response. Grant money was secured; negotiations and compromise were sustained until the complex of necessary alliances was formed; an interim administrative structure was created, with the consortium taking the lead for a two-year period in order to give the project time to become institutionalized; an innovative and unusually successful computer-based learning center, emphasizing also the affective dimensions, was established; and incentives were used to secure commitments for support from every critical element of the community, including the private sector, educational institutions, social service agencies, and neighborhood leaders.

Now, several years later, the learning center is well established and highly respected among employers, who hire the students when they leave the center. Its acceptance and success is confirmed by the waiting list of people wanting to get into the program. The center was supported earlier by the Fund for the Improvement of Post-Secondary Education (FIPSE), is currently underwritten by the Job Training Partnership Act (JTPA), and is administratively a part of Trident Technical College, the two-year technical college in the consortium. The center will soon be relocated in the new technical-school campus that is about to open on the East Side, just across the street from the small-business incubator.

The presence of the technical school in the neighborhood is a concrete illustration of the improved image of the East Side and will offer residents access to postsecondary education and to the skills training essential for the economic health of the individuals and for the community at large. Overall, the consortium has worked to diminish traditional alienation, to remove institutional barriers to cooperation, and to help to create new forms of community interaction now that interdependencies are acknowledged and accepted.

Working with the Schools and Others

Somewhat comparable to the corporate/educational linkage cited immediately above is the business/educational linkage whose aim is to help the public schools to cope with problems of school management, teacher preparedness, and student performance. Although one impetus for this dimension of collaboration is the improvement of the quality of those students entering postsecondary institutions, an even more compelling inducement is the receptivity within the business community to approaches for partnership projects with public schools. The immediacy of the payoff, in terms of assistance both to the community and to current and future employees, is profound. Linkages around such projects serve as fertile settings for our postsecondary institutions to build and to expand these relationships and partnerships.

During the summer of 1984, the consortium and the Work/Education Council, building on a similar program that has been successful for nearly 10 years with precollege teachers and counselors, began a pilot project for principals. In the ongoing program, teachers and counselors are placed for six weeks in entry-level jobs in local businesses and industries. Here they gain experiences intended to expand their exposure to, and realistic understanding of, authentic work-site settings. They spend one day each week in sessions that are designed to encourage individual and group reflection on the implications for the educational process.

In order to assist principals who are striving to manage their schools more effectively, the pilot project was designed to give them broad exposure to a diversity of upper-level managers operating within their own work settings. The participating principals spent one week in each of four companies and one week in the Medical University of South Carolina, a consortium institution.

The management approaches and styles in every situation were markedly different. Principals were provided opportunities to discuss what they observed, to reflect on and evaluate their experience, and to compare their own management styles with those of their hosts in half-day seminars at the end of each week. There was a consensus among the principals at the conclusion of the program that their skills were improved, their perceptions were broadened, and their imaginations were stimulated. In fact, the reactions of the participants were so positive that the initial program was refined and subsequently offered to a larger group.

Many other coordinated ventures between higher education and business are subsumed under other headings, such as co-op partnerships, work-study internships for students and faculty members, simulations, sabbaticals, executives in residence, required volunteer work, career days, task forces, and maintenance roles. These ventures may be linked with such other agencies as the Work/Education Council, the Industry-Labor Education Council, the JTPA and the Private-Industry Council (PIC), the National Association for Industry-Education Cooperation, the Education Commission of the States, and the National Alliance for Business. Suffice it to say that they provide unusual opportunities for consortial involvement, with each opportunity exhibiting peculiar advantages and problems too numerous to catalog fully.

Advantages of Business–Higher Education Cooperation through a Consortium

It might be worth enumerating some of the general advantages and problems that arise in the process of consortial venturing between business and higher education.

A CONSISTENT APPROACH

A consortial effort unifies the approach and produces an integrated and more comprehensive program, with improved results. The efforts of several colleges separately engaged with the same companies tend to be unrelated, duplicative, tentative, and less productive than desired. A unified approach removes the ad hoc character of many student and staff activity involvements. This is particularly true in partnership programs for economically disadvantaged, high-risk students.

AN IMPRESSIVE COLLECTIVE RESOURCE

In a community striving to enhance its economic base, higher education can be a stronger element in marketing itself as a significant resource if it presents itself as a consortial model. When talking to a corporate executive searching out the area as a possible plant site, mentioning a consortium's faculty of 1,200 and its expertise and research resources is much more impressive than talking about 6 or so separate faculties that range from 68 to 300.

To put it succinctly, the whole is much more than the sum total of its parts, and the presentation of a community's integrated educational establishment gives the impression of a richer and much more diverse system. After all, a liberal arts college is a liberal arts college, and five liberal arts colleges seem to add up to one duplicated five times. But when a representative from a high-technology industry learns that among this consortium's institutions there are five specialists in artificial intelligence, for instance, a noticeable expression of interest is immediately detected.

MORE, AT LESS COST

Indirect costs of business companies are typically much higher than those of public and private educational institutions, which offer not only their facilities but also the research expertise of faculty members and students dedicated to the study of the human condition and its problems, who give much time and effort merely for the satisfaction derived from helping to shed some new light on problems in the area of human development and human relationships. Experience suggests that more is available and is offered at a lesser cost when implemented within a consortial structure.

A BROADER FUNDING BASE

Besides a broader organizational base, a consortium can provide a broader funding base. Particularly for businesses not accustomed to supporting higher education, the consortium appears to appeal in a manner not very different from that of the United Way. Often colleges and universities working with companies produce new funding possibilities that, if pursued by one or the other separately, would not be productive. Through working together there emerge new funding networks (i.e., an order of new sponsorships), along with a new public image of industry and education coordinated in joint undertakings that directly benefit the community and each other.

Furthermore, consortial interaction with business tends to foster mutual respect between institutions of higher learning that are working together in the same program, with the same cooperating businesses. Such networking provides a more sharply focused "real-world orientation" that provides a better basis for further cooperation and mutual concern when shared by education and business. In addition, this may augment independent research and development funding for company-sponsored projects at colleges and universities.

OPPORTUNITIES FOR INNOVATION

Consortial interaction in projects with business presents an opportunity for innovation and experimentation otherwise resisted by colleagues on a single campus, particularly when such plans call for extending programs beyond campus. Innovation poses the threat of precedent setting and suggests that something needs to be improved. A consortial effort with business increases the chances of risk taking being accepted, because it is risk taking with a partner accustomed to risk. This provides that "real-world orientation" necessary to persuade enough academic persons to venture. Consortial interactions with business increase the chances for innovation and experimentation among those on campus.

BETTER COMMUNICATIONS

Communications are improved with business because of consortium relations. In terms of time and dollars saved and energy conserved, the chances of communicating effectively through one agency are much better than through ten simultaneously. It stands to reason that as the numbers of individually involved agencies increase, the chances for misunderstanding, duplication, fragmentation, and low productivity increase.

A MODEL OF COOPERATION

Successful cooperation among institutions seems to promote cooperation and to propagate healthy attitudes conducive to further cooperation—a bit different from competition, which most often breeds antagonism, contempt, and distress, hardly the attitudinal ingredients for community action of lasting quality. The consortium model of education is a good one for cooperation with business: i.e., it is a win-win and lose-lose model wherein both win, or both lose. It certainly is exemplary of the character and spirit such enterprises should wish to foster in joint endeavors.

A BROADER PERSPECTIVE FOR BOTH PARTNERS

A consortial approach helps to minimize the turf-oriented perspective that dampens and defeats so many joint projects and accentuates the possibilities for utilizing the diversity of its people, among whom visionaries can be identified and assembled in common tasks. Likewise, this approach can bring the parties in business with similar qualities into a linkage with those so recognized in academe. The result can be a broader perspective for both academe and industry, eventually producing transition within a community. Also, bureaucratically encumbered structures are less likely to emerge.

DEVELOPING NEW KNOWLEDGE

Colleges and universities continue to be the primary source for new knowledge, new discoveries, and new concepts. Partnerships of these institutions with those of the corporate world make for very suitable and readily adaptable modes of transmission immediately beneficial to society at large. In addition, it should be more cost-effective for industry to rely on a tax-exempt educational structure for such transmissions than to continue to develop separate programs of its own within the private tax sector.

A COMMITMENT TO THE COMMUNITY

Colleges and universities working in consort with one another, and in partnership with businesses, stand as concrete evidence of joint commitment to community or regional development and can come to symbolize a bulwark of strength and ingenuity in the promotion of, and service to, that community. Because such a consortium has a broader perspective and political base, more extensive linkages, and greater and more diverse human resources than any of its member institutions, and because its modus operandi is cooperative and not competitive, built on mutual respect and understanding, what it generates or instigates should be more realistically oriented. Business can contribute significantly to education as a partner to one of education's critical touchstones of realism, the consortium.

Some Potential Problems

Let us turn now to the potential problems of this business/higher education relationship. What business expects of the academy is a structure and a modus operandi that reinforce community and that maintain the autonomy, politically and philosophically, of the parties engaged in the cooperative enterprise. It is imperative that education deal in styles befitting an educational model: a model that espouses openness, not secrecy; truth and understanding, not misinformation; trust, not suspicion; full partnership, not minimal compliance; the use of conflict for creative cooperation, not for control and spoils; and the sharing of power by all parties to the mutual benefit of all parties, not balance of power. This is the image of the consortium that best reflects the educational component of a business–education enterprise and the image that most likely will extend itself effectively to its business partners.

Of course we can hardly say that what we know as academe today evolved out of a system of thought or philosophy of learning wherein means and ends were clearly contrived or enlivened by a clarity of mission or commitment. Admittedly the changes that take place within academe evolve out of discordant traditions—out of the internal conflicts of interests and external collisions with other social institutions, out of the emergence of new needs and new resources or disappearing resources, and out of the interplay of ideas and ideals with the frequently unmanageable conditions of human nature.

Then again, we are reminded further that colleges and universities are truth seeking, truth telling institutions and that the questions posed are critical to the meaning conveyed in their heritage and to the perpetuation of society through that heritage: its social and cultural values; its moral vision; its accumulated wisdom (which embraces the struggle for justice, the case of the less-fortunate, and the liberation of the oppressed); the compassion to share oneself; and the pleasure to gain back oneself. All of this constitutes the truth of meaning—the meaning that grows out of our understanding and knowledge of human relationships, human problems, and human destiny.

This being the case, a most aggravating source of friction arising from the implementation of a business–education co-venture is the problem of "turf"—that is, when the consortium is perceived by one or more constituents as an intruder into territories claimed as exclusive domains. Such claims are often couched in expressions suggesting competition in public relations, fund-raising, and program. Of course the final sequel is a series of questions about the authority of a consortium to represent its members to any business in a projected joint enterprise.

To say the least, this is confusing to business partners. These attitudes have an impact on partnerships particularly at the point where cooperating with business requires risk and on-the-spot decisions, which in the operation of business means placing authority at the level where the action is. This is consistent with the task-oriented, tangible-return approach of a business enterprise but less than tolerant of the academy's governance model, depicted as the traditional faculty conclave in which every individual has his or her say on every matter.

Another aspect to which we must be alert is posturing. The educational enterprise tends to avoid issues by regulating, by getting its organization in shape to face the issues, and then by further regulating itself to avoid confrontation. It behaves somewhat like the military establishment, which is always preparing itself so as to avoid what it hopes it will not have to face. Business, on the other hand, prepares by moving to meet the problem—by regarding the problem as an invitation to a solution. These differences in posturing for action may present problems for interaction.

Attitudes are another problem area. The college or the university approaching the corporation is often perceived as "coming with hat in hand": i.e., coming only when it wants something. Also, when partnerships of one sort or another are suggested, it is usually expected that those within the corporation will play junior-level roles in a project designed by those in academe to ends primarily academic—albeit with the condition that the corporation underwrites the costs as an expression of the worth to the corporation of identification with the academy: "prestige at a price."

These attitudes do not prevail in every instance, but they are provoked too frequently. Fortunately the consortium exists to do together what cannot be readily accomplished alone, and by the very purpose of enhancing and maintaining cooperation it insures sharing in the planning and evolving of a project. A consortial format provides a leveling influence to nonproductive attitudes that discourage and sometimes stultify healthy relationships; the consortium keeps the focus on the success of the project and not on who brings what to the project, and it is always pressing for sensitivity and flexibility.

Disappointment also takes its toll in cooperative undertakings between business and education. On many occasions, representatives of industry and education work out good plans, only to have them cancelled because the educational institutions within the consortium will not agree to slight adjustments in structure or procedures necessary to the implementation of the plan. Also, more than a few programs have been arranged for faculty research, leaves, or sabbaticals within industry, only to have little or no interest shown in them—even when the months of planning had been based on an expression of strong interest. This is least likely to happen when a group of presidents of participating educational institutions lends its verbal endorsement, which is communicated directly to the faculties by the provosts or deans.

Success in Business–Education Cooperation

There are other advantages and problems, but suffice it to say that the advantages outweigh the problems. The model of cooperation between business and education presented by educational consortia, as in the case of the Charleston Higher Education Consortium, is a productive one. The settings seem complex, primarily because too little energy has been concentrated in this model.

To be successful in our joint undertakings, we are going to have to define learning more in terms of experience than in terms of data. We probably must behave differently, becoming a bit less objective and less dedicated to regulatory process. We must become more sensitive—and more open to confrontation. We must be more tolerant of uncertainty and less fearful of losing identity. We must, finally, become more cognizant of our role of sharing values in a social-change process in which we are expected to survive change.

Rather than competing with each other within the educational establishment at points where we touch concerns with business and industry, it would seem better to cooperate with one another in pursuance of the goals we share with the world of production and trade. There is a great deal at stake—not only savings of great sums of money, but the smooth transition of society and the traditional contributions we are best prepared to provide for guaranteeing a smooth transition, preferably along the lines of enlightened self-interest.

Expanded partnerships of education with business, particularly those on the order of the educational consortium, are and should be a signal of what the trends portend. Certainly such effective approaches for dialogue and cooperation between the corporate and educational sectors need to be explored more vigorously.

—8—

School/College Collaboration

DONN C. NEAL

During the last few years, schools and higher education institutions have begun to rediscover one another. After too many years when they were isolated from and ignorant of each other, schools and colleges have come to realize how important they are to one another. Questions about the quality of education in the schools (and, more recently, at the college level as well) have strengthened the awareness of the need for good communication and for collaboration between the two sectors.

As Americans have reassessed how well our two educational systems are performing, they have also begun to rethink how these systems can work better together. The College Board, the National Commission on Excellence in Education, and more than a dozen other groups that have addressed the issue of quality in education have cited the importance of school/college collaboration. There is a growing recognition that how schools and colleges cooperate may be critical to the achievement of quality at both levels, and there are encouraging signs that such cooperation is increasing.

The higher education consortium can play a unique and vital role

The Pittsburgh Council on Higher Education (PCHE) is a multi-purpose consortium that includes the ten colleges and universities in Allegheny County (Pittsburgh), Pennsylvania. Established in 1966, PCHE enables its member institutions to share information and to strengthen their diverse educational programs, as well as to enhance the intellectual, cultural, and economic attractiveness of Pittsburgh.

127

in fostering school/college collaboration by facilitating communication, by helping the partners to identify common goals, and sometimes by hosting cooperative ventures. This chapter will describe some areas where collaboration between schools and colleges seems most promising, the advantages and disadvantages of using a consortium to institute this cooperation, and some strategies for bringing about successful collaborative activities.

The Reasons for Cooperation

It might be useful to start with some of the reasons why the schools and higher education should invest in cooperation with one another—and an investment, of time and energy as well as of funds, it will certainly be. As with any form of cooperation, both partners must be able to foresee some benefits from the partnership. The consortium can play a constructive role in encouraging school/college collaboration only if it knows the potential benefits, abstract and practical alike, that can flow from the partnership. Why, then, should these two sectors cooperate?

All of us, whatever our roles in education, have a stake in quality at all levels of our two systems. Education must excel, from beginning to end, if we are to have an informed and responsible citizenry and a humane and progressive society. All of us also profit or suffer as education (in the broadest sense) rises or falls in popular esteem. Education is truly a continuum—the "seamless web," as Ernest Boyer has called it—and we all have more that unites us than we have that separates us. Higher education cannot afford to sit complacently on the sidelines when the schools take their lumps any more than it can afford to be across the scrimmage line administering some of those lumps.

More selfishly, colleges and universities need a strong and successful school system because higher education is a major consumer of the product of the schools: well-educated graduates. Only as the schools improve can colleges and universities themselves do a better job of educating their students.

In addition, education is today increasingly recognized as a priceless resource in economic development. Communities across the nation expect education to support economic revitalization and growth. Paradoxically, though, many Americans have lost respect for education: the popular perception is that all of us in education are not doing the job in preparing graduates for a place in modern society. This dichotomy is not a healthy one for all of us in education, and if it grows the pressures to "reform" our two systems so that schooling concentrates on practical outcomes may sweep aside some of the precious educational values that we share.

The demographic facts of life for the 1980s and 1990s compel us as a society to get more out of less. There are simply fewer young people to educate, and all Americans are hostage to them: if these young people do not furnish the intellectual capital, social leadership, and economic security that our society needs, everyone will suffer. Too many talented young people do not aspire to a career or job that requires the advanced knowledge, broader perspective, and special skills that come only through education. Too many of these young people plan their futures poorly, if at all. Too many of them, consequently, become wasted assets for our society. During the next two decades especially, we cannot afford to squander these invaluable resources. A challenge of this magnitude can be met only by all of us in education, working together.

It is, moreover, wasteful for schools and higher education institutions to teach the same skills and content, whether these are actually mastered at an early level (and then unnecessarily duplicated later) or else not mastered in the schools (so that they must be compensated for at the college level). Beginning with a comprehensive review of what is taught throughout the entire American educational system, we must work toward a division of labor between schools and colleges that is based upon the most appropriate sequence of content, difficulty level, and specialization of function.

Since colleges and universities train virtually all of the schoolteachers in the United States, higher education has a particular obligation to insure that teachers have the most suitable, most satisfying, and most effective training, both before and during their classroom careers. Nothing will have such a powerful influence on the quality of teaching in the schools as the colleges and universities where teachers receive both their initial and most of their advanced training.

Intense and sometimes bitter competition for a limited supply of educational dollars has sometimes made for friction between the schools and colleges, especially at the state level. We cannot afford the luxury of this division today, when the resources are often so much scarcer: schools and colleges must learn how to coalesce their efforts.

All of these forces make education today more accountable than ever before. Without cooperation between schools and colleges, we simply are not acting very intelligently. Our interests are not only compatible but complementary, and by working together in common cause we can achieve mutually valuable benefits. What is more, schools and colleges—perhaps to the surprise of some in both sectors—can actually learn something from one another.

There are, to be sure, numerous barriers to meaningful school/college collaboration. These include the dead hand of inertia; skepticism, even outright opposition, on the part of key individuals; the absence in many cases of someone with the responsibility, written into a job description, for seeing that action is taken and that productive cooperation has a real chance to succeed; turf and status issues that get in the way; parochial attitudes that prevent some people from looking beyond the campus or the school building; the absence of clear incentives and rewards for cooperative initiatives; and the danger that rhetorical commitment will take the place of true commitment, with a subsequent disappointment of the hopes that were unrealistically lifted at the outset of the relationship.

People of good will can overcome all of these barriers so that cooperation is achieved, but a victory of this nature takes a sense of realism, some hard work, a lot of patience, and skillful leadership. We cannot let potential barriers keep us from trying. We must begin.

Forms of School–College Collaboration

Let us turn to some of the specific forms of cooperation that schools and colleges have found useful and see how interinstitutional cooperation through a consortium brings to this collaboration an important added dimension. Individual colleges and universities all over the United States are already active in each of these areas, as are many consortia, but there is more to be done. These examples hardly exhaust the possible forms of cooperation, of course, and a consortium that takes the initiative in school/college collaboration is likely to discover many unexpected dividends as well.

CONSULTATIONS ON TEACHING APPROACHES, CONTENT, AND CURRICULA

Schoolteachers and college faculty members share numerous instructional interests and needs, and they should exchange views on these topics on a regular basis. In some areas of the country, "alliances" of teachers from all levels in education have come together, in several academic disciplines, for this purpose. Through formal means like these, or informally, teachers are able to wrestle together with issues each must address: how a field of study, like mathematics, is organized; how social history is integrated into traditional history; how laboratory skills are taught; the state of the humanities today; and similar topics. As professional contacts and respect grow, these teachers may begin to discuss the concepts and techniques that each uses, or that each needs in order to become more effective. Discussions of how they can collaborate in order to strengthen one another's knowledge and skills are likely to follow.

College faculty members can be especially helpful in providing content updates to their counterparts in the schools, in return gaining a better understanding of what their own students have been taught as a foundation for their college studies. Conversations begun in this way can flower into thorough joint analyses of how the content at both levels can best be integrated. A better comprehension of what each level of education is expected to accomplish, and, ultimately, a better articulation path for students, result from discussions like these.

With relatively static teaching corps at both levels, these opportunities for mutual growth should be welcome for the reinvigoration that they will provide. Teaching methods, course content, and curricular strategies all can be refreshed and improved by this form of cooperation.

It is unlikely that any single college or university can supply all of the intellectual and pedagogical expertise that a school district may want, and the prospect of bearing alone an unpredictable number of requests for assistance may actually deter some campus leaders from offering to help. In addition, most colleges and universities have developed different kinds of strengths, and by working together they can put the best of what they offer at the service of all the schools in the region.

A consortium can help by bringing school districts into contact with most or all of the colleges and universities in the area. Concerted action will mean not only that the schools will have available the kind of assistance that they need but that the higher education institutions will share in the opportunities for collaboration and improved instruction that will result. While the colleges and universities avoid destructive and duplicative competition by pooling their resources, the schools have a larger, more balanced, and more highly diversified pool to draw from.

A consortium can perform a brokering function, matching the particular needs of the schools with the special strengths of the member institutions. A well-informed and impartial agency like a consortium thus can play a vital role in facilitating effective communication and coordination in instructional areas. In addition, consortia can sponsor alliances of classroom instructors from both levels, bringing together on neutral ground sufficient numbers from each level to insure real diversity.

For the members of the consortium, a bonus of these academic discussions with the schools will be a more profound understanding of the similarities and differences within their own number. This understanding might give an impetus to broader and more imaginative forms of academic cooperation among these colleges and universities, since they will appreciate one another's strengths and weaknesses better than before.

CONSULTATIONS ON REQUIREMENTS, COURSE EQUIVALENCIES, AND TESTING

Similarly, schools and colleges can consult more than they now do on these matters so that the two systems function as harmoniously as possible—and without nasty surprises in policy changes and clashes in standards. When colleges drop or add foreign language requirements, raise or lower English proficiency levels, or change expected preparation standards in the sciences, they have an enormous impact on schools. When the schools tighten or relax their graduation requirements, either independently or in response to new state regulations, they cause significant consequences for higher education. All of this calls for increased communication and perhaps even for outright negotiation.

The College Board and others have sought to establish at least the gridiron for some understandings about academic preparation, and so a starting point already exists. The consortium can assist in this process, too. As a vehicle for interinstitutional cooperation, it can bring its members into systematic and disciplined interchange with schools, especially if the schools themselves are represented through an intermediate unit or similar administrative unit. Better communication, smoother articulation, and fewer collisions between separate courses of action can result from this dialogue.

While improving their relationship with the schools, colleges and universities will once again profit from the greater knowledge of one another that the cooperative effort requires. As they get to know each other better, they will come to respect their individual differences and learn how they can complement one another more in their academic programs.

COLLEGE COURSES IN THE SCHOOLS

No magic line divides what is best taught in the schools and what should be postponed until the college years. The customary divisions often inhibit good learning, occasionally lead to duplicated instruction, and sometimes leave advanced students in particular with too little challenge at a time when their school careers should be climaxing. Some colleges and universities have accepted the invitations of school districts to supplement high school instruction with college-level courses taught in the schools. Sometimes this is done by college faculty members who visit the schools, and sometimes (as in Project Advance) by high school teachers whom the college or university has trained to provide college-level instruction. More of this kind of cooperation should develop out of the consultations described in the preceding section of this chapter.

Adult and continuing education represents yet another opportunity for closer collaboration between the schools and colleges. In many areas, both levels mount extensive programs for adults, and some cooperation may already be taking place. A coordinated program would help to avoid needless duplication and would provide the community with a richer and more diverse assortment of challenging courses.

Whether the audience is composed of high school seniors or adults, a consortium can make the situation better. Working together, colleges and universities can select the best of their courses and instructors for the rewarding duty of teaching in the schools. A concerted approach relieves the district of a confusing and incomplete array of college-level instruction that forces a school administrator to choose among the institutions. The advantages of eliminating deleterious competition among the colleges and universities are obvious.

This is another opportunity for the consortium to serve as a broker, packaging and coordinating college-level instruction in the schools. It can also negotiate, within its membership, the automatic acceptance of this instruction (so long as it meets certain standards) so that high school students who enroll in these special courses can be assured of receiving college credit anywhere in the consortium. Joining forces to serve the broader community by teaching both teenage and adult learners may enable the members of the consortium to learn still more about one another and how they might coordinate their educational programs better.

SPECIAL PROGRAMS FOR ADVANCED STUDENTS, MINORITIES, AND OTHERS

In a similar way, special academic programs can profit from a multi-institutional focus, especially if these are closely correlated with the developed strengths of the members of the consortium. Summer programs in the arts or the sciences, accelerated opportunities for minority students, and developmental programs for students who are making slower progress all can be enhanced through shared responsibility or, at least, joint sponsorship.

If these programs are jointly created and advertised under the aegis of the consortium, they are likely to have more visibility and credibility than they would under that of a single institution. Collective programs of this sort are also likely to achieve a high level of consistency and to serve the largest possible constituency while they continue to broaden the base for academic cooperation among the colleges and universities of the consortium.

VISITS TO SCHOOLS BY COLLEGE FACULTY MEMBERS

This source of enrichment for the schools also benefits the college faculty members who make the visits. By spending some time in the schools—lecturing, leading discussions, talking with teachers, and exploring how the school operates—the college faculty member brings a new and probably richer understanding of the content to everyone he or she touches. At the same time, the faculty member, who must rethink his or her subject matter for presentation in these surroundings, is likely to carry away from the experience a new and more tangible grasp of the nature and quality of instruction at the school level, and probably some fresh insights into the subject matter as well.

Individual colleges and universities have sometimes volunteered their faculties for this service, but a consortium will have a more comprehensive resource to publicize and use. Compiling the catalog of faculty resources offers the members yet another opportunity to discover one another's academic strengths, which might lead to a higher degree of collaboration at the collegiate level. (The collective "speakers' bureau" may have additional uses in community service as well.)

IN-SERVICE EXPERIENCES FOR TEACHERS AND ADMINISTRATORS

We have an aging group of schoolteachers; in most districts, the average time in service is already well over a dozen years, and this will continue to increase. Schoolteachers, in addition, do not always have sufficient opportunity to pursue advanced work in their disciplines, and so they have been unable—despite their best individual efforts—to keep up with the often rapid developments in those disciplines. Institutes in content areas, intensive summer courses, laboratory experiences, seminars in human development during the adolescent years, skill building programs, and the like are urgently needed in many districts. Sometimes these needs are being partially met through in-service opportunities, and, of course, many teachers do pursue their continued intellectual and professional growth on their own, but we can do more.

Colleges and universities have an opportunity to assist in this process by devising—in close collaboration with school districts, naturally—an array of stimulating and valuable in-service offerings for teachers, and by strengthening in-service programs where they already exist. A consortium and its diverse membership will be a vital asset in creating such in-service programs, and interinstitutional sponsorship of the initiative will give it greater visibility and credibility. If the members of the consortium agree to accept each other's in-service offerings for credit, teachers can sample from the richness of the collective resource in constructing coherent and exciting individualized programs.

There is an even more urgent need in many districts for training activities that will help school administrators to become more professional and more efficient. The possible activities range from seminars on personnel-evaluation techniques to training in leadership skills to tips about writing proposals for funding. The collective resources of the colleges and universities that cooperate through a consortium to provide these services for administrators are inevitably larger and more complete than those of any single institution.

The interaction that takes place when representatives of the member institutions work together may lead to new forms of cooperation within higher education as well. In addition, the stimulation of creating and leading these in-service programs may be an important source of challenge and growth for many college and university faculty members and administrators. Some of the in-service programs that emerge may be adaptable for other clienteles, including some that are within higher education itself.

TEACHER EDUCATION

Attracting capable and committed persons into the teaching profession and training them to be as competent as possible is an area where the schools can make a major contribution to the effectiveness of higher education. The schools know a great deal about what makes a good and successful teacher, and colleges and universities can draw more deeply upon this wisdom than they now do. The theory and practice of teaching both can be strengthened when schools and colleges work together on what is, after all, one of their principal intersections: teacher education.

Those colleges and universities that award teaching certificates might agree upon rigorous common standards, the specialized training experiences that a prospective teacher should have, and ways of monitoring and influencing state regulations and standards in teacher education. Special efforts to recruit and train teachers in critical areas like science and mathematics also are improved through collaboration because of the increased visibility that it offers. Some greater rationalization of teacher-education offerings at the collegiate level might also result from this cooperation as the participating institutions share their fresh approaches to pedagogy, their information about new teaching materials, and their valuable but unfilled student-teacher placements.

Here again, the consortium can be a powerful force for building communication and cooperation. Since it does not offer any teacher-education courses of its own, the consortium can serve as an impartial mediator to bring the cooperating parties into touch with one another and to moderate their inevitable differences. At the same time, the consortium can also facilitate and even host the collective endeavors that may grow out of these contacts.

PRECOLLEGIATE COUNSELING

Few people (including most guidance counselors) think that schools do an adequate job of acquainting young people and their parents with the opportunities they must evaluate in planning for the future. Career counseling, academic preparation, and the selection of which kinds of postsecondary education to consider—all of this happens less thoroughly and less effectively than it should. Overworked counselors, a lack of reliable information about careers, uninformed or indifferent parents, the imposition of extraneous tasks on top of counseling duties, and the absence of a sound context for decision making plague precollegiate counseling today.

Colleges and universities play a key role in augmenting the knowledge of counselors and in developing the skills they use in their profession, and there is much opportunity for cooperation in this area. Colleges and universities can make readily available to counselors more pertinent information about their respective academic strengths, about financial aid, and about other matters to which prospective students and their parents should have access; these institutions should also work with counselors to see that this information reaches those who need it most. Colleges and universities also can draw better relationships between their academic programs and career preparation, the world of work, and the changing economic nature of our society so that counselors and those they advise can be more informed about these topics.

Counseling does not take place in a vacuum: public attitudes toward education and the role of college are also influential. By working with the schools, opinion leaders, parents, civic organizations, and others, colleges and universities can help to shape public thinking about education. In this way, they can assist in building greater awareness of the importance of postsecondary schooling and in combating well-entrenched low levels of aspiration for college. The high drop-out rate in many areas is a special problem that ought to be addressed cooperatively too.

Information about colleges and universities is valuable only to the degree that it is comprehensive and objective, and the odds increase that these goals will be met when a neutral body like a consortium organizes this information. In addition, when colleges and universities speak together about such broad issues as financial aid and career planning, they are sure to command a larger hearing and are less likely to be seen as grinding an institutional axe. A collective approach to the continuing professional education of counselors is another opportunity, like programs for teachers and administrators, to bring the campuses' various intellectual and research resources to bear on a common problem.

While colleges and universities are working together in this area, they will also learn a great deal about some broad issues (economic change in the region, for example) that affect them as much as they do the schools. The members of a consortium will bring to the discussion of these topics many different perspectives, greatly enriching the topic for all who participate.

RECOGNITION OF EXCELLENCE IN TEACHING

The dedication, professionalism, and effectiveness of the best in American schoolteaching is not as widely appreciated as it should be, and colleges and universities can lead the way in rectifying this situation by honoring excellence in teaching. The consortium is an ideal vehicle for this recognition: by uniting the higher education community and mobilizing its collective prestige, a consortium can bring special meaning and visibility to the celebration of superior teaching.

Collectively recognizing excellence in the schools will reflect well on higher education. In addition, the process of defining and identifying excellent teaching will enable colleges and universities to focus on the outcomes of teaching, including their own, and on what they as well as the schools do well. Exchanging conceptions of quality in teaching and applauding generally acknowledged excellence on the campuses will be salutary by-products of the common tributes to good teaching in the schools.

DEVELOPING COALITIONS BEYOND EDUCATION

Education, whatever the level, exists in a world of political realities where alliances of interests are often crucial. Schools and colleges must work in harmony not only with one another but with all kinds of groups—businesses, civic organizations, governments, and others—to achieve mutual goals. Individual schools and colleges have sometimes built these alliances, but rarely do they work together to do so. Pooling their efforts should make them more effective.

A consortium, already a proven instrument for establishing closer ties between higher education and other sectors of the community, can be useful here too in helping schools and colleges to construct tripartite alliances with these noneducational organizations so that common responses to shared needs can develop. Working with the schools in this manner may place colleges and universities into fruitful contact with groups to which they would not otherwise have ready access, since most school districts have, of necessity, cultivated some powerful political allies.

Pittsburgh as a Case Study

No consortium can do all of these things, but every group of colleges and universities can do something to advance school/college collaboration. The colleges and universities in Pittsburgh have been active in several of the areas that this chapter has described, not only individually but through the Pittsburgh Council on Higher Education (PCHE).

Through a series of conferences and seminars, college faculty members and local teachers met to explore the changing nature of the humanities and how each group is reconsidering this field. Those who participated exchanged ideas on content issues in the humanities, their respective teaching approaches, and some new materials in the humanities. PCHE also hosted one of The College Board's early discussions of academic preparation for college. Both events helped to strengthen communication between the schools and the campuses.

Since PCHE is engaged in a community-wide effort, using the acclaimed television series "The Constitution: That Delicate Balance," to increase understanding of the United States Constitution, it seemed natural to include the schools in the project. A grant from Alcoa Foundation made it possible for the consortium to purchase multiple sets of the thirteen programs, and several of these sets have been loaned to intermediate units and larger school districts in the region. In addition, college faculty members and high school teachers have taken part in joint seminars on the topics covered by the programs and on how to use the programs themselves effectively in the classroom, and so they have learned together. This cooperation is continuing to develop during the bicentennial of the Constitution.

PCHE has also sponsored for four years a highly successful enrichment seminar for science and mathematics teachers from schools in the Pittsburgh area; nearly 100 teachers have participated. One of the members of the consortium, Duquesne University, furnishes the instructor and awards graduate-level credit, and another local foundation, the Buhl Foundation, launched the project by underwriting most of the costs for three years. During the course of the six-month seminar, the teachers visit many of the leading scientific and medical establishments in the Pittsburgh area and hear presentations from key researchers who work there. In addition, the program arranges for summer internships for a limited number of teachers, who thus receive not only valuable content updates but firsthand research experience in local laboratories and workplaces.

Since the Pittsburgh public schools have a nationally recognized teacher center, the consortium is sometimes asked to make contacts between the teachers who are retraining themselves and college or university faculty members who have special knowledge. Even more of this occurs less formally as the consortium helps individual teachers or districts to locate experts on particular topics. PCHE is also playing an active role in designing a "principals' academy" that will help school administrators to sharpen and develop their managerial skills.

Precollegiate counseling is another area where cooperation through the consortium has occurred. PCHE regularly sponsors the Pittsburgh College Fair, one of the largest in the nation, which succeeds in good part because college and high school representatives have worked together on it. The consortium has also arranged for generic financial aid seminars, both in the schools and in the community at large.

The members of the Pittsburgh consortium are sensitive to larger issues that affect education. PCHE has hosted a task force that examined attitudes toward education in western Pennsylvania, which has an unusually low percentage of high school graduates who attend college. In addition, PCHE helped to sponsor a series of seminars on broad social and economic changes that loom for western Pennsylvania. This series, by focusing on "the changing world of work and academe," has done much to acquaint campus and school leaders alike with the implications of these changes for all of education.

In many of these projects, the consortium has served as a catalyst for bringing higher education into closer touch with other community groups. PCHE also enabled college presidents and school superintendents to meet—often for the first time—and to discuss how their respective institutions could forge closer working relationships with one another, and with others in the region.

One should not make too much of PCHE's ventures, for they are only beginnings that will need careful cultivation in order to succeed. They do demonstrate anew, though, that a consortium can be an effective vehicle for school/college collaboration. There are plenty of opportunities for it to choose from. The consortium can stimulate the discussion of mutual issues; can link those with needs and those with information or expertise; and can sponsor certain collaborative projects. Given time, and encouragement from leaders at both levels of education, these initiatives can flourish.

The Advantages of the Consortium

Few colleges and universities are already deeply involved in school/college collaboration, and so the members of a consortium are not likely to see consortial initiatives as an interloping activity. Indeed, the members quite possibly will welcome these initiatives as another logical service that the cooperative agency they created *should* perform.

The consortium, in order to survive, has become proficient at facilitating—and perhaps even prodding along—cooperation between and among colleges and universities. It is used to managing the kind of political give-and-take that will be necessary to make school/college collaboration succeed. The consortium likely has experience coordinating or even brokering activities that involve higher education and other groups in the community, so reaching out to the schools probably will not require the consortium to alter its mission or governance. In view of the fact that schools are used to working with coordinating bodies, the two groups ought to be able to understand one another without too much difficulty.

Consortial decision making is typically of high quality, since any activity on the consortium's part requires long and thorough consultation with all of the members, a clear statement of the rationale for action and the purposes to be achieved, explicit authorization of any co-venture, and a thorough review of the results. The argument for the involvement of many disparate minds is a familiar one that need not be rehearsed here. This kind of decision making helps to check impetuous and unsupported initiatives and to avoid premature or unduly optimistic commitments, either of which will doom school/college collaboration by disillusioning the schools.

The power of example that functions within a consortium's membership may accelerate school/college cooperation. Since not all colleges and universities change at the same rate, some have been quicker than others to recognize the need for and the benefits of cooperation with the schools. Communication (and, inevitably, comparison) within the consortium can bring the trailing members along faster than they would move otherwise, can alert some of the members to needs that they would not otherwise perceive, and can even stimulate some friendly rivalry to be the most helpful to the schools.

The solidarity that the consortium offers is an asset that cannot be overestimated. When most or all of the higher education institutions in a certain area undertake a school/college project together, reach an agreement with the superintendents in the region, or work with the schools in a broader alliance, they make a powerful statement about themselves. On the one hand, they contradict the suspicion that they are indecisive or at one another's throats; on the other, by working together they signal their willingness to make a united and effective response to a critical community need.

A consortium serves its members as a neutral, disinterested, and therefore safe mechanism for dealing with the schools. An experimental venture through the consortium involves less risk to the institutions: the politics in school districts is highly charged, and colleges and universities may see clear advantages in insulating themselves somewhat by working through a third-party agency like the consortium. The schools and the community will also benefit from this neutrality. School administrators will appreciate being approached by a group of higher education institutions, instead of by one institution after another. They will realize that colleges and universities have considerable self-interest invested in the cooperation, and by dealing with the institutions collectively they can avoid the appearance of playing favorites. In short, neither colleges nor schools have to choose among potential partners or risk offending someone by making a choice when the consortium serves as a linkage between the two groups. Nor do community leaders (foundation heads, business executives, local politicians, etc.) who will be drawn into the collaboration have to choose partners, either, since all of the players in the game are already colleagues in a single, unified effort.

A comprehensive approach like this cannot help but have a special attraction for foundations and other funding sources. The consortium is not only all-inclusive and impartial but well situated to make a real difference in the quantity and quality of the cooperative programs. The funder is, in fact, likely to be especially interested in the larger impact that it can achieve by concentrating its support through the combination of institutions that the consortium includes.

Public support for collaborative initiatives will prove important in the long run, and the consortium offers the partners in school/college collaboration the opportunity to secure wider public awareness of what is being done together. This kind of joint endeavor is still rare enough to merit notice, and the partners can use the consortium to publicize their activities.

For all of these reasons, interinstitutional cooperation through a consortium brings a new and powerful dimension to school/college collaboration. Working together through this cooperative vehicle, colleges and universities have a greater chance of achieving their own goals, advancing the cause of collaboration, and making a real difference in the quality of education.

Barriers to Successful Cooperation

Interinstitutional cooperation is hardly a panacea in school/college collaboration, any more than elsewhere, and working together through a consortium does have some significant limitations and drawbacks. Any school/college initiative should take these matters into account when the purposes are identified, when the strategy is set, and when efforts commence.

The administrators and faculty members of the colleges and universities that belong to a consortium typically give only a fraction of their attention and (more importantly) of their loyalty to the consortium. Quite naturally, they preserve these mostly for their own institutions. In practical terms, this means that a consortial venture will be successful only when it truly represents an area in which the institution's goals and needs can be met through joint action. Few institutional leaders will contribute money, time, or energy to a consortial venture unless there is a direct payoff for their own colleges and universities.

The consortium's staff must therefore be clever enough to identify and develop endeavors in those areas where sufficient institutional goals and needs intersect (although not every member of the consortium need be involved in every one of its activities). Such endeavors, moreover, must promise clear and direct benefits to these members or else the consortial initiatives will meet with too little support, and even overt opposition. Nothing exempts school/college initiatives from this fundamental principle of interinstitutional cooperation.

A consortium, typically a voluntary organization, is by nature a rather fragile vessel. With all of its potential, it is still relatively undeveloped in its goals and priorities, and it may be rather inexperienced in facilitating cooperative ventures. Because many of the consortium's member institutions have probably made only tentative and limited commitments to the concept of interinstitutional cooperation that the consortium represents, they may not view it as a natural vehicle for collaboration with the schools. It will be important for campus leaders and the consortial staff to make the case for consortial initiatives in this area, where the consortium is unlikely to have been active before now.

Insofar as one motive for cooperation with the schools is increased enrollments, the degree to which the members of the consortium compete with one another for potential students will complicate the school/college collaboration they are trying to achieve. Fortunately, this competition is (sometimes surprisingly) restrained in most consortia, but it is a factor to consider. Competition for public recognition of overtures to the schools, if it were to get out of control, might also seriously diminish the consortium's effectiveness.

The consortium's main attributes are communication, coordination, and facilitation. It is often less successful as an actor. Nor does it have any independent authority: as a derivative organization, it cannot compel its members to share information, to undertake collaborative ventures, or to follow through at the institutional level—even when a consensus has been reached. The fact that the consortium cannot undertake any initiatives without authorization and assistance from its members means that it is only as good as they are, and an ineffectual consortial staff can squander even this asset.

The multiple layers of institutional and interinstitutional authority that a consortium must penetrate in order to have its members agree upon a proposal and to commence a project together can seem stifling. Although this process contributes to sound decision making, as we have seen, the bureaucratic hurdles can be daunting and time-consuming, at least, and the compromise solution that emerges from a consensus can be less than creative. To many outsiders, a consortium may appear indecisive or timid because of the formidable challenges involved in pulling its disparate members together.

The fact that numerous imaginative and exciting cooperative ventures—including school/college alliances—have been formed under consortial banners proves that these limitations and disadvantages, while worth bearing in mind, can be overcome. In addition, an effective program of school/college collaboration may help the consortium to gain a renewed sense of purpose and energy that will actually deepen the commitment of its members and enable it to become more effective in other areas as well. School/college collaboration thus represents a rich opportunity for the consortium itself, even beyond the substantive value of the specific projects that will result from the initiative.

Strategies for Successful Collaboration

What are the best strategies for cultivating successful school/college collaboration? How can cooperation between and among higher education institutions make these strategies more effective? How can a consortium help? This chapter has already offered some answers to these questions, but some general remarks are in order.

A school/college partnership must be a genuine one: the two partners must listen to one another, set aside judgments (and perhaps some unfortunate previous experience as well), and look for ways to help one another. School leaders often know what many of their solutions are, and they usually have a pragmatic grasp of how higher education can assist them—even if they are not always convinced that colleges and universities are inclined to furnish that assistance. Higher education leaders must cultivate a willingness to listen to their colleagues in the schools and then to act without prescribing. At the same time, campus leaders are acutely aware how their institutions' other missions and peculiarly decentralized nature work against marshalling them to help the schools. School leaders must realize that most of their solutions will have to come from within, and from partners outside of education. The more realistic the expectations, the more likely the partnership is to succeed.

We should not pretend that self-interest is not a factor in school/college collaboration. There are, of course, numerous altruistic reasons for cooperation, but unless both partners anticipate benefits they are unlikely to give more than lipservice to the concern. Neither schools nor colleges can afford to waste time and energy, not to mention resources, on sham and posturing. This mutual self-interest should be acknowledged, identified in detail, and even celebrated throughout the collaboration. Reviewing the self-interest each partner is seeking will be a convenient measuring stick for whether or not the partnership is working well.

Stereotypes that inhibit a truly collaborative spirit should be aired and then attacked. Even well-meaning persons in schools and colleges do not always perceive one another as colleagues. The former sometimes think that college professors and others on campuses are arrogant and poorly informed about the schools. Many people in higher education, on the other hand, have a tendency to look down upon the quality of instruction in the schools and to underestimate the professionalism of those who work there. (The unionization of teachers in many areas may have contributed to this feeling among the typically unorganized faculty members and administrators of higher education.) These stereotypes are widespread, whether they are articulated or not, and so they must be realistically addressed as collaboration gets under way.

Administrators—superintendents and presidents in particular—play key roles in getting collaboration started, in financing projects, in building public awareness, and in maintaining momentum. Unless they signal their own commitment, communicate their affirmative attitudes, and explain their objectives to their subordinates, little will be done. Even the most ambitious and well-meant collaborative initiatives will not get far, though, unless those actually in the classrooms develop some meaningful professional relationships. Special efforts must be made, therefore, to involve both institutional leaders and teaching staffs in the collaborative plan and to give both groups a sense of ownership for what it will do.

The challenge of expanding effective school/college collaboration will test the abilities of people on both sides, and so the two partners should draw upon their ablest and most energetic administrators and faculty members—not those who, for some reason, merely have the time available. For colleges and universities in particular, this may mean shifting institutional priorities (and thus rewards) away from research and publication and into an area of "service" that has not always been valued as highly as these other endeavors.

School/college collaboration has a tendency to falter after the initial burst of energy and enthusiasm has expended itself and when the difficult, unglamorous work of hammering out agreements and lining up resources has begun. There is much to be said for locating the responsibility for generating, monitoring, and expanding school/college contacts in a key office, close to the president (or dean) or to the superintendent (or principal).

These duties should become an explicit part of someone's job description. This person should have incentives for taking the initiative, should get regular encouragement from superiors, and should be evaluated on how well he or she has done in developing collaborative ventures. The person responsible for managing the cooperative effort should be well informed about the institution's activities, strengths, and ethos, and should know how to capture the attention of the school or campus. In the end, as with most things, dynamic and resourceful leadership can make the difference in whether or not the collaboration succeeds.

Interinstitutional cooperation possesses abundant advantages in each of these areas—in opening lines of communication; in identifying the factors of self-interest each partner brings to the topic; in combating stereotypes that can inhibit cooperation; in involving administrative and teaching staffs to the fullest; and in deepening the institutional commitment to collaboration. The consortium provides a neutral table around which the participants can sit. The constructive rivalry of colleges and universities can be harnessed to encourage them to put forth their best efforts.

In the process, the members of a consortium learn from the experiences of one another. Collectively, they can be more ambitious in what they seek to achieve, and together they can afford to invest more resources. The consortium, by consolidating its members' strengths and energies, can act as a sort of balance wheel to insure that the schools have the benefit of a well-rounded, consistently delivered, and exceptional program of collaboration with those members.

Conclusion

Unless school/college collaboration increases during the next two decades, all of us in education will suffer, and interinstitutional cooperation through a consortium can play a vital and unique role in building productive examples of that collaboration. The best strategy, as it is so often, is to get started where the opportunity is greatest. Those searching for a way to stimulate or accelerate cooperation between the schools and higher education may find in the consortium an immediate and useful device for doing so. Existing consortia can undertake cooperative ventures, and new consortia can be formed with this kind of activity as a central goal. Either way, every aspect of education will benefit, as will our communities and our society as a whole.

—9—

Public and Government Relations

JOHN W. RYAN

Public relations as a form of communication plays a prominent role in our society by providing a framework, through a variety of techniques and means, that promotes a better understanding of issues that affect each of us to one degree or another. The central purpose of all such activity is to influence and shape the basis of our everyday perceptions and attitudes in a way that is mutually beneficial to the source delivering the message and to its intended audience.

Public relations serves a useful function in society by expanding the process of communication through the dissemination of information that might not otherwise be as readily accessible to individuals. The availability of information provides the public with an opportunity to make informed judgments on issues that are relevant to its interests.

As a vehicle for promoting change, public relations has at times been misunderstood and misused by its practitioners. Legitimate efforts to persuade the public on various issues have had adverse effects and consequences, undermining the credibility of the very group or organization seeking to gain understanding and support. The success of

The Worcester (Massachusetts) Consortium for Higher Education, with membership that includes ten colleges and universities, was established in 1968. Its resources are further enriched by 13 associate member organizations, primarily specialized and cultural institutions. The consortium provides numerous opportunities for student participation and community involvement.

147

any public relations campaign can be attributed primarily to a solid grasp and application of several underlying principles.

How Does Public Relations Succeed?

There are several fundamental elements that are essential to ensure that the aims of a public relations initiative meet with a degree of acceptance and success. These include planning, organizing, and (most importantly) achieving a basic understanding and sound application of the principles of communication. Communication is a strong force and, when effectively channeled, can serve as a potent catalyst for achieving desired goals in any setting.

Communication is innate with each of us. Without it, we could not exist as a civilization. In its most basic form, communication serves as the vehicle for imparting information, ideas, and attitudes to others in a variety of ways. The manner in which we communicate can be as elementary as a glance or may extend to a very sophisticated and elaborate performance that employs a multitude of aids. Each of us, on a daily basis, is subjected to thousands of external stimuli that affect our senses and emotions. This condition has a significant bearing upon our interpersonal relationships and how we view things. For example, our ability to smile communicates certain underlying feelings and conveys a message to others.

As complex as interpersonal communication is, communicating to larger audiences is even more complicated and presents formidable challenges for even those most skillful in the process. A significant part of the difficulty in relating to large groups lies in the diversity and makeup of others who are the intended targets of a message. All of us have views on issues concerning which we may or may not be in agreement. If a message is broad or controversial, we react to it accordingly. The divisiveness that occurs from such a situation only serves to reduce the credibility of the communicator.

Good communication focuses upon what to say and how to say it. The message that one wishes to get across must be simple and yet have substance. A complicated statement only serves to muddy the waters and to create uncertainty and confusion in the mind of the listener. It has often been said that repetition is a tool of learning. The appropriate use of such a technique has a positive and desired effect upon any audience. The success of many major American corporations in promoting their products serves as ample testimony to this method.

When applied to any setting, communication in its many forms is the main force for achieving the goals of an effort and of reaching the public. It is within this context that public and government relations in a cooperative setting should be viewed.

The Limitations on Collective Action

Consortia, by their very nature, seek to provide a neutral forum that will afford participants an opportunity to communicate and that will, it is hoped, lead to productive dialogue and increased interinstitutional cooperation. The aims of consortia, although noble, are sometimes inherently in conflict with the nature of academe, where cooperation is not the generally accepted norm.

Part of this dilemma stems from a reluctance on the part of institutions to view collaboration as a legitimate means of reinforcing and introducing new dimensions and breadth to the existing framework. Consortia are seen by many in an academic environment as ancillary in nature and not necessarily vital to the mission and goals of institutions. Cooperation is viewed as fine to the extent that it does not excessively intrude or disrupt the educational process or modify the character of institutions.

There are other factors that tend to diminish collective efforts. The diversity of colleges and universities in a consortial arrangement at times presents unique problems. Some of them are public, and some are private; some are small, and some are mammoth; some are well endowed, and others exist at the margin; some enjoy national reputations, whereas others have a more local appeal. It is obvious from the pluralistic nature of academic institutions that, at times, mutually cooperative interests do not converge. Although complementary to each other in many ways, the aims and needs of each institution are not necessarily synonymous.

Institutional status and prestige is another area that tends to inhibit cooperation. Institutions that are endowed with adequate resources, superior students, and outstanding faculty are less likely to share their advantage, since there is very little to be gained. In part, this situation may be attributed to the competition for scarce resources and to ambiguities that develop over goals and priorities. Perhaps the factor that can have the greatest debilitating effect on cooperation is a marginal commitment on the part of institutional leaders. If enthusiasm and a spirit of agreement are not apparent among the chief executives and are not promulgated in vigorous fashion, then the likelihood of success in developing and implementing a coherent plan of action to promote new endeavors will usually be minimal.

The Advantages of Speaking Together

Despite these potential limitations, the current state of higher education provides consortia with many opportunities for achieving their mission and goals. Much that is beneficial can be accomplished through collective efforts that focus their attention on those problems and concerns that presently exist and have been forecast for higher education in coming years, as well as those areas where common interests prevail.

Today higher education may be faced with more uncertainties than in the past. First and foremost is the projected decline in the number of prospective students during the coming decade. Many observers have predicted that by the early 1990s there will be a dramatic decline in the traditional applicant pool throughout the nation. Such a situation, if it materializes, will obviously have a profound effect on colleges and universities. If one adds to this the prospect of increasing costs in personnel, books, and other instructional materials, as well as the uncertainty of energy costs and the deferred maintenance and deterioration of aging physical plants, it becomes readily apparent that financial problems will continue to plague higher education in the coming years.

As a labor-intensive industry, the higher education community cannot assume that the implementation of new technologies and increased investments will lead to reduced costs and will provide comparable excellence in the educational product. The necessity of keeping pace with an expanding knowledge base (through the development of new programs to satisfy student and faculty interest) will exert more financial pressure. Such a scenario should not lead one to pessimism. Instead, it can and should serve as a catalyst for launching a revitalized effort in institutional planning and cooperation. Such circumstances present a unique opportunity for institutions to share information, to increase collaboration, and to mount joint initiatives.

There are obvious advantages in speaking together. The opportunity for open discussion with colleagues can provide different perspectives and lead to the development and implementation of new joint services and programs that are economically viable and that capture the best of all parties. Increased communication can also promote better understanding of educational offerings and needs, which can lead to greater public support of education and to institutional stability.

Institutions can also find greater security and can reduce long-range risks by sharing information and resources rather than by traveling separate routes. Those institutions that follow an independent path limit themselves. They remove themselves from exploring new opportunities that might have a positive impact upon their institutions. In essence, coming together is becoming a quid pro quo for institutional vitality and renewal.

Melding Individual Interests into a Common Voice

Establishing and maintaining a unified public relations program and approach presents a unique opportunity and challenge for those who wish to develop new and creative initiatives. In order to accomplish the tasks posed in such an arrangement one must have an appreciation and understanding of the process of communication and group dynamics. Both of these elements constitute essential cornerstones in blending individual interests into a common voice.

Another major factor in determining whether a creative and viable program in a collective arrangement can be implemented rests in large part with the geographic proximity of institutions in relation to one another within a community. Colleges and universities that are close to one another are blessed with an advantage, since close working relationships can be facilitated, physical resources can be shared, and the image of a combined effort can be reinforced in the public eye.

This is not to suggest that an effective consortial public relations program cannot be mounted in settings where institutions are at some distance from one another; the task, however, will be somewhat more formidable and challenging if this is the case.

Many professional practitioners view public relations as an art to be used only in those instances where the greatest advantage or impact can be gained. Others view it with a wider degree of latitude. Wherever good public relations resides, however, it requires a grasp of the purpose and aims that one seeks to achieve and an analysis of the audience that one wishes to influence.

The ability to inform and educate the public in regard to one's case is not an easy task. Much of the difficulty encountered is related to the complexity of societal interests and the intense competition among various organizations and groups that are simultaneously seeking recognition from the media in presenting their stories.

At the outset, it should be noted that public relations is not an activity that is or can be isolated from the media. Instead, it shares an interdependence with the media. In order to have the potential of securing its most dramatic impact, any serious public relations effort must rely heavily upon the media for whatever degree of success is achieved.

The reasons underlying this linkage are basic. Public relations campaigns are aimed at reaching the broadest possible audience. The various media provide the access point for obtaining this goal. Conversely, the media are dependent upon public relations for information that might not otherwise be available.

Media, in general, are always searching for news that has human interest and an angle that will stimulate their readers and viewers. Educational news, for the most part, is viewed by the media as "soft" news—that is to say, it is not seen as newsworthy and thus does not enjoy top priority. Such major issues as the rise and decline of SAT scores or institutional rankings always receive attention, since they have a broad flavor and have an impact upon millions of citizens. Run-of-the-mill stories, though, do not have the same appeal and are disposed of accordingly. There are no guaranteed prescriptions to ensure that every public relations effort will be successful. There are, however, certain characteristics that lend themselves to the probability of success in a consortial arrangement.

Public relations offices at colleges and universities vary in purpose, size, budget, and sophistication. Some of them are blessed with all of the requisites for fulfilling their individual role and mission with a high degree of effectiveness and success; others, for a variety of reasons, are dreadfully ill-prepared for maintaining even a modest effort. It is within these extremes that a blend of resources can be utilized to establish a meaningful public relations program in an interinstitutional context.

It is essential to note that each institution, whatever its condition, has something to offer and must be given the opportunity to contribute to a joint effort. A degree of commitment and enthusiasm on the part of public relations directors in working together toward a common goal must be apparent. Additionally, the participants involved need to sense that there are benefits to be gained by cooperating with one another. If such is not the case, then the ability to capture the best of all parties is diminished and the ensuing effort will have lost some of its vigor.

It is also significant to recognize that what might work in one setting may not be effective or appropriate in another environment. One of the basic elements in a successful public relations program lies in being familiar with and acutely aware of the mission, goals, and characteristics of each institution within a cooperative framework. Each college or university possesses its own identity, and its priorities may be completely different from those of another institution. Although elementary, this distinction is often ignored and can lead to an uneasy fragmentation of interest among the parties involved if it is not perceived initially.

It should also be noted that there is a difference between institutional and consortial public relations. A consortium is a loosely bound confederation of competing interests. Its members view their interests—and justifiably so—to be of prime importance in presenting their case to the public. There are areas, however, when it is in the best interests of all that the consortium umbrella be used.

A good example of this is in the preparation and distribution of an impact study focusing on those interests that will provide citizens with a better understanding of the role of colleges and universities, demonstrating their collective significance to the vitality of the community.

Many people are unaware of the tremendous impact that colleges and universities have in their community. The impact goes far beyond the number of individuals employed by the institutions or the substantial investments the higher education institutions make in land, buildings, and scientific and instructional equipment. It includes such areas as faculty and staff members who serve the community in a wide range of appointed or elected positions; students who serve the community in a variety of appointed or elected positions; students who, through intern programs or as volunteers, work with local schools or with social agencies serving the aged and handicapped; and the library holdings of the colleges and universities, which exist as an important community resource. If each institution were to develop its own report, this would entail much duplication of effort and resources and would result in a more modest statement than one that effectively portrays the totality and economic benefit of higher education to the community. In this instance, the sum is greater than the parts and has a more profound effect upon community perceptions and attitudes.

Another joint public relations opportunity lies in the area of cooperative recruitment. Every region of the country seeks to acquaint others with its unique and special characteristics, which include institutions of higher education. For colleges and universities in a collaborative setting, the opportunity for broad exposure can be increased, through cooperation, in a variety of ways.

Institutions can reinforce their image in a collective fashion through the publication and distribution of attractive materials that focus upon the assets of their area and, more importantly, that underscore the educational opportunities available on their respective campuses. Such an approach is not only economically more viable but also increases the level of interest and student inquiry from other than the traditional markets where student recruitment usually occurs. A videotape production that captures the spirit of colleges and universities in a consortial arrangement is also useful in stimulating prospective student interest. The costs of distribution to wide audiences are negligible when compared to the potential of attracting larger applicant pools from a broader mix of students.

Marketing and public relations techniques can also be enhanced through a joint admissions effort that enlists the support of high school guidance counselors. In many communities, guidance counselors play a prominent role in suggesting colleges to students. On occasion, they may not be familiar with certain colleges. By providing a tour for guidance counselors through a planned sequence of events, colleges can promote greater understanding of, and appreciation for, their institutions. The group effort can be continued and sustained through periodic newsletter mailings, which focus on new programs and other areas that would be of interest to guidance counselors.

Another area that presents an occasion for all parties to come together is the tackling of major issues and concerns that affect colleges and universities. Such activity might include federal and state legislative initiatives, long-range planning relating to interinstitutional interests, and public health problems that are common to all, which include such issues as alcohol and substance abuse, AIDS (Acquired Immune Deficiency Syndrome), and other concerns. The concept of strength in numbers provides for a more informed approach in seeking solutions, due to the diversity of resources available. There is also greater leverage in addressing issues that have an impact upon all institutions.

Community Public Relations

A high concentration of colleges and universities in a community is a definite source of strength in the promotion of public relations, because citizens take pride in their institutions and can readily identify with them in a collective sense.

Whatever direction a consortial public relations campaign takes, it is essential that its scope be integrated with as many facets of community life as possible in order to gain maximum impact. Colleges and universities should not be viewed as isolated academic groves but instead be perceived as dynamic and vital parts of the intellectual, cultural, economic, and social fabric of the community.

There are a number of vehicles available for promoting an effective community public relations program within a consortium framework.

Billboard advertisements that convey a simple message tied to the community (such as "Every great city has at least one college; Mayberry has ten") offer a novel way of drawing attention to institutions. Not only do they serve to reinforce the presence of the colleges and universities as a significant part of the community, but they also serve as an aid in student recruitment and they bolster civic pride.

Regional and local magazines are very useful for getting the message across, as are such traditional media as news stories, radio features, and television coverage of significant campus events. The format might include roundtable discussions of timely topics that relate to citizen interest (such as economic forecasts), interviews with faculty members who have authored noteworthy books, and in-depth profiles of significant research developments in emerging areas such as biotechnology, robotics, and medical advances. The focus of all such activity should aim at informing the public in areas that will be beneficial to them and that will favorably reflect on colleges and universities.

In addition to the standard forms of communication in reaching the public, colleges and universities by their very nature and presence can provide a number of services to a community. Either collectively or individually they can share their resources with individuals and groups. They can offer use of their facilities to community members or organizations, allow their library collections to be available through an interlibrary loan program, and offer citizens (the elderly and the unemployed, for instance) an opportunity to pursue a course of study on a space-available basis without charge. All of these possibilities serve the best interests of the community as well as the colleges and universities.

The stimulation of civic interest and involvement in college activities is another dimension that is significant for the success of any public relations endeavor tied to colleges and universities. Though not necessarily interested in pursuing a course of study, community members may wish to attend a concert, play, or lecture. The publication and distribution of a common monthly calendar of campus cultural events that are open without charge to the public encourages positive town–college relationships and allows citizens numerous opportunities for enjoyment.

Another way of presenting the collective interest of colleges and universities to the public is available through the sponsorship of a series of events in conjunction with National Higher Education Week. An advertising campaign that focuses upon a theme can effectively marshall all resources in a productive and stimulating fashion. Symposia, cultural activities, and special events provide a useful way of fostering a greater awareness of the contributions of higher education to a community. The collective format of activities can readily be encouraged through promotion by the media, the chamber of commerce, and local and state governments through special recognition and legislative proclamations.

Colleges and universities in a collaborative arrangement are also in a unique position to serve as catalysts for effecting social change within a community. Every community has certain needs, and the willingness and ability of colleges and universities to be responsive to those needs serves a mutually beneficial purpose. A good example of a joint and concerted effort would be the seeking of change and improvements in neighborhoods that may be under stress. Neighborhoods are the lifeline of any community, and improving their condition through various forms of assistance is a sound investment. Formal partnerships between higher education institutions and neighborhood schools, as another chapter in this volume shows, is another way colleges and universities can make a contribution to neighborhoods. Such initiatives only serve to strengthen the identity and pride of the neighborhoods served; they can also lead to a higher level of appreciation by the public toward the role of colleges and universities.

Another pressing need in every community is the availability of reasonably priced rental housing to accommodate citizens. Through a joint effort, colleges and universities can play a pivotal role in addressing this need by working closely with local government and responsible citizens' groups to improve this condition. The scope of involvement can range from sharing faculty expertise to the acquisition of land and rehabilitation of existing property that can be dedicated to the fulfillment of this need.

A collective approach can also be adopted with respect to the development and preservation of the environment. For instance, water quality is becoming a major public issue and concern in many communities. By enlisting the best minds of scientists and researchers from colleges and universities and municipal agencies, a joint program for improvement can be mounted and implemented through research that will identify problems and seek solutions. A water-testing program and conferences devoted to water quality issues can also serve as valuable supplements.

Similarly, emerging new technologies pose potential risks for millions of individuals nationwide. In this regard, several member institutions of the Worcester Consortium have recently established a collaborative effort to address this situation.

The New Technologies Safety and Health Institute (NTSHI), a program of the consortium, has developed an independent scientific capability to study, gather, and disseminate information and to provide risk assessment in new technologies in order to anticipate and minimize the occupational and environmental hazards that may evolve from products and processes.

The institute will serve as a major resource base for information and referral on hazards associated with new technologies. This role will be complemented by a broad base interdisciplinary research program that will study new technologies such as microelectronics, biotechnology, video display terminals, and selected polymers.

Education and training in hazard assessment and management will be another thrust of the NTSHI. Programs will be developed and tailored to the specific needs of industry groups, small business, labor, and communities at large. Finally, an annual multidisciplinary conference will be held to address issues relevant to the assessment and management of hazards related to new technologies.

The establishment of the NTSHI will serve the academic and scientific community through research and education; provide the public sector with information and training; and serve business and industry, their employees, and their labor unions through up-to-date information and hazard-management strategies.

The NTSHI represents a good example of a collaborative effort that can be beneficial to the public interest and can have a positive effect in addressing problems related to the environment.

Another area where opportunity exists for joint endeavors is relations with business and industry. The presence of many institutions of higher education in a community offers the business community an opportunity to draw upon a significant amount of professional expertise and resources that can readily assist them in seeking resolution to their problems.

An easy way of facilitating college/business partnerships is through a strong working relationship with the local chamber of commerce. Sponsored events that focus upon linkages between business and academic leaders are an effective way of accomplishing this. Joint meetings with college presidents and top corporative leaders are also very useful in establishing agendas and priorities for addressing major community issues. The joint approach provides strength in terms of resource allocation among all parties and exhibits a strong commitment toward achieving desired goals.

Another area where a combined effort can be beneficial to various sectors of the community is through the establishment of a common speakers' bureau. There is a tremendous amount of talent available from colleges and universities that can be tapped by business and industry for its purposes and those of the community. A speakers' bureau can provide a ready resource of highly trained experts who are willing to share their knowledge.

Other avenues where collaborative public relations efforts can be fruitful is through a coordination of effort with the convention and visitors' bureau. Through joint planning efforts, colleges and universities in a community can be previewed through promotional literature issued by the visitors' bureau. Additionally, campus tours of educational landmarks and the development of special-interest programs for visitors can provide an ongoing exposure for colleges and universities.

In a similar vein, the development of a job exposition in conjunction with an organization such as the local chamber of commerce provides fertile ground for showcasing a community and its higher educational establishment to regional and national companies who are seeking well-prepared individuals to serve their needs. An exposition can not only increase the visibility of a community but it can also provide a number of direct student-employer contacts that might not otherwise be available to potential graduates and employers.

The ability and willingness of institutions of higher education in a local setting to come together and to provide community service through a sharing of expertise and resources with all sectors of a community represents one of the greatest assets available to any municipality. The adoption of a combined public relations approach not only casts a favorable light on colleges and universities but benefits all segments of community life by giving a richer and deeper meaning to the term *partnership.*

Operating in Legislative Forums

Advocacy in legislative forums embodies many elements that have a commonality with public relations. Those engaged in the process must be good communicators, have the ability to analyze and perceive issues, and be adept in making their case. There is a parallel between government and public relations. Both activities are aimed at eliciting support for one's position. Government relations focuses upon issues and strategies. Public relations, though similar in intent, serves as the vehicle for implementation of the strategy through the utilization of communicative techniques that will assure a successful outcome.

The representation of higher education in local, state, and national arenas is an area that can provide a sense of excitement and challenge, as well as its share of frustration and disappointment for those with unrealistic expectations.

Legislators at all levels, by and large, are very dedicated, informed, and industrious individuals who exercise their responsibilities with a high degree of commitment and professionalism. They listen and respond to useful and informed suggestions from citizens and various groups. They also possess keen insights and are very pragmatic in seeking solutions to problems and concerns that have an impact upon their constituents. Their degree of success and effectiveness is measured in large part by their efforts and public perception. To say that their job is easy is a gross understatement. They are constantly subject to public scrutiny and endure pressures from all sides. Their role is an endless balancing act.

The process of enacting legislation to serve the needs of the nation, state, or community in the best manner is not an easy task and is at best imperfect. All competing interests feel that their case is unique and worthy of special consideration. It is important to remember that, despite one's finest efforts in organizing and presenting an informed and convincing case, the legislative process ultimately yields to compromise. It is not a perfect system, but one that seeks the best under all given conditions.

Legislators are besieged daily with requests from various groups and citizens, all of whom seek special interests. A typical day in the life of a legislator consists of sitting in committee meetings listening to countless hours of testimony from witnesses who present compelling cases for their causes. It is obvious that this daily routine can lead to information overload and, at times, to fuzziness on matters under consideration. Thus, legislators appreciate people who can present the facts in a clear, concise, and meaningful fashion in order to clarify issues.

One of the greatest shortcomings of interest groups, in the eyes of legislators, is their inability to supply concrete and current information from which legislators can make informed judgments on matters related to public policy. Higher education is no exception. Several legislators have publicly commented that what is needed most from the higher education community is more information rather than self-serving rhetoric.

Many individuals view government relations as a rather mysterious process that is often characterized by secrecy and intrigue. This is far from the case. Advocacy is fundamental to the political process. It has been suggested that the process is very similar to techniques used in marketing a product or commodity. It basically consists of knowing your subject, knowing whom you are dealing with, and telling your story in a simple, straightforward fashion. If your case is worthwhile, and you present it properly, your chance for success will be heightened.

Success in achieving one's goal in the legislative process comes by making one's case in a cogent manner that is clearly backed up by facts. What makes an impression on legislators is not saying what is important but proving it. Emotional arguments serve no useful purpose. Nothing is gained by being pushy or persistent. If anything, the case for support of an issue has been damaged.

Representation of higher education's interests to governmental bodies is an interactive process that requires a practitioner to have good political instincts and interpersonal skills, as well as a solid grasp of the ways legislative bodies function. Also essential is a well-defined strategy to ensure the ultimate success of an effort.

The implementation of a strategy in making a case for support of an issue should be intertwined with grass-roots support whenever possible. The reason is quite clear. In the context of higher education, an issue such as student financial aid impacts heavily upon many constituents in a personal way. To a member of Congress, *grass roots* translates into votes and warrants serious attention.

There are many public relations techniques available to encourage and solidify grass-roots support for an issue. One of the most common is the placement of an advertisement in appropriate media urging citizens to contact their legislator regarding the issue under consideration. An ad campaign that focuses upon the question of fairness is usually effective in gaining legislative support.

Letter campaigns, telegrams, and telephone calls are also useful vehicles for getting the message heard. It has been suggested on many occasions that when you have legislators by the grass roots, their minds and hearts will follow.

The process for enacting legislation is one that can be characterized as fraught with ambivalence, structure, and parliamentary delay. Major decision making in the legislative branch originates through committees, and it is at this point that interest and information relative to a proposed bill or program meets its initial test from legislators.

Perhaps the most influential individuals that one should contact prior to embarking on a strategy are one's local representative and staff members. Legislators at all levels of government tend to lend a sympathetic ear to constituent concerns. They are also in a position to offer various types of introductions to other officials in the legislative and executive branches who can prove to be beneficial. They may even propose active intervention.

Staff members are also key players—perhaps more so than they are given credit for. They play a prominent role in the development and review of a significant amount of legislation. In addition to providing their professional expertise and counsel, they also offer many recommendations that are incorporated into legislation. In a sense, they serve as "the eyes and the ears" for legislators. Thus, one of the first steps in promoting a workable legislative strategy is to establish strong working relationships with committee staff members.

Coupled with the necessity of cementing relationships with staff is that of identifying legislators who, for various reasons, might be supportive of one's interests. There are many obvious choices.

In addition to one's own representative, there are the members of such key committees as appropriations and various education committees. Other possibilities include those members who are supportive of education, based upon their past voting record, as well as those representatives who may have children of their own enrolled in a college or university.

When a pool of potential supporters is identified, it is important to establish a procedure for continually informing legislators and staff members of developments. One of the most common complaints of legislators and staff is that they rarely hear from members of the higher education community. This can be rectified by inviting legislators to the campus to see what is occurring. Those who avail themselves of the opportunity are usually pleased with what they learn. Periodic visits to legislative offices also provide an ongoing dialogue that can lead to greater support of one's case.

Common problems serve as a useful framework for adopting common solutions, and it is in this regard that the development of a collective approach can be very effective in seeking to gain understanding and support. Government relations as a group effort can provide many opportunities and advantages. The implementation of a unified program can lead to greater recognition of institutional interests by drawing upon the strengths of all parties involved in an effort. A collective approach also provides for a higher degree of credibility of institutional interests, since it reflects a concern that is common to all rather than unique to one.

Legislative breakfasts are a useful technique for gaining understanding and support of group interests. Most legislators that represent areas with a large concentration of colleges are usually disposed to discuss issues in this type of forum since it brings together many people under one roof and can lead to productive solutions to common problems.

Of equal importance is the ability to involve other constituencies within the community in support of one's case. A joint approach that includes a strong commitment from community and business leaders strengthens the position of institutional interests. More credibility is established when backing comes from another party that views the interests of colleges and universities as germane to community interests.

In most areas where there is a concentrated presence of colleges and universities, the mutual interests of the academic and business communities are fundamentally intertwined. Each sector reinforces the other in an economic sense. Many business and community leaders serve as members of college or university boards of trustees and are very instrumental in assisting in institutional advancement efforts. Their interest and concern for the success of higher education is manifested by their degree of tangible commitment and leadership in affecting appropriate linkages that will be beneficial to the college or university. By generating the support of the business community in a collective effort, a genuine interest is apparent and presents an even more convincing case to legislators.

A good illustration of this can be seen in the recent establishment of a biotechnology park in Worcester. The linkages between community, colleges and universities, and local government in laying the groundwork and working together toward such a development received strong endorsement and support from federal and state legislators. When fully completed, the park will add further economic strength to the community through increased opportunities for thousands of citizens. It will also enable Worcester colleges and universities to enhance their research capabilities and develop new programs to prepare individuals for careers in this emerging area. Finally, the biotechnology park will serve as a focus for potential discoveries that may have major scientific and medical impact upon countless number of citizens throughout the nation.

The degree of success obtained from a cooperative government-relations endeavor rests heavily with establishing agreement among all parties involved in an effort. The ability to enlist support and unify all parties requires a high level of organization and cultivation of various groups. The fruits of all such activity can provide a valuable and meaningful experience for those so engaged.

—10—

The Challenge of
New Technology

DIANA T. STRANGE

Perhaps no other challenge to higher education is as perplexing to most of us, or as radical, as the challenge of new technology. The new technology has invaded our society and our lives to the extent that it affects virtually everything that we do. One retail store, Williams-Sonoma, even sells a programmable toaster!

In his well-known book, *Player Piano,* Kurt Vonnegut, Jr., describes a society in which decision making has been given over to machines. The system he describes, which penalizes creativity and imagination, mirrors our fears of what society may become if we allow ourselves to come to depend on these technologies. It is in the context of these fears—still at work 20 years after Vonnegut wrote this book—that we face questions about how we in higher education will do our business in the information age. Indeed, these questions are so fundamental that we very likely will need to make radical responses.

This chapter will describe some of the challenges to higher education that we are already facing as we move into the world of new technology.

The Northeast Consortium of Colleges and Universities in Massachusetts (NECCUM) is a voluntary consortium, incorporated in 1981, that includes among its members 11 institutions of higher education in the region north of Boston. Major programs include cross-registration, cooperative computer-based library services, collaboration with area schools, and improved access to college for linguistic minorities.

These changes cut at the very root of higher education, and we are powerless to halt them. Steven Muller, president of Johns Hopkins University, has said that we are "already in an environment for higher education that represents *the most drastic change* [emphasis mine] since the founding of the University of Paris and Bologna and the other great universities some eight or nine centuries ago" ("The Post-Gutenberg University" in *Colleges Enter the Information Society,* 1983–1984).

The magnitude of these challenges demands innovative solutions. What kind of environment encourages innovation? To what extent do these challenges demand cooperative endeavors? Is there a role for consortia as colleges and universities face these challenges? What are some of the opportunities for collaboration that these challenges present?

Challenges to Education

The term *new technologies* calls to mind first of all the now almost ubiquitous computer. Although we cannot ignore other new technologies (the laser videodisc, satellites, television, cable, microwave technology, fiber optics, etc.), it is the development of the silicon chip, the integrated circuit—in short, the computer—that has had so dramatic an effect that we now speak of "The Information Age" or "The Postindustrial Society": a new era.

The very earliest computers were used as powerful research tools. When computers were first introduced to higher education, however, they came as aids to administrators in the form of large CPUs (central processing units) designed to handle data bases, including student records, course listings, and payroll information. Even the advent of computing to assist with these functions was greeted with suspicion. Now registrars, financial aid officers, admissions directors, and vice presidents for administration and finance all are familiar enough with computing to be writing and marketing original software. The *Chronicle of Higher Education* recently reported that administrators at Stanford University have done just that with a program called MOZART, which projects attendance at musical performances.

During the last decade, colleges and universities have felt enormous pressure to get on the new-technology bandwagon. Many of them have decided to purchase systems without having faced clearly the question, Why computers anyway? Marc Tucker, former director of the Project for Information Technology and Education, observed in the November/December 1984 issue of *Change Magazine* that it is "external pressure rather than any compelling vision of how computing might improve learning [that] is bringing computers to most campuses." Hence the dissatisfaction and distrust that is often associated with this new technology. In fact, Tucker asserts that "among those in the deepest trouble are likely to be those who buy this technology without thinking [the] issues through, for they will have simply added to their costs, which may just put them at more of a disadvantage than those who have done nothing at all."

Most colleges and universities have spent considerable energy in recent years developing programs and resources to train technicians and to render students and faculty members "computer literate." In *Global Stakes* (1982), James Botkin, Dan Dimancescu, and Ray Stata argue that higher education has failed to meet its responsibility to train sufficient numbers of engineers and technicians to meet the employment needs of the rapidly growing high-technology sector of our economy. Even so, many institutions have responded by allocating disproportionate resources to the growth and development of technical training programs.

Some colleges and universities have heeded the call for computer literacy by requiring computer programming courses of all graduates; others have instituted plans that will provide a computer for every student; still others have implemented professional development programs to serve faculty and staff members.

Future Implications

During the past several years, we have all witnessed so many changes resulting from the impact of new technologies that few people argue anymore that computers will have no more effect than television did on how we do higher education (an argument I have heard more than once). But now most students and many faculty members are familiar with computer data bases, word processing, electronic mail, and so on. Even skeptics of a few years ago are scheming to acquire personal computers for their homes and offices. In fact, more and more educators have come to view the impact of the new technologies on education as inevitable and essentially radical.

The following six statements describe the radical nature of the impact of the new technologies on education; educators must come to grips with the implications of these challenges in the academy:

- The new technologies have shifted the importance of the written word in favor of sound and images.

- Research is done differently.

- Retraining is as important as preparation for a career in the first place.
- Most workers will depend on computers in some way or other within a very few years.
- Large data bases make information readily available.
- The personal nature of the technologies has put the learner in charge.

THE WRITTEN WORD IS BECOMING LESS AND LESS IMPORTANT

Remember when television was new? Prognosticators predicted that television would change the world of education. Educational television would replace the classroom, reading machines would replace teachers, and so forth. Although predictions that television would change the way we teach have not come to pass, it is certainly true that television and other new technologies are changing the way we learn. The importance of the written word has shifted to images and sound.

By the time a child begins school, powerful ideas have been learned without "hard copy." "We are going to have to teach people by the use of images, and we are going to have to legitimize that process," warns Steven Muller. The way people learn has changed, and we educators, by and large, have not recognized these changes in the formal environments we create to encourage learning—in our colleges and universities.

RESEARCH IS DONE DIFFERENTLY

Scholarly research "has been liberated from the printed page," writes Patricia Battin, former vice president and university librarian of Columbia University ("The Library: Center of the Restructured University" in *Current Issues in Higher Education,* 1983–1984). Traditionally, the role of libraries, according to Battin, has been basically archival. The new technologies have developed new capacities for creating, saving, and accessing information, and these "capacities no longer require links to physical objects in stationary collections."

This new environment, not bound by physical and geographic constraints, demands a link among the "multiplicity of scholarly re-sources . . . into an easily accessible system," Battin states. Research, writing, and even publishing will be done electronically. Large bibliographic data bases are being made available to scholars by for-profit companies. More and more scholars have access to personal computers. Increasingly scholars are producing material in machine-readable form. The missing ingredient is the "organizational capacity for on-line . . . distribution," Battin asserts.

RETRAINING HAS BECOME AS IMPORTANT AS THE FIRST ACQUISITION OF SKILLS

The rapid proliferation of information and the almost incredible rate at which new generations of technological advances appear will require virtually every worker to seek retraining during his or her work life. In the postindustrial society (characterized by the computer and the cathode ray tube), educators cannot turn out "finished products." The half-life of an engineer today is about five years. "The necessary proficiencies are not static, but highly dynamic," writes Ernest A. Lynton in *The Missing Connection Between Business and the Universities* (1984). Furthermore, the number of youth entering the work force will radically decrease during the next two decades, placing even more demands for retraining on older workers already in the work force to do jobs formerly held by youth just entering the market.

Colleges and universities, in the main, continue to see the training of young people for entry into the world of work as their principal function. Educators have not yet claimed as central to the missions of our institutions the retraining function. For the most part, we have left this function to the private sector. Lynton urges educators to accept education "as a lifelong, recurrent process" and to begin to make the changes necessary to facilitate that process.

TECHNOLOGY HAS CHANGED HOW WE GET WORK DONE

We see computers at airline reservations desks, at the checkout line at the grocery, at the automobile inspection station, in banks, at stockbrokers' desks, in hospitals, and in campus registration lines. It is not difficult to imagine a time when it will be as common to see computer terminals on every desk as it is to see telephones. Louis Robinson, director of university relations for IBM, cited these data in a presentation at a higher education conference in 1983:

- Over 50% of those now employed in the United States are in an information activity.

- In the United States today, there is a computer terminal for every 48 jobholders, including nurses, air traffic controllers, newspaper reporters, stockbrokers, and accountants.

• By 1990, 70% of those employed in the labor force in the United States will have some knowledge of how a computer works just to be able to hold their jobs.

How will changes such as these in the world of work affect the world of education?

LARGE DATA BASES MAKE MOST FACTS READILY AVAILABLE

In the introduction to *Gutenberg II,* David Godfrey suggests that by the year 2000 we will be living in a society in which all information will be available in all places at all times! In the early days of the "Information Age," when we spoke of computers we meant machines that do arithmetic: i.e., compute. Today, computers do arithmetic less than 5% of the time; instead, they are most commonly information processors. Steven Muller points out that for a very long time educators have equated learning with memorization and reading. The computer, with all this information stored in huge data bases, has become a memory enhancer.

Muller asks, "Are we going to insist that students recall data in their own minds when in real life later they are going to use the computer for that data?" Is it not more important to know what data you need, how to get it, and what to do with it when you have it? And if this is so, then educators need to be much more deliberate about helping students learn how to access available information, how to analyze its usefulness, and how to organize it to address problems. It becomes much more important to know how to frame the questions than to be able to recite facts.

THE NEW TECHNOLOGIES PUT THE LEARNER IN CHARGE

All these technologies, from television to computers to laser videodiscs, are combining to make learning more important than teaching. In "Technology and Education: Some Strange Thoughts" (The Alden Seminars, 1984), John Strange notes that the new technologies "will challenge the very nature of our educational institutions" because they are

• interactive, allowing users to communicate almost as if they were communicating with another person

• integrated, combining video, audio, data manipulation, etc.

• portable, making it possible to use the technology anywhere, anytime

• personal, belonging to individuals, to be used without permission, intervention, or scheduling by others

The most important aspect is the personal. The learner is in charge. This does not imply the elimination of the educational system or its teachers. It does, however, make the teacher more of a coach and less of a trainer whose students perform complex tricks. This is precisely the role prescribed by Theodore Sizer in *Horace's Compromise* as the ideal for the best teaching/learning situation. Ithiel de Sola Pool of MIT called it the "individualization of instruction."

If the written word is not supreme; if scholars no longer need to communicate only through hard-copy publications; if the world of work changes faster than the world of education; if retraining becomes equal in importance to "education"; if students no longer need to memorize facts; if students can take charge of their own learning—how will higher education change to respond to these challenges?

We are still in awe of this technology that we do not understand. In the Brown University *Alumni Monthly,* a campus official wrote, "We are looking at a massive change in intellectual society. If you aren't scared about the implications of this change, how it's going to revolutionize teaching and research, you're not thinking." Ernest Lynton writes, "The growth of higher education and the economy's dependence on highly skilled human resources, as well as on effective technology transfer, has *rendered the ivory tower obsolete* [emphasis mine]." Seymour Papert of MIT says, in *Mindstorms* (1980), "I believe that the computer's presence will enable us to so modify the learning environment outside the classroom that much . . . will be learned, as the child learns to talk, painlessly, successfully, and *without organized instruction* [emphasis mine]." Most of us have not taken the time to imagine what our institutions must be like in the context of an information age.

John Strange, in a paper delivered as a part of the Alden Seminars, predicts that these changes are likely to take place in education, and soon:

> We currently deliver instructional material which has been prepared, in most cases by an individual teacher, to classes of students enrolled in an educational institution. In the not too distant future we will have instructional material prepared by groups of people, and these "instructors" will often not be the employees of educational institutions. The instruction will be delivered directly to the learner. He or she will buy the software, rent the laser disc, buy the video tape, access the course through computer communication techniques. We will deliver instruction through private entrepreneurs who will act as intermediaries between the "software" and the student. . . .

Muller predicts that such challenges will require us to become different in four fundamental ways. We will, he says, have different clients; we will have different delivery systems; we will deliver different content; and we will approach the enterprise in a different style.

Our clients are already older, and they come to our institutions with different resources and different needs from our traditional 18–22 year-old student. Many of these students will not be new to higher education. They will hold degrees and will be reentering the system not seeking advanced degrees, but in search of the latest information in a career area or seeking a body of knowledge entirely new to them. These clients will not be the traditional full-time student but will be full-time workers seeking part-time training and education.

The new technologies, some predict, will create more leisure for most of us. The new student will come to higher education for personal enrichment to enhance this increased leisure. In short, "we are going to serve a clientele which is adult, which wants to participate in education for a variety of reasons, professional and personal," according to Muller.

These new students will require new services. Interactive communications will be economically feasible by the end of this decade. Students who are workers and parents will require services delivered in the work place and in the home. Courses cannot be taught only in neat 15-week modules, delivered in 3 classroom contact hours per week. If learners do not come to us, and we must go to them, we will need entirely new structures for both delivering and evaluating learning.

The content of our services will have to change. Up until now, we have largely equated learning with memorization of facts and reading. With the availability of the computer and its capacity for storing and retrieving large amounts of data, we cannot continue to examine students principally on their ability to recall. If we are serious about teaching people to solve problems, we are going to have to look carefully both at the content of our courses and at the methods by which we examine students to determine their success. Since learners have become accustomed to images and sound as sources of learning, educators will be challenged to teach people using images and sound. The computer combined with videodisc technology, for example, provides an incredibly powerful teaching and learning tool not yet explored by educators.

New clients, new services, and new content demand new ways of operating. Muller suggests the answer to the questions raised by the new technologies may well be radical. "There may be an answer . . . and [it] is that 3000 disparate institutions in the United States, each of which is marked by an unquenchable desire to survive and a parochialism to match, may actually have to become serious about *sharing*."

Can the Consortium Help?

The new technology's challenge to higher education is that we must change. In fact, changes are occurring; how we manage those changes will be the challenge. Change requires innovation. We must create environments that will allow for innovation. We need to be willing to take risks, to ask questions, to look at the roots of our institutions, to dare to have the vision, and to work to make it real.

Rosabeth Moss Kanter, in *The Change Masters* (1983), describes conditions that encourage and inhibit innovation. Her audience is the corporate sector, but her insights are particularly useful for educators. Kanter defines innovation as "the capacity to change or adapt." Innovation seldom occurs in an environment where people say, "We've never done it that way before." Kanter cites Marshall McLuhan's description of "driving into the future, while looking out of the rear view mirror." I hope this is not higher education.

According to Kanter, innovators approach problems with "the willingness to move beyond received wisdom, to combine ideas from unconnected sources, to embrace change as an opportunity to test limits." She further asserts that it is in "team oriented, *cooperative environments* [that] innovation flourishes [emphasis mine]." She describes segmented systems as environments that discourage innovation.

What Kanter says about other organizations is true of colleges and universities; they are historically segmented from one another, and each is fiercely independent:

> Each is assumed to stand or fall independently of any other anyway, so why *should* they need to cooperate? . . . The system is designed to protect against change and to ensure that individuals have sufficient awe and respect . . . to maintain their role in it without question . . . . Individual segments may develop good, innovative ideas, but there is little impetus or mechanism for transfer of this knowledge from one segment to another.

Does this description seem apt for higher education? Kanter uses it to describe a highly segmented industry unlikely to be innovative.

There are in higher education few mechanisms for crossing over these segmented institutional barriers to create the unusual, unexpected alliances that Kanter says are necessary for the emergence of innovators whom she calls change masters. If "cooperative environments" are needed to encourage innovation, as Kanter prescribes, then the consortium deserves some careful attention by educational leaders.

The Consortium: One Solution

Admittedly, consortia have infrequently been used deliberately in the past as mechanisms to break down barriers. In fact, one of the first things you may hear about the difficulty of organizing an effective consortium is what is commonly called the "turf issue." Nevertheless, the consortium can be a tool to enhance the member institutions' capacity for cooperation. In choosing to participate in a consortium, college and university leaders choose to break out of the limits of the segmented system.

If we are going to consider organizing a consortium to address the challenges of the new technologies, it is important to consider both the strengths and the limits of consortia. The consortium is merely a tool available to educators. It is not a ready "fix," or a good thing in and of itself. To determine the applicability of collaboration toward a solution, educators need to be clear about the nature of the problem, the options available (which include cooperation) for addressing the problem, and the costs and benefits of each. Collaboration must be around issues important to institutional mission. Goals should be clear and should enhance, not threaten, institutional autonomy. Nevertheless, to commit institutional resources in time and energy to cooperation is risky and requires at least sharing of some turf, if not loss of it.

The key to a successful collaboration is leadership and the imagination necessary to articulate the vision. The consortium gives the members an environment outside the traditional limits of our highly segmented educational system, described by Kanter as inhibiting innovation. Patricia Battin, in her call for a restructured university, prescribes cooperation as the solution: "The new communications technologies will require an extraordinary and unprecedented *cooperative* effort. . . . *The scholarly community must transcend its cherished autonomy and create organizational mechanisms which will support effective cooperative activities in its own best interests* [emphasis mine]."

Some Consortium Examples

There are many examples of consortial efforts being made to address the new technology's challenges to higher education. The *1983 Consortium*

Directory lists, among the more than 130 entries, at least 45 consortia involved in some way in promoting or using new technologies. Some of the examples cited below are new consortia, begun for a particular purpose; others are consortia of long standing (some special purpose and others of a more general purpose) that have chosen projects to address aspects of this challenge. Some represent innovative approaches; others are more traditional.

The challenges of images and sounds are growing as the interactive cable, microwave, videodisc, holography, and other technologies become more sophisticated, more affordable, and more available. The TAGER Television Network of the Association for Higher Education of North Texas was started in 1980 to share academic resources and to deliver programs to business, industry, and schools in the area. Some 70 cable systems in the region served by the consortium's members were expected, by the end of 1985, to be carrying campus-originated programming.

Kentuckiana Metroversity operates two cable channels 18 hours a day. The Virginia Tidewater Consortium for Continuing Education owns and operates a 24-hour cable channel, through which it is "able to reach over one million people." In Boston, the cable television franchise agreement required the establishment of a higher education consortium to help the cable company and the city plan for higher education access to the system. The Boston Consortium for Cable-TV includes among its members most of the colleges and universities in the greater Boston area.

The International University Consortium for Telecommunications in Learning, housed at the University of Maryland, is a national network of nearly 20 higher education institutions, broadcast stations, and cable systems from Massachusetts to California that provides complete bachelor's degree programs to adults. The Public Service Satellite Consortium provides its members access to its National Satellite Network for distribution of programming, teleconferencing, and the like.

The new scholarship, as described by Battin, requires new ways for distributing information. Battin predicts new models for libraries that will depend on cooperative activities. Consortia are already changing how scholars and libraries function. Many general-purpose consortia (including Five Colleges, Inc., and NECCUM in Massachusetts) have initiated computer based library networks among their members. The Atlanta University Center created a consolidated library long before the "computer revolution," and its members continue to cooperate to provide better research facilities for faculty members and students.

EDUCOM and EDUNET are national networks, by now familiar to most educators, that extend the resources of large, very powerful, and very expensive computers. They provide to their members access to computer resources for research, electronic mail and conferencing, administrative services, consulting services, publications, etc. With the advent of personal computers, these large networks become most useful for large research projects that require the capacity of this kind of equipment.

Recently the *Chronicle of Higher Education* reported on a "Star Wars consortium," organized among seven universities with an award from the Department of Defense, to undertake research and development of a small computer using "optical signal processing." This kind of research consortium will be seen more frequently as we proceed into the "Information Age."

Large information data bases are more and more available through commercial vendors, such as the SOURCE. Users can get information about everything from economic trends to airline schedules. Consortia are creating their own data bases, some on a national scale and others locally. OCLC, the nationwide network and data base of library holdings, is familiar to many educators (see Chapter 4 for more on this subject).

SPHERE, a consortium of 11 colleges and universities in Spokane, Washington, created as a community service a local data base of the members' continuing education courses, as well as a listing of shorter term, noncredit seminars, workshops, and presentations. NECCUM is working on a similar service. The Communications Consortium, housed at MIT, is using conferences, workshops, publications, and a data base of information and programming to inform its members about new technologies and is consulting with them on planning for new communications technologies.

Consortia are helping colleges and universities to provide the retraining that the rapidly changing workplace is making necessary. Efforts to develop third-party brokering mechanisms to facilitate retraining are being tried. The Corporate-Education Exchange in Boston, under joint sponsorship of business and educational institutions, was one such effort. With the sponsorship of a large Kellogg grant, another, more successful effort was initiated by the New Hampshire College and University Council. The New Hampshire Continuing Education Network made the consortium the broker for access to retraining opportunities. In Philadelphia, under the umbrella of the Compact for Lifelong Educational Opportunity (CLEO), the Business and Education Center has been operating, on-site in an industrial park. The center brings the resources of its member colleges and universities to the workplace, providing degree programs as well as personal improvement workshops.

Schools of engineering at 21 universities have organized a consortium, the National Technological University, to provide graduate-level programs to meet the continuing education needs of practicing engineers and scientists. The first series of seminars was telecast over a two-week period in early 1985. These courses, which are taught by professors of affiliated universities, were made available, for a fee of $1,000, to any college or university with satellite reception equipment; rental arrangements were also possible.

The biggest challenge for the consortium (and higher education), however, is the effort to explore the new role for educators in a learner-controlled environment. Here are some selected developments, reported in the *Chronicle of Higher Education* during the past year or so, that illustrate the kinds of alliances we can expect. In July of 1984, it was reported that the Inter-University Consortium on Academic Computing was organized by Carnegie-Mellon University (CMU) and 14 other institutions—public, private; small, large; university, liberal arts—nationwide "to develop and evaluate education software." John P. Crecine, then chair of the consortium board and senior academic vice president at CMU, said, "If a University like CMU has to write all the education software we need to revolutionize education on our campus, there won't be a revolution on our campus." The consortium had met with three major computer companies to advocate a common operating system to facilitate software exchange.

Early in 1985, the *Chronicle of Higher Education* reported two new consortia. Eight universities, working with an $8 million grant from Air Force funds, had organized the Artificial Intelligence Consortium. These universities, all in the northeastern United States, hope to raise additional funds from other sources in order to "develop a strong computer-technology center in the Northeast." And the very next week, it was reported that the City University of New York had been the first of three universities to join a new consortium being organized by Wadsworth Professional Software, Inc., publishers of STATPRO, a statistics package for the IBM PC. Six other institutions were strongly considering membership, it was reported. Members of the consortium agreed to purchase two copies of STATPRO at half-price and to test and help develop new software—a sort of "software-of-the-month" club.

Twenty-four colleges and universities were, by mid-1984, members of the Apple University Consortium; by now there are undoubtedly more. Apple offers hefty discounts in exchange for commitment to its products and expects users to become advocates and developers of new software. Digital and IBM have encouraged similar user networks.

In March of 1984, the development of physics, chemistry, and biology laboratory courses on an interactive, computer-programmable videodisc made news in the *Chronicle of Higher Education*. The courses, developed by the University of Nebraska Videodisc Design/Production Group under a grant from the Annenberg/Corporation for Public Broadcasting project, have been tested under a cooperative arrangement with six other higher education institutions and a preparatory school.

The Barriers to Cooperation

If we are successfully to encourage innovation, Kanter warns, leaders must find ways to break out of the hierarchy that controls institutions, to share information freely, and to make available the tools necessary to do the job. Many institutions of higher education operate in a highly structured administrative model, with clear reporting lines. Even faculty councils have their place in the hierarchy of higher education. On our campuses, most people have defined, limited responsibilities, and few have a broad perspective.

The consortium can be the only context in which people of various levels, from within several segments—even several colleges and universities—work together to solve a problem. Too often, information is hoarded, especially between colleges, but often also within a given institution. It is important that information be available. Communication between policymakers and doers is key. Networks must be established and nurtured. The consortium, again, can be the medium in which communication among nontraditional sets of people can take place.

Finally, as Kanter warns, limited tools for getting the job done will certainly limit success. Too often there is little or no access to the money, time, or training required for the task. Historically, the consortium is viewed as a frivolous extra, and most consortia have few of these tools. The successful ones have adequate resources.

Conclusion

The advent of the new technologies has challenged higher education to make new kinds of responses to new clients, to new content, to new methods, and to new styles. These challenges call on leaders to create conditions conducive to innovation. Innovation requires collaboration in situations where the barriers of hierarchical organizational structure, of hoarded information, and of limited resources can be broken.

The consortium operates on the edges of higher education. If it is on the edge (outside the hierarchy, but connected to the key people); if it has access to information; and if it is endowed with sufficient support, it can be an effective tool for educators eager to participate in the changes brought about by the new technologies.

In short, the consortium clearly has the potential to be an environment conducive to the innovation that higher education needs in order to meet the challenges of new technology—if educational leaders are able to lead the way.

—11—

Consortia as Risk-Takers

JON W. FULLER

The very act of cooperation among academic institutions is risky, which is perhaps why they are so likely to focus their cooperation on relatively safe areas—joint purchasing, cross-registration for students, and professional camaraderie among nonacademic administrators—activities that emphasize the easily understood (though not always so easily realized) economies of scale that consortia offer.

There is also a potential for consortia to undertake much more exciting challenges: to be on the cutting edge of issues and to relate to the academic heart of their member institutions. Consortia not only allow colleges and universities to do that which is familiar in a more cost-efficient way, but they can open up new possibilities as well.

The Great Lakes Colleges Association

This chapter draws largely on the collective experience of the Great Lakes Colleges Association (GLCA) and describes some case studies of

The Great Lakes Colleges Association (GLCA) was created in 1961 by the 12 undergraduate, liberal-arts colleges that constitute its membership today. GLCA sponsors off-campus study programs, professional development programs for faculty members, conferences, and exchanges of comparative data. GLCA also engages in collective admissions activities and represents the interests of undergraduate liberal arts education.

how this consortium has enabled its members to innovate successfully
and efficiently. Its beginnings in 1961 rank it among the most venerable
of consortia and, by general consent, among the most successful as
well. GLCA was created by 12 independent liberal arts colleges: DePauw,
Earlham, and Wabash in Indiana; Albion, Hope, and Kalamazoo in
Michigan; and Antioch, Denison, Kenyon, Oberlin, Ohio Wesleyan, and
The College of Wooster in Ohio. That membership list has been
unchanged throughout GLCA's quarter century of operation.

In creating this consortium, the founders were consciously imitating
the Associated Colleges of the Midwest (ACM), a group of similar
institutions in states just to the west of GLCA's territory, which had begun
consortial operations in the late 1950s. Although there are important
distinctions and differences, these two associations have shared much
the same development and success, and these two midwestern consortial
twins have pioneered that next level of cooperation in higher education:
collaboration between consortia.

GLCA was born in what was, for its members, an expansive and
optimistic time. Indeed, one motive of some of the association's founding
presidents was to find a way to resist the lure of enlarging their institutions,
while still taking advantage of the new educational opportunities that were
then developing and that seemed to require a larger base of support.

Off-Campus Study

One important opportunity, which the leaders of the GLCA colleges
wanted to seize, but which seemed to require significant enlargements
of faculty size and student enrollment, was the study of the non-European
world. These colleges shared with most American colleges and universities
an almost exclusive focus on the history, literature, and thought shared
by Western Europe and the United States. Several GLCA colleges had a
long-standing involvement with China and Japan (a legacy of missionary
activity in earlier years), but this affected the curricula of the colleges in
only peripheral ways.

The task, however, was a daunting one. For a small college to take
seriously the teaching of Asia, Africa, and Latin America seemed to require
an expansion of faculty and library resources, and an increase in student
enrollment, that the GLCA schools did not wish to undertake, even though
such physical expansion might well have been possible in the "Golden
Years" of the 1960s.

The consortium looked like a way to expand educational vision and scope, without enlarging the size of the individual member colleges. The founding presidents agreed to pool and coordinate their efforts to attend to these "new" parts of the world. It seemed almost reminiscent of the Congress of Berlin: faculty and administrators of the GLCA colleges divided responsibility for developing educational resources and opportunities about each part of the non-Western world. Individual colleges were designated as "agent colleges" for the consortium, each with its own particular geographic area.

Many of the GLCA assignments drew on the special institutional connections of particular colleges with particular parts of the world. So, Oberlin became the agent for China (realistically limited in those days to Taiwan and Hong Kong); Earlham became the agent for Japan; Wooster took the lead in India; Antioch developed resources about Latin America (creating the still flourishing Centro de Estudios Universitarios Colombo-Americano [CEUCA] in Bogota); Kenyon took responsibility for the Middle East, focusing on a program at the American University in Beirut; while Kalamazoo developed unique opportunities for GLCA undergraduates to study in African universities.

The dream was a bold one, and there were failures along the way, together with notable successes. But the consortium allowed the GLCA colleges to take these risks, drawing on individual institutional strengths and interests, and reinforced by the collective resources of all twelve. Their joint venture in international education attracted significant outside support, particularly from the Ford Foundation. This not only allowed individual institutions to develop unusual strengths in their assigned parts of the world—Earlham's faculty and library resources, focused on Japan, are still among the best in the nation—but also made available the full range of resources to faculty and students in all 12 colleges. A faculty member at Earlham, interested in Africa, could look to the programs and resources at Kalamazoo for support; a student at Hope, with a wish to study in the Middle East, could enroll in a GLCA program at Beirut, administered by Kenyon.

By banding together to take on the challenges of truly global education, these colleges were able to put themselves in the first rank in American higher education. They could meet virtually any student interest in any part of the world, through programs in which each college had a stake and over which it could help to exercise quality control. An otherwise lonely area specialist on a small college faculty could be regularly linked to colleagues at other colleges who shared the same enthusiasm, and who could offer tangible assistance—access to special library collections, to visiting speakers and performers, and to film (and, more recently, video) resources for teaching.

Because these were shared ventures, moreover, the inevitable defeats and disappointments—such as the necessity to close the GLCA program in Beirut as political conditions there deteriorated—did not mean the elimination of international opportunities for the students and faculty of the agent college. Changing faculty interests and college priorities also led eventually to closing GLCA's own program in India, although those study opportunities were sustained through ACM's continuing India Program.

Gradually the same logic that had led these colleges to cooperate in development of opportunities for study abroad was extended to the development of several domestic off-campus programs, including an arts program in New York, a science program at the Oak Ridge National Laboratory, a unique liberal arts program in an urban setting through the GLCA Philadelphia Center, and eventually to cosponsorship (with ACM) of the Newberry Library Program in the Humanities.

To some extent, these off-campus study opportunities represented an application of that basic strength of any consortial venture: economies of scale. A small college may have only one or two students a year whose interest in Japan is sufficient to make them want to spend a year studying there. By joining with other colleges in consortial sponsorship, the opportunity can be offered year after year, maintaining enrollments large enough to make the program viable.

GLCA's international ventures (and later its domestic off-campus programs as well) were not just more-of-the-same kinds of educational opportunities that were offered in campus classrooms. These programs have fruitfully combined elements of formal study with the best aspects of experiential education. Such combinations were less troublesome and difficult in a consortial setting than they would have been had they been developed and sponsored on most of the member campuses. There was a reassurance in sharing responsibility for a program with a group of peer colleges. There was a greater tolerance for experimentation away from the home campus.

This does not suggest that consortial programs lack standards or rigor. In fact, the demands of consortial sponsorship generally require more frequent and careful evaluation and agreement about educational value than is demanded for offerings on campus. But cooperation among a group of institutions both makes programs economically possible (by ensuring sufficient enrollment) and also allows a greater range of experimentation and risk.

Faculty Development

GLCA's move into the area of professional development programs for faculty illustrates the same advantages of consortial activity, focused on a quite different audience. As "faculty development" began to be talked about in higher education conferences and publications in the early 1970s, it was greeted with a substantial amount of skepticism on campuses such as those in GLCA, which generally take a conservative and cautious posture toward the new and the "trendy" in education. Faculty development seemed too much like the pedagogical preoccupations of elementary and secondary teacher training. In its concern for individual growth and development, it impressed some as being too reminiscent of encounter groups of the late 1960s.

At the same time, many faculty members and administrators believed their institutions could be strengthened by explicit attention to teaching and to the growth and development of individual faculty members. Again the consortium provided a way for the GLCA colleges to sample these new possibilities before making a full institutional commitment to them.

GLCA's move into faculty development as an area of consortial activity was significantly encouraged by a major foundation grant: almost half a million dollars from the Lilly Endowment. The grant allowed faculty and administrators of the GLCA colleges to experiment and sample the various forms of faculty development programming that were then emerging. Over the three-year span of the grant, the consortium sponsored some relatively conservative and traditional programs, such as conferences focused on teaching in a particular discipline, or on seeking grant support for individual research projects. It also explored more risky elements, including workshops on personal growth and career change, as well as exploration of new and potentially controversial teaching areas, such as women's studies. Individual colleges were encouraged to develop their own on-campus approaches to faculty development: some established workshop programs for faculty; some formed faculty study groups to explore the literature of student development; and others designated a tenured faculty member as a teaching consultant to help colleagues assess and improve their own teaching on a confidential basis.

Faculty professional development has remained a major area of consortial programming for GLCA. The Lilly Endowment grant was an almost textbook example of successful foundation support for educational change. The new resources of the grant allowed the colleges to experiment together, trying out the possibilities suggested in the faculty development literature as well as some locally created variations. The requirement for increasing financial commitment by the colleges, in the form of matching dollars, prepared them to sustain that effort after the grant ended.

What the GLCA colleges have sustained includes an annual series of 8 to 10 faculty conferences and workshops: some focused on teaching in a particular discipline, such as psychology; some on an interdisciplinary opportunity, such as teaching about nuclear issues; and some on other aspects of faculty professional activity, including workshops for department chairs and workshops on grant support for research.

Despite the skepticism about pedagogy, the GLCA colleges also offer an annual workshop on teaching and course design. The practical focus of this one-week workshop, in which each faculty participant works on a particular course (either being revised or being prepared for the first time), allows a comfortable and relevant consideration of such issues as course objectives and planning, alternative methods of presentation of material, and assessment and evaluation. The enthusiastic reports of past participants when they return to their campuses has kept annual workshop enrollment at capacity in recent years. Again the GLCA colleges were able to work together to develop and sustain a valued professional opportunity for their faculties, whereas suspicion and controversy would probably have doomed such efforts on most of their campuses, had they undertaken such activities individually.

Women's Studies

The experimentation allowed by the Lilly Endowment faculty development grant led directly to the development of consortial exploration of a new and controversial curriculum area—women's studies. This was initially the topic of just one of a series of workshops conducted under the Lilly Endowment faculty development program. But it drew an unexpectedly large and enthusiastic response, which led to faculty proposals for a larger and more ambitious GLCA Women's Studies Conference. That conference, undertaken largely with financial support by the individual colleges themselves, drew more than 100 participants, including students and administrators as well as faculty members. Despite the silent hopes of some administrators that sponsoring a conference would satisfy the interest and allow the consortium and most of the colleges to go on to other topics, it proved to be the beginning of a major consortial activity.

An enthusiastic women's studies committee, including faculty from every campus, was formed and soon developed a funding proposal for a major consortial program in women's studies. This time, it was the Fund for the Improvement of Post-Secondary Education (FIPSE) that provided the crucial financial support to allow the development and experimentation that was needed.

The GLCA women's studies conference became an annual event (now attracting more than 200 participants each year—most of them attending their first women's studies event). The FIPSE grant led to additional support from the Lilly Endowment to develop a National Summer Institute in Women's Studies. Over three years, that institute made its own contributions to the field of women's studies nationally. It also sustained the GLCA program long enough for it to make a successful claim on continuing support from the colleges themselves. In 1981, the presidents of the 12 member colleges agreed to increase their consortial dues in order to maintain the GLCA women's studies coordinator as a half-time consortial staff position and to fund the continuing work of the GLCA Women's Studies Committee.

GLCA's collective venture in women's studies has served the consortium and all of its colleges well. The consortium has gained support and involvement from an enthusiastic group of faculty members on each campus. Each GLCA college now has women's studies as an established part of its own curriculum, represented in ways appropriate to the style of that institution. The consortium has always been careful to respect institutional autonomy and the distinct traditions of each college. Some GLCA college catalogs list a women's studies major, some a minor, and some have courses that are identified as "women's studies" courses. On other campuses, the courses are listed under individual departments, although they also address the growing body of scholarship by and about women. From a situation a decade ago, when women's studies was represented by only a handful of experimental courses on a few of the campuses, and by the fearful hopes of a few faculty members, it is now a presence on all 12 GLCA campuses—even at Wabash, which remains one of the few colleges for men in the country.

The development of GLCA's women's studies program demonstrates another advantage of a consortial approach to risky topics. The colleges were able, through the consortium, to explore and test a new and potentially exciting field, with each college eventually finding an approach that was comfortable and appropriate for its faculty and students. Learning about this new field was sped up because each college could learn readily from the others. There was a regular and comfortable means of communicating common experiences and concerns. Further, acceptance of new ideas was made easier by the approval of faculty at other colleges. Faculty were more comfortable about unfamiliar and potentially controversial material when they knew that it was being used and accepted at other GLCA campuses.

GLCA's approach to women's studies has brought with it collective attention to issues about the status of women as faculty members and students, along with attention to new research and teaching possibilities. In this aspect, too, the colleges learn from each other. Hiring guidelines and policy statements on sexual harassment are shared among faculty and administrators. Each college could move ahead faster, and with more confidence, because it could draw on the experience of the others.

The power of example within a consortium has a greater intensity than do examples offered at national higher education conferences or in magazines or journals. In the course of operating a consortium, presidents and deans and faculty leaders come to know their counterparts at other colleges. They work together on a variety of projects. They come to know the special strengths and traditions of each of the member institutions. They develop personal trust. This allows them to learn from each other more confidently and efficiently. They come to recognize which aspects of the experience of others reflect special local institutional conditions, and which aspects might be applied to their own situation and needs.

The Problems of Untenured Faculty Members

The special problems facing untenured faculty members have provided yet another opportunity for GLCA to help its colleges deal with a significant issue that would have been much more difficult for them to take on individually. The tensions and anger that can focus on the status of untenured professors are obvious enough on most campuses, and the usual reaction is to preserve what remains of those important values of community and collegiality by avoiding any general and full discussion of the situation. Untenured faculty grumble among themselves, and senior professors lament with their contemporaries about the difficulties of getting to know younger colleagues. Various policy modifications may be adopted in response to specific concerns, but a full exploration of this tender topic is usually avoided.

The frustration and anger connected to this topic became evident to GLCA's consortial staff several years ago. In their role as "inside outsiders," staff members of a consortium like GLCA often hear faculty and administrators talk about problems and concerns with a freedom they cannot feel with their own immediate campus colleagues. Consortial staff can be relied on to understand the local situation, but they are not part of it, and so they make good informal consultants about many problems. They often can report experiences from other campuses that can be directly helpful. These many quiet conversations on the member campuses can lead consortial staff to identify problems shared by several of the colleges, which might then make a collective response appropriate.

The first extended discussion of the problems of untenured faculty came at a meeting of GLCA's academic council, which brings together faculty representatives from all 12 colleges. Several untenured and recently tenured faculty who were present found the setting one in which they could express their frustration and anger more openly and forcefully than they had ever felt able to do with senior colleagues on their own campus. They described the pain of uncertainty about procedures and standards, and their resentment that they were required to meet far more rigorous tests than had ever been faced by the same older faculty who now served as their judges. In response, several senior faculty expressed their anger about the assumption by some junior faculty that their senior colleagues were less able and less qualified because the earlier procedures for awarding tenure had been less rigorous and elaborate.

Following that discussion by the academic council, GLCA's vice president took on development of a proposal that would allow the consortium to take up the problems faced by untenured faculty and would allow the coordinated exploration of possible solutions. Proposed drafts were circulated widely for comment and suggestions from faculty and administrators. Finally, formal approval was given by the deans' council and by the board of directors, and a request for support was submitted to the Fund for the Improvement of Post-Secondary Education.

Staff at the Fund responded with characteristic helpfulness and understanding, despite the inevitable uncertainty and tentative nature of the proposal, and a grant was made to GLCA in 1982, allowing the consortium to explore a variety of approaches to this problem. Workshops that drew together both tenured and untenured faculty from each campus proved very useful. Junior faculty were reassured by open discussion of their problems and concerns. Senior faculty were able to listen, without defensiveness, to junior faculty who were not from their own campus and then could apply their new understanding of the general problem to the conditions at their own college.

In addition, there was a systematic comparison of the 12 colleges' formal policies related to faculty evaluation and tenure. On any campus, there is a tendency to think that local policies and practices are essentially similar to those of other institutions, whether they are or not. Most faculty members and administrators have extensive knowledge and experience only of their own college and its procedures. Systematic comparisons with similar institutions can help identify which practices are a response to broad trends in higher education, and which are the result of local traditions and choices and the influence of specific personalities. Such comparisons can also prompt recognition that particular policies may be having a very different result than was intended.

GLCA's examination of college tenure policies provides an example of how this comparison can be effective. It became evident that the practice, adopted on several GLCA campuses, of designating certain faculty positions "not tenurable" was increasing anxiety and uncertainty, although the policy had been intended to make the situation as clear and certain as possible, and thus to reduce anxiety. Despite the intention, there was always the possibility that conditions would change, making tenure possible for those in "not tenurable" positions. Those junior faculty thus experienced the same anxiety and hope for security that weighed upon colleagues occupying formally tenurable positions. At the same time, the junior faculty at these colleges felt their group divided into unequal classes, reproducing many of the general tensions between tenured and untenured faculty and reducing the possibilities for mutual support within the untenured group. Because the issue was difficult to discuss, and even more difficult to think about apart from the involvement of specific individuals, none of this was as clear on a single campus as it became when examined in a consortial context.

An important result of the tensions found on every campus between tenured and untenured faculty was a breakdown in the usual patterns of socialization for junior colleagues into the practices and expectations both of the profession generally and those of their own campus in particular. Open conversation between senior and junior colleagues was more difficult than it had been when tenure was not a major issue, and individuals in both categories were less willing to risk the development of close friendships that could make a negative tenure decision even more difficult and painful.

To compensate for this loss, GLCA developed a "mentoring" program, which paired a junior faculty member from one GLCA college with a senior faculty member from another college. These voluntary relationships were complicated, of course, by the distance between GLCA campuses, but that geographic distance was sometimes less difficult to overcome than was the social distance that had emerged between tenured and untenured faculty members on the same campus.

One other element of the consortial program was the collection and dissemination of information about career patterns and tenure results for junior faculty on all 12 campuses. On a single campus, the unhappiness caused by a difficult tenure denial can influence the perceptions of all faculty members at that college. The distress of a single specific decision will overshadow several positive and therefore less notable tenure decisions. The combined consortial data revealed that, despite more rigorous and demanding standards, junior faculty still were granted tenure more often than not, and those who were disappointed by tenure denials almost always remained in the profession if they wished, finding permanent faculty positions elsewhere.

GLCA's program to address problems of untenured faculty is another clear example of a consortium helping its colleges to take risks that they would find difficult and therefore would be unlikely to take, acting alone. Many of the issues connected with the predicament of untenured faculty seem "too hot to handle," and faculty and administrators prefer to endure unspoken tension and even hostility rather than risk a full discussion of the problems. The consortial setting provides a neutral setting for such discussion, which is made easier by participation of faculty from several colleges. The pros and cons of particular policies can be considered without the additional emotional barrier of senior people feeling responsible and defensive about particular decisions they had taken, or of junior people fearing that too much candor might threaten their own careers.

Tensions about tenure decisions and evaluation of junior faculty are real and inherent in the current state of higher education. No consortial program could make all of the problems go away. But a consortial approach has allowed the GLCA colleges to take the risks of reexamining their individual policies and practices while avoiding the hazards of confrontation and defensiveness about specific past decisions that are likely to inhibit such reexamination within a single campus. It has been possible to reestablish mutually advantageous and satisfying relationships between individual senior and junior faculty members by helping them make connections across campus lines. The member colleges have retained their full autonomy, and they continue to follow individual and different practices in dealing with tenure and evaluation. But each college has identified changes that improve its own situation, and the individual faculty members who participate in consortial programs find some relief from the isolation and anxiety of their own campus.

Area Studies

One more advantage of cooperation is illustrated by a recent development in GLCA's history. Working together, institutions in a consortium can more readily make connections to other institutions and other organizations. In GLCA's experience, this is well represented by the recent development of the Program for Inter-Institutional Collaboration in Area Studies (PICAS), through which the 12 GLCA colleges are joined together with the 13 of the ACM and with the University of Michigan.

PICAS allows the language and area studies centers (funded by federal support) located at the University of Michigan to enrich the international education resources of the 25 GLCA and ACM colleges. Faculty from the colleges receive support to spend from six months to a year as fellows-in-residence at one of the Michigan area studies centers, or to make shorter visits of even a few days to consult with experts and to use the university's specialized library resources.

The program also organizes conferences, focused on various areas of the world, to bring together faculty from the ACM and GLCA colleges and from the University of Michigan. Faculty at the colleges benefit from the research resources of the university, while university faculty learn from counterparts at undergraduate colleges where the focus on teaching issues is stronger. Undergraduates also have opportunities to receive support for summer language study, or for short visits to the university to use library and other area studies resources.

All of this collaborative activity is coordinated and facilitated by the executive director, who serves as a member of the university staff, and is supported by an advisory committee representing both the university's centers and the participating colleges.

The basic idea of PICAS proved to be very appealing to the foundations to which it was presented. The funding has been shared by the Ford Foundation, the Mellon Foundation, and the Glen Mede Trust. The need to strengthen the international dimension of the colleges' curricula was readily recognized, and the proposed activities responded directly to that need. Cooperation among 25 colleges, located in 8 states, had its own appeal, which was greatly enhanced when these undergraduate colleges were joined with a major research university. Cooperation between these independent colleges and a large public institution also made the proposal more attractive.

To be sure, such collaborative arrangements might be possible and attractive for any combination of undergraduate colleges that want to link themselves to a major research university around an area of mutual interest. But it was much easier for two established consortia to make such connections. The first set of questions had already been answered: i.e., Which institutions would be involved? How could their interests be determined? and Who is to represent them in the required negotiations?

Because the two consortia were already established, it was possible for their presidents to respond promptly to the first suggestion of the University of Michigan's interest in such an ambitious collaboration. There was a clear and manageable process for consultation with all of the institutions, and for them to give the necessary formal approval to the idea. As established and ongoing organizations, GLCA and ACM could readily absorb the costs connected with development and presentation of a major proposal. The necessary travel, telephone calls, and clerical support could be paid for from the consortial operating budgets, eliminating another issue that would have made a similar development much more difficult (and hence less likely) for an ad hoc grouping of colleges.

All this illustrates again the general point that consortia can be instruments for collective risk taking by institutions. The exploration and development of any new idea, particularly one which would require outside support for implementation, requires real financial risks. These risks are more readily undertaken and funded by an established organization.

Conclusion

GLCA has enabled its member colleges to explore many other possibilities for collaborative action that have not—at least not yet—been funded and implemented. Those include shared facilities for scientific research, a collaborative program for retirement planning, a joint graduate program, and a journal for publication of faculty research. But the colleges benefit from having a ready means to explore various possibilities for cooperation, including those which are not found to be feasible, cost-effective, or able to command necessary outside support.

Colleges and universities are generally well served by procedures and traditions that make them behave cautiously and undertake new ventures slowly, if at all. The complexity of campus governance systems requires that change come at a manageable pace. Collegiality is central to the academic enterprise, and it is an important value to protect.

But these familiar and useful conservative qualities are sometimes too effective and unnecessarily limit the change and steady adaptation that institutions also need. Consortia can offer a manageable way to explore possibilities that might seem dangerously different from the established traditions of their member institutions. Decision making can actually be quicker and more flexible for a consortium than it is for most institutions. Institutional reputations, while still invested in the activities of a consortium to which they belong, are less at risk in collective than in individual enterprises. Consortia can thus allow their members to take more risks with fewer costs and to enjoy greater possibilities for benefit than would be possible for those institutions acting alone.

—12—

The Limits of Cooperation

DONALD A. JOHNSON

The chief executive officer of a consortium must be an eternal optimist. Anyone who has "been there" knows the advantages that accrue from having such a mindset. It means that you face challenges with confidence. It means that you bring a work ethic that says "Things can be done." It means that success is expected. Molding educational and institutional diversity into an organization with common goals requires a positive, confident attitude. Constraints and roadblocks exist everywhere; this chapter examines a few that inhere to educational consortia. But the constraints and barriers need not remain problems that retard progress in business, industry, or consortia. Developing interinstitutional cooperative programs is a challenge that can be met even within the parameters identified in this chapter.

The first and most pervasive reason why the consortium will not solve every problem in higher education is the fact that in our society—from child-rearing practices to Olympic competition, and from bake-offs to presidential races—competition is not only condoned, but rewarded and encouraged. Institutions of higher education foster that same competitive

The Quad Cities Graduate Study Center is a voluntary academic consortium of nine colleges and universities in Illinois and Iowa. Its primary purpose for nearly 20 years has been to provide a vehicle and focus for organized, cooperative graduate study opportunities. The center, which is funded equally by the two states, offers 11 master's degree programs.

stance and have learned to live with oftentimes ruthless competition for faculty members, for students, and for federal, state, and private dollars.

Such competition is the real institutional battle—one that makes football and basketball contests pale by comparison. Asking an administrator at one college or university to cooperate with counterparts from other higher education institutions is asking something that is alien to the attitudes and values absorbed since birth. One reason, then, that consortia have not flourished in the higher education community is that they run counter to the grain of higher education. Competition is a given; cooperation is a variable that one can accept or reject.

But such competition need not be directed at another person or institution. One of the challenges for the consortium leader is to develop an entrepreneurial and innovative spirit that will thrive in such an environment. The sense of excitement and reward that comes with successful ventures thus help to counter the frustration of going against the grain.

In 1980, the *Chronicle of Higher Education* printed a "Point of View" essay written by the then chairman of the board of the Association of Governing Boards of Universities and Colleges. In this article, "The Crazy Dream of a College Trustee," Robert Lewis called cooperation exotic yet practical. Yet, with too few exceptions, he wrote, administrators have no serious objection to keeping interinstitutional cooperation a secret. It has been kept a secret when it should have been touted: the dream has not been translated into action. For a consortium to succeed, it must have the support of the several institutional administrations. Administrators must not keep their consortial memberships a secret but, rather, they must publicly support the work and mission of the consortium. A president can exert powerful leadership in this process.

Autonomy is a term that consortium directors hear frequently in connection with the failure of cooperative ventures to gain support. Typically those who believe that consortia, by their very nature, undermine institutional autonomy are the ones who apply the term. Larry Rose recently wrote that the major constraint to cooperation is the matter of autonomy. Some observers, including Fritz Grupe, have argued that cooperation actually strengthens autonomy by avoiding the greater threat of cooptation.

Consorting is not a step toward consolidation, although the question of institutional independence and autonomy is one that consortium directors are constantly made sensitive to. The threat of consolidation is perceived as real by institutional leaders, although some of them may be willing to sacrifice a limited amount of autonomy if essential programs are not endangered.

Hannah Kreplin and Jane Bolce outline four potential impacts on consortia of the concern over autonomy: these include (1) an institution's fear of a drain on its resources; (2) prohibitive decision making procedures on one or more campuses that prevent true cooperation; (3) possible support for weak programs; and (4) the lack of reward for faculty participation.

An additional constraint emerges from the diversity of missions of the institutions involved in cooperation. Differing missions may mean different kinds of faculties and student bodies, and so there may be few opportunities to cooperate. For example, a "Big Ten" university and a liberal arts college may have little in common in which they can cooperate. Likewise, a regional university and a school of design may also have little in common. The diversity of missions can be used as an excuse not to cooperate—or it can be a reason to cooperate.

Diversity of mission may suggest that the institutions are significantly different and therefore have no natural areas of cooperation. One must also recognize, though, that their very differences make the opportunities to complement one another obvious. For example, a land-grant institution could provide some seminars or courses in land and water conservation to strengthen that component of the biology department in a liberal arts college. The liberal arts college, in return, could provide some options in foreign travel or other culturally enriching options. Another example is where a community college and a liberal arts college jointly offer life-long learning opportunities to the public, each drawing upon their respective strengths to do so. Cooperation can mean as little as respecting one another's domains.

Students of the interinstitutional movement and consortia have identified other potential barriers to cooperation. Grupe lists eight major difficulties that must be confronted. These include maintaining neutrality and balance among member benefits, developing a new perspective on educational quality within the multi-institutional setting, establishing realistic expectations, and exceeding the mere form of cooperation. Dan M. Martin cites certain persistent errors by consortia that impede interinstitutional success: undue emphasis on reducing costs, inadequate attention to the whole range of possible action, and the mismatching of membership and mission. Judith S. Glazer, finally, pinpoints what she believes is another major constraint: consortia are very complex organizational units that run counter to institutional tradition.

Consortial arrangements thus have not been the panacea for higher education: the dream still needs some reality therapy. Even with the realism that this perspective brings, though, we must ask what factors have inhibited the growth of interinstitutional cooperation and consortia.

Even though the work of the consortium's staff is meant to serve the member institutions, this work is not always conveyed in a meaningful way to faculty members, students, and others. Too often the work is not widely publicized. Consortium directors and boards need to print and distribute to their various constituents newsletters, annual reports, and the like. Because consortia lack a public relations and information thrust, the consortium concept is not viewed as an integral part of each member institution—the consortium is seen merely as a group to contract with for specific services. Just as a substitute in a bridge game or a golf foursome is nice, but not cherished, so the consortium staff and their work rarely receive full acceptance by the members.

Related to this, but raising another problem, is the fact that the policy leadership, for most consortia, is provided by a presidents' council. A "presidents' club" will probably evolve from that structure unless the consortium staff is very skilled at directing and prodding presidents—an exceedingly dangerous duty. The staff and the faculty members of the institutions must be involved, at appropriate tasks, so that the verbal commitment of the presidents is translated into some type of institutional service: teaching, research, or public service.

Many times interinstitutional cooperation through a consortium has been touted as a good thing but fails because it lacks a clear-cut mission or charge from the organizers. It is a truism that management theory is very explicit about goal-setting. For one's personal life, for industry, for sales, for institutions, or for truck drivers, having a goal is mandatory. And yet the demise or failure of many consortia to produce can be attributed entirely to their lack of a well-defined mission.

As we have noted, some mission statements are so narrow or conservative as to provide little direction or no challenge. One consortium's mission was to make education accessible by delivering it to the student wherever he or she might be. The "open university" as a concept is commendable, but as a mission statement it is so general as to give no direction; it is, therefore, ineffective. Consortia require some visionary people in leadership positions, but their missions must also be specific enough to provide guidance. A consortium could, therefore, find it a real asset to include on its policy board some representatives from business, industry, or the community.

Not only is the composition of the policy board of critical concern; so, too, is the consortium director. The leader of a consortium must not be merely the solution to a personnel problem, such as how to give work to an unemployed or underemployed faculty or staff member. The chief executive officer of a consortium must have some entrepreneurial attitudes and skills as well as some administrative experience. Without a few years of experience on a college or university campus, he or she will be severely handicapped. The experience the consortium director will have gained by having served on a curriculum committee or in a faculty senate, by having survived a budget hearing, or by having written a college or university's research proposal for foundation or federal funding—any of these will be crucial for the insights that they bring to the consortium director.

Too often the director of a consortium's program comes to these duties from one of the institutions involved, which means that he or she has to struggle with several questions of loyalty. In many instances, moreover, the director has this assignment along with many (maybe all) of the institutional responsibilities previously held. A director cannot have (nor be perceived to have) biases for or against any of the member institutions. This perception is almost impossible to allay if the director still has numerous duties at one institution or even draws a salary from that institution.

The final section in this chapter, focusing on factors affecting cooperation, will address some of the "strawmen" of consortia: problems or issues that are trumped up. From the perspective of a single institution, some issues appear to be significant, but these same issues can evaporate when they are examined objectively.

The first strawman is inertia. A body at rest tends to stay at rest. If an institution, business, or industry has had minimal or no cooperative ventures, it naturally asks why it should risk this approach now, especially with the economy depressed as it is in many areas of the United States. I view it the other way, however: our economy will no longer allow us to "go it alone." For example, the need for research and development continues, both on campus and in industry. One way that will allow both is to have academic institutions and industry collaborate in the research and design function.

How can the strawman of inertia be overcome? First, trust must be established between the parties involved. Trust is developed by getting to know one another, both professionally (by comparing programs or research emphases) and personally. Friends trust one another; without trust, there can be no cooperation. Trust may be translated in this context to confidence in and respect for another person or for an institution's academic integrity. Trust may be developed directly by groups studying each other's curricula, or through the less-pressured exchange of views possible on a retreat; it may be developed indirectly in such social settings as student-faculty receptions or the fairways of a golf course.

Another means of overcoming inertia is to take small steps with short-term consequences. It took the Quad/Cities Graduate Study Center two years of tentative growth and gradual acceptance before it was incorporated. The development was slow, but it takes time to build trust and confidence. Even then, it was decided that the center would be a three-year experiment. Institutions and board directors were willing to risk supporting this new model for higher education only when there was a definite end point. This pilot project has now completed 18 years of academic cooperation and has been used as a model nationwide. Just as a cross-country or marathon runner works up to a 10,000-meter or 25-mile performance through a series of shorter runs, so a consortium must overcome inertia by taking small steps, building a base for trust.

The second strawman can best be described as tokenism. Everyone disdains tokenism—until it comes to cooperation among institutions. Colleges and universities readily cooperate in the use of computers or in an interlibrary exchange. It is easy to see the wisdom of joint purchasing agreements and cooperative lecture or arts series. But, as E. Jefferson Murphy has said, interinstitutional cooperation is not a natural form of behavior. For this reason, cooperation is initially pro forma instead of substantial. Far more frequently, administrators and faculty members look with real skepticism on cooperation with colleagues in other institutions.

Cooperation is generally easier in administrative functions than in academic programs. Administrators are more hierarchically organized and thus more likely to follow directives than are faculty members, who typically function more autonomously. As a result, some faculty members will make a token commitment to cooperate because it is a "good thing to do," but gaining their real cooperation takes a strong commitment and vigorous leadership.

The final strawman I want to identify in this section is that of "turf." I am reminded of Ardrey's book. *The Territorial Imperative,* which explains how animals stake out claims on certain portions of the forest. In the academic world, *turf* may include the geographic section of the state that institutions claim to have a responsibility to serve, or certain disciplines (e.g., professional schools), or a stratum of students' motivation and abilities. Turf claims, no matter what the domain, are great inhibitors of cooperation. In a few states, Pennsylvania and Virginia for example, there are real geographic boundaries, but in most states those lines are artificial barriers. It seems that too often institutions want to protect their acreage rather than serve their constituents.

One can survive—even actually flourish—amid all the limits on interinstitutional cooperation. The advantages of increased opportunities for students, or the chance to provide new or better services than the individual institutions can provide alone, must be kept in focus so that limitations and barriers do not paralyze us. The analogy of charting a course for a yacht comes to mind. The captain must be aware of reefs and shoals but, at the same time, look to the distant harbor. The captain steers around the reef so that he can deliver the treasures from the hold. So, too, the consortium director must steer around such limitations so that the advantages the consortium provides, as a vehicle for interinstitutional cooperation, may be delivered.

Bibliography

MARK W. POLAND

Introduction

Literature on consortia and cooperative programs of colleges and universities has tended to be, until fairly recently, anecdotal in nature. Many of the pieces available were written by consortium administrators and practitioners about their own experiences. Now, however, there is some "hard" research available that sheds light on consortia and their operation. Interestingly, this research often validates the anecdotes.

The Council for Interinstitutional Leadership (CIL) sponsors conferences on cooperation from which much important literature springs. CIL publishes an informative newsletter for its members and maintains a modest professional library at its headquarters in Kansas City. Dedicated to enhancing cooperation among colleges and universities, business and industry, and governmental agencies, CIL is an excellent source of information, both written and oral, about consortia.

The single most comprehensive collection of citations on cooperation is *Interinstitutional Cooperation, Consortia, and Regionalism: Comprehensive Bibliography #3 (with citations to 1983)* by Fritz H. Grupe (published by CIL and available directly from them). This book contains hundreds of citations of books, articles, and research papers on this subject, and it is an excellent research tool for the student of cooperation in higher education.

The references listed below are a representative sample of the body of literature available. Annotations are included for many of the citations. This collection includes some of the better writing available and is a good starting place for further research. Most citations contain their own useful bibliographies.

201

The combination of Grupe's compendium and this reference list should provide the researcher with a good body of literature on cooperation.

ALDRICH, HOWARD and SERGIO E. MINDLIN, "Interorganizational Dependence: A Review of the Concept and Reexamination of the Findings of the Aston Group," *Administration Science Quarterly,* 20, pp. 382–392 (September 1975).

AXFORD, ROGER W., "Improving Adult Teaching by Consortium: Cost Effectiveness plus Cooperation," *Phi Delta Kappan,* 62, no. 3, pp. 212–213 (November 1980). This article describes an Arizona consortium that embraces colleges and universities as well as public television stations and public service organizations. Axford indicates that, through this consortium, telecourses and materials can be produced and delivered to continuing education students throughout the state in a cost-effective manner.

BEHM, ROBERT J., *Community College-University Cooperation and its Benefits,* 1983. (ERIC Document Reproduction Service no. ED 238 484)

BERDAHL, ROBERT O., *Statewide Coordination of Higher Education,* Washington, D.C., American Council on Education, 1971. Berdahl examines the issues surrounding coordination/cooperation among state institutions of higher education. He suggests that states might need to develop "suitably sensitive mechanisms" to control unnecessary duplication of effort among their institutions in order to use their limited resources more efficiently and effectively. Although Berdahl deals with the issue of coordination, there is much valuable information· for those interested in cooperation among colleges and universities.

BRADLEY, JR., ALLAN P., *Academic Consortium Effectiveness: An Investigation of Criteria,* Ann Arbor, University of Michigan. Unpublished doctoral dissertation, 1971. Bradley's dissertation is in two parts. Part one is an investigation into those factors that tend to encourage the effectiveness of a consortium. Part two applies these criteria to two consortia considered to be effective. Bradley concludes that, to be effective, a consortium must fulfill its members' needs, and he suggests ways that these needs can be met.

BURKE, PETER J., "Consortium Administration in Higher Education." Paper presented to the Annual Meeting of the American Educational Research Association in Los Angeles, April 1981. (ERIC Document Reproduction Service no. ED 201 279)

CARNEGIE COMMISSION ON HIGHER EDUCATION, *The More Effective Use of Resources: An Imperative for Higher Education,* New York, McGraw-Hill Book Company, 1972.

CARUSO, BARBARA and KATHERINE LORING, "Out of Necessity: National Summer Institute in Women's Studies, the Great Lakes Colleges Association," in *Women's Place in the Academy: Transforming the Liberal Arts Curriculum,* Marilyn Schuster and Susan VanDyne, eds., Totowa, N.J., Roman and Allanheld, 1985.

CLARY, WILLIAM W., *The Claremont Colleges: A History of the Development of the Claremont Group Plan,* Claremont, Ca., Claremont University Center, 1970.

Clary outlines the factors that led to the founding of the Claremont Colleges consortium (considered to be the first higher education consortium in the United States) and the programs and activities in which it has engaged over the years.

CONNERS, JR., M. AUSTIN, THOMAS J. DIENER, LEWIS D. PATTERSON, HOWARD W. JOHNSON, and NORMAN McCRUMMEN, *Guide to Interinstitutional Arrangements: Voluntary and Statutory,* Washington, D.C., American Association for Higher Education, 1974.

DOLCE, PHILIP C., *The Consortium Approach: Preserving College Decision-Making,* 1981. (ERIC Document Reproduction Service no. ED 220 934)

EASTMOND, NICK, *Starting a Regional Consortium in Instructional Development: Lessons After Four Years of Experiential Learning,* 1981. (ERIC Document Reproduction Service no. ED 207 593)

ELKIN, JUDITH L., *The Great Lakes Colleges Association: Twenty-One Years of Cooperation in Higher Education,* Ann Arbor, Great Lakes Colleges Association, 1982. (ERIC Document Reproduction Service no. ED 261 591)

This monograph is a detailed description of the Great Lakes Colleges Association. It includes chapters on the history, governance, and programs/activities of the consortium.

FEHNEL, RICHARD A., "The National University Consortium: An Assessment," *Journal of Continuing Education,* 30, no. 4, pp. 21–23 (1982).

GLAZER, JUDITH S., "Designing and Managing an Interuniversity Consortium in a Period of Decline," *Journal of Higher Education,* 53, no. 2, pp. 177–194 (March/April 1982).

Glazer discusses graduate level consortia and offers guidelines for their design and management.

GOODE, JOHN and MARY ELLIS, *The Basics of Managing a Consortium: Things Everyone Should Know,* Chapel Hill, N.C., John Goode and Associates, 1981.

GRUPE, FRITZ H., "Founding Consortia: Idea and Reality," *The Journal of Higher Education,* XLII, no. 6, pp. 747–762 (June 1971).

GRUPE, FRITZ H., *Managing Interinstitutional Change: Consortia in Higher Education,* Potsdam, N.Y., Associated Colleges of the Saint Lawrence Valley, 1975.

These two works by Grupe outline the practical aspects of cooperation. Grupe suggests ways that colleges and universities can avoid the disappointments that can come from idealistic expectations of cooperation. He notes that "expectations for a consortium's success should be tempered by the knowledge that innovations of any type are always high risk." To overcome these idealistic expectations, Grupe offers his opinions on some of the "nuts and bolts" necessary to set up and operate an effective consortium.

GRUPE, FRITZ H. and KATHLEEN L. SUKANEK, *Together We Do More: Cost-Effectiveness through Interinstitutional Cooperation,* New York, Carnegie Corporation of New York, 1981. (ERIC Document Reproduction Service no. ED 207 373)

HERSHFIELD, ALLAN, "The National University Consortium—One Year Later," *Change,* 13, no. 8, pp. 43–45 (November/December 1981).

JAMES, THOMAS O'CONNER, "The Costing of a Consortium Project," *Business Officer,* pp. 26–28 (June 1979).

KEYSER, JOHN S., "The Oregon Consortium for Student Success: Mobilizing to Improve Retention," *Community and Junior College Journal,* 52, no. 4, pp. 24–26 (December/January 1981–1982).

KONKEL, RICHARD H. and LEWIS D. PATTERSON, *Sharing Collegiate Resources: The New Challenge,* Washington, D.C., Council for Interinstitutional Leadership, 1981. (ERIC Document Reproduction Service no. ED 210 968)

Based on the proceedings of the National Invitational Conference at Wingspread on sharing resources in the 1980s, this monograph's chapters include: "Benefits and Potential of Resource Sharing," "Structures and Policies to Achieve Resource Sharing," and "Action Agendas to Achieve Cooperation and Sharing."

KREPLIN, HANNAH S. and JANE W. BOLCE, *Interinstitutional Cooperation in Higher Education: An Analysis and Critique,* Berkeley, University of California, 1973.

Although published in 1973, Kreplin and Bolce's examination of the benefits and drawbacks of cooperative endeavors is still relevant to those who must debate this issue today.

LAMDIN, LOIS, "Changing Through Cooperation," *Change,* 14, no. 8, pp. 27–29 (November/December 1982).

LICK, DALE W., "The Human Factor in Successful Interinstitutional Cooperation." Paper presented at the Wingspread Conference on Interinstitutional Resource Sharing, March 1981.

Lick offers concrete and practical proposals to enhance cooperation among colleges and universities.

MARTIN, DAN M., "The Academic Consortium: Limitations and Possibilities," *Educational Record,* 62, no. 1, pp. 36–39 (Winter 1981).

MCKEEFERY, WILLIAM J., *Cooperative Arrangements Between Private and Public Colleges,* Wayne, N.J., William Patterson College of New Jersey, 1978.

MCKEON, THOMAS L., *A Case Study of the Legislative Policy Decision Which Established Consortia for the Coordination of Continuing Higher Education in Virginia,* Charlottesville, University of Virginia. Unpublished doctoral dissertation, 1976.

McKeon's research into the political factors influencing the establishment of Virginia's statutory Consortia for Continuing Higher Education provides a view of the types of forces that affect statutory consortia and their missions.

MCPHERSON, K.S. and N.R. WYLIE, "Teaching Psychology at the Small Liberal Arts College: A Two-Day Conference," *Teaching of Psychology,* 10, no. 3, pp. 144–146 (1983).

MEREDITH, CHARLES, "Strengthening Interinstitutional Cooperation While Protecting Institutional Autonomy." Paper presented at the Wingspread Conference on Interinstitutional Resource Sharing, March 1981.

MITZMAN, BARRY, "Cooperation in the Pacific Northwest," *Change,* 12, no. 4, pp. 59–61 (May/June 1980).

MOORE, RAYMOND S., *Consortiums in American Higher Education 1965–66: Report of an Exploratory Study,* Washington, D.C., Office of Education (Department of Health, Education, and Welfare), September 1968. (ERIC Document Reproduction Service no. ED 051 728)

Although Moore's work is 20 years old, it still offers a benchmark against which consortia today can be measured.

MURPHY, E. JEFFERSON, "Consortia for Interinstitutional Cooperation: A Case Study," *Business Officer,* pp. 22–24 (October 1981).

NEAL, DONN C., "I Have Seen the Future, and It Is OBAD," *The Journal of Continuing Higher Education,* 31, no. 3, pp. 2–5 (Summer 1983).

Neal, in an article of "prophecy," describes telecommunication programs consortia could undertake.

NEAL, DONN C., "Interinstitutional Cooperation in Continuing Education," *The Journal of Continuing Higher Education,* 33, no. 2, pp. 11–14 (Spring 1985).

NEAL, DONN C., "New Roles for Consortia," *Planning for Higher Education,* 12, no. 2, pp. 23–31 (Winter 1984).

Neal suggests that consortia, through "imaginative cooperative relationships," can provide college and university planners with flexibility, resources, and efficiency in a time of retrenchment.

NEAL, DONN C., "What a College Should Expect When It Joins A Consortium," *The Chronicle of Higher Education,* February 20, 1984, p. 96.

The consortium administrator/director and staff must be politically astute, diplomatic, and patient, according to Neal. The consortium serves its membership and must be sensitive to their needs and desires.

NEAL, DONN C., D.K. SNELL, S.E. BROOKS, and NEIL R. WYLIE, "Inter-institutional Sponsorship of Off-Campus Programs," in *Proceedings of the Seventh Annual Conference on Quality in Off-Campus Credit Programs: Today's Issues and Tomorrow's Prospects,* Manhattan, Kans., Kansas State University Press, 1985.

NEFF, CHARLES B. and JON W. FULLER, "Organizing International Programs: The Experience of Two Consortia," *Liberal Education,* 69, no. 3, pp. 273–283 (Fall 1983).

Neff and Fuller, both experienced consortium administrators, offer some insights into two consortias' international programs.

NIEBUHR, JR., HERMAN, "The CLEO Story: An Alternative to Decline," *Planning for Higher Education,* 10, no. 3, pp. 1–4 (Spring 1982).

NOWAK, PHILLIP and JEFFREY PFEFFER, "Joint Venture and Interorganizational Interdependence," *Administrative Science Quarterly,* 21, pp. 398–399 (September 1976).

NOWIK, NAN, "Workshop on Course Design and Teaching Styles: A Model for Faculty Development" in *To Improve the Academy: Resources for Student, Faculty, and Institutional Development,* M. Davis, M. Fisher, S.C. Inglis, and S. Scholl, eds., Orinda, Calif., John F. Kennedy University, 1983.

OFFERMAN, MICHAEL J., *Factors Leading to the Termination of Three Consortia of Higher Education Institutions: A Case Study,* DeKalb, Northern Illinois University. Unpublished doctoral dissertation, 1985.

Offerman's dissertation provides some valuable "lessons learned" to those involved in consortia. His conclusions offer practical suggestions for avoiding the pitfalls three "failed" consortia encountered.

PAREKH, SATISH B., *A Long Range Planning Model for Colleges and Universities,* New York, Phelps-Stokes Fund, 1975. (ERIC Document Reproduction Service no. ED 116 519)

PATRICK, RUTH, *Guidelines for Library Cooperation: Development of Academic Library Consortia,* Santa Monica, Calif., System Development Corporation, 1972.

PATTERSON, FRANKLIN, *Colleges in Consort,* San Francisco, Jossey-Bass Publishers, 1974.

This seminal work should be required reading for anyone involved in a consortium. Patterson offers his views on a kind of cooperation that is both realistic and attainable.

PATTERSON, LEWIS D., *Benefits of Collegiate Cooperation,* University, Ala., Council for Interinstitutional Leadership, 1979.

This monograph lists ways colleges and universities have been able to save money through cooperative projects and activities (e.g., cross-registration, library and media cooperation, group purchasing, cooperative academic programs).

PATTERSON, LEWIS D., *Consortia in American Higher Education,* Washington, D.C., ERIC Clearinghouse on Higher Education, November 1980. (ERIC Document Reproduction Service no. ED 043 800)

PATTERSON, LEWIS D., *Costing Collegiate Cooperation: A Report on the Costs and Benefits of Interinstitutional Programs with Consortium Case Studies and Guidelines,* University, Ala., Council for Interinstitutional Leadership, 1979.

This document is a comprehensive study of 38 cooperative programs at 25 consortia. Each program is analyzed for its cost-effectiveness. The benefits of cooperation beyond cost savings are also discussed.

PATTERSON, LEWIS D., *Survival through Interdependence: Assessing the Cost and Benefits of Interinstitutional Cooperation,* Washington, D.C., American Association for Higher Education, 1979. (ERIC Document Reproduction Service no. ED 183 116)

Included in this monograph is a chapter that discusses the role cooperation will play in the future for higher education.

PETERS, GIB, "A Consortium Approach to the Utilization of Television for the Delivery of Instruction to Business and Industry," in *Communications Technology in Education and Training,* Silver Springs, Information Dynamics, Inc., 1982.

REED, BETH, "Transforming the Academy: Twelve Schools Working Together," *Change,* 14, no. 3, pp. 30, 35–37 (April 1982).

Reed's paper looks at how a consortium (Great Lakes College Association) has developed its faculty development approach to women's studies.

ROZANSKI, MORDECHAI and ANN KELLEHER, "International Education Consortium: A Case Study," *Educational Research Quarterly,* 8, no. 1, pp. 100–107 (1983).

SCOTT, HARRY, "Consortia in Higher Education: A Sober Reflection," *Educational Record,* 58, no. 4, pp. 429–433 (Fall 1977).

Scott notes that consortia may not be the solution to every problem, and colleges and universities must carefully and completely evaluate cooperative activities before engaging in them.

SMITH, FAYE MCDONALD, "E Pluribus?," *Change,* 11, no. 7, pp. 18–20 (October 1979).

THOMPSON, WILLIAM J. and GEORGE M. SIMMONS, "Graduate Education Wins in Interstate Rivalry," *Chemical Engineering Education,* 17, no. 4, pp. 182–183, 194 (1983).

TOPPE, CHRISTOPHER and PAUL BRUBAKER, *An Evaluation of the Small College Consortium, 1977–78. A Title III Project. Part I: Survey Results,* Washington, D.C., Systems Research, Inc., 1978. (ERIC Document Reproduction Service no. ED 161 311)

WAGNER, RICHARD D., *Strategies for Interinstitutional Cooperation: The Experience in Illinois,* 1981. (ERIC Document Reproduction Service no. ED 216 646)

WALKER, HAROLD E., "Cooperation: Voluntary vs. Statutory," *Planning for Higher Education,* 2, no. 1, pp. 1–4 (Feburary 1973).

WAREHAM, N.L., *The Report on Library Cooperation, 1984,* Chicago, Ill., Association of Specialized and Cooperative Library Agencies, 1984.

WEAST, PHILIP GRAHAM, *A Profile of Interinstitutional Cooperation Among Public and Private Institutions of Higher Education in Georgia,* Athens, University of Georgia. Unpublished doctoral dissertation, 1981.

WHETTEN, DAVID A., "Interorganizational Relations: A Review of the Field," *Journal of Higher Education,* 52, no. 1, pp. 1–28 (January/February 1981).

WYLIE, NEIL R. and JON W. FULLER, "Enhancing Faculty Vitality Through Collaboration Among Colleagues," in *Incentives for Faculty Vitality,* Roger G. Baldwin, ed., San Francisco, Jossey-Bass Publishers, 1985.

YOUNG, JAMES H. and RAM L. CHUGH, "Working Together: A Blueprint for Inter-Institutional Cooperation," *AGB Reports,* 26, no. 3, pp. 41–46 (May/June 1984).

ZEMP, JOHN W., *A Model Continuing Education Needs Assessment/Response System in Science and Engineering: Summary Report,* Washington, D.C., National Science Foundation, 1981. (ERIC Document Reproduction Service no. ED 214 790)

This report outlines a model of comprehensive needs assessment and follow-up that consortia of colleges and universities can use when seeking to serve industry's continuing education needs.

ZIFF, HOWARD, "Sharing at the Five Colleges," *Change,* 12, no. 4, pp. 62–64 (May/June 1980).

ZIGERELL, JAMES, "Consortia—A Growing Trend in Educational Programming," *Educational and Instructional Television,* 14, no. 2, pp. 43–47 (February 1982).

Index

Albany Medical College, 84
Albion College, 180
Alcoa Foundation, 139
Alden Seminars, 168–69
Alfred University, 103
American Council on Education, 1
American Library Association, 64
Annenberg/Corporation for Public
    Broadcasting, 176
Antioch University, 180
Apple University Consortium, 175
Ardrey, Robert, *The Territorial
    Imperative,* 198
Artificial Intelligence Consortium,
    175
Aspen Institute, 11, 114–15
Associated Colleges of the Midwest,
    19, 39, 180, 182, 190–91
Association for Higher Education of
    North Texas, 4, 23
Association of Governing Boards of
    Universities and Colleges, 194
Atlanta University Center, 2, 34, 173
Augustana College, 65–66

Baptist College at Charleston, 113
Battin, Patricia, 166, 172–73
Bibliographic Retrieval Service, 69
Bishop, Jake E., 82, 90, 94
Boston Consortium for Cable-TV, 173
Boyer, Ernest, 128
Bryant, Douglas, 62
Buhl Foundation, 139

California Statewide System,
    University of, 68
Carnegie-Mellon University, 175

Charleston, City of, 11, 116
Charleston, College of, 114
Charleston Higher Education
    Consortium, 11, 111–18
Chemical Abstracts, 69
Chicago Academic Library Council,
    64
Chronicle of Higher Education,
    174–76, 194
Citadel, The, 114
City University of New York, 175
Claremont Colleges, 2, 34
Clark College, 103
College Board, The, 127, 132, 138
College Center of the Finger Lakes,
    9–10, 97, 102–106, 108–109
Colleges of Mid-America, 7, 61
Colorado Alliance of Research
    Libraries, 75
Columbia University, 166
Commerce Business Daily, 69
Communications Consortium, The,
    174
Compact for Lifelong Educational
    Opportunity, 174
Consortia
    characteristics, 2, 26
    definition, 1, 26
    growth, 2, 33–34
    leadership and staff, 28–29, 42–44
    objectives, 3, 25–31, 46
    roles, 25–31
    "third-party" role, 4, 23–31
Control Data, 116
Cooperative Libraries in Consortium,
    64
Cornell University, 103

211

Corning Community College, 103
Corporate-Education Exchange, 174
Council for Interinstitutional
    Leadership, 25, 82
Crecine, John P., 175
CUADRA Associates, 69

Dartmouth College, 114
Denison University, 180
DePauw University, 180
de Sola Pool, Ithiel, 169
DIALOG, 69, 73
Digital Electronic Corporation, 175
Directory of On-Line Data Bases, 69
Duke University, 66
Duquesne University, 139

Earlham College, 180–81
Educational and Institutional
    Cooperative Service, Inc., 82
Educational Resources Information
    Center, 69
EDUCOM, 173
EDUNET, 173
Evergreen State College, 102–103

Federal Trade Commission, 95
Five Colleges, Inc., 4, 33, 39, 92, 94,
    173
Fletcher, C. Scott, *Toward the
    Liberally Educated Executive,*
    113
Ford Foundation, 181, 190
Fund for Adult Education, 113
Fund for the Improvement of Post-
    Secondary Education, 56, 104,
    117, 184–85, 187

Garfield, James, 50
Glazer, Judith S., 195
Glen Mede Trust, 190
Godfrey, David, *Gutenberg II,* 168
Great Lakes Colleges Association, 18,
    39, 179–91
Grupe, Fritz, 194–95

Hampshire Interlibrary Center, 66
Harvard University Library, 62
Hevener, Carl J., 95
Hewlett-Packard, 102
Hope College, 180–81
Hopkins, Mark, 50
Hudson-Mohawk Association of
    Colleges and Universities, 8–9,
    79–81, 83–92, 94
Hudson Valley Community College,
    84

IBM, 167, 175
Illinois Educational Consortium, 91
Interinstitutional cooperation
    in academic areas, 3–6, 24–25,
        33–46; *see also*
        Interinstitutional cooperation,
        in taking risks; in professional
        development
    barriers, 41–42
    benefits, 33–34
    cross-registration, 35–36
    disciplinary meetings, 44
    faculty exchanges, 36–37
    incentives, 45
    joint academic programs, 37–41
    joint appointments, 38
    joint degrees, 39
    joint departments, 39–40
    with business and industry, 9–12,
        97–117, 119–24; *see also*
        Interinstitutional cooperation,
        in government relations
    barriers, 122–24
    benefits, 98–99, 107–108, 119–22
    in Charleston, 111–19
    cost-effectiveness, 120
    in economic development,
        115–17
    in education and training,
        97–110
    in liberal education seminars,
        113–15
    in research opportunities, 111–12

in school-college collaboration,
    117–18
conditions for success of, 26–31,
    43–45
cost-effectiveness of, 25, 34;
    see also Interinstitutional
    cooperation, with business
    and industry; in joint
    purchasing; in professional
    development
general limits of, 20–21, 193–99
in government relations, 16,
    158–62
    advocacy in legislative arenas,
        158–61
    involving other constituencies,
        161–62
    techniques, 160–62
    in Worcester, 162
in joint purchasing, 8–9, 79–96;
    see also Interinstitutional
    cooperation, cost-
    effectiveness; among libraries
    of academic services, 93
    anti-trust considerations, 94–96
    barriers, 91
    benefits, 79–81
    among hospitals, 83
    in HMACU, 84–91
    measuring savings, 89–92
    process, 82–89
among libraries, 7–8, 61–77
    in acquisitions, 66, 74–75
    in automation, 66–69
    benefits, 62–63, 73–76
    in cooperative planning, 75
    in cooperative training, 75
    in data base access, 69–70
    in expertise sharing, 76
    in interlibrary loan, 63–65
    in joint purchasing, 73–74
    in learning resources sharing,
        70–71
    in resource sharing, 74
    in shared access, 65

in union lists, 65
in new technologies, 16–18,
    163–76
    barriers, 176
    benefits, 171–72
    cooperative initiatives, 172–76
    implications of new
        technologies, 165–71
in professional development,
    6–7, 47–59; see also
    Interinstitutional cooperation,
    in taking risks
    barriers, 49–50
    benefits, 47–49, 52–53, 57–59
    in conferences, 49–53, 55
    in consultants, 50–55
    cost-effectiveness, 52–53
    disciplinary meetings, 57
    grants, 53–54
    in Kansas City, 53–56
    referrals, 51–52
in public relations, 15–16, 147–58
    barriers, 149
    benefits, 150–51
    in community service, 155–58
    in cooperative promotion,
        153–55
    process, 151–53
    in Worcester, 156–57
between schools and colleges,
    12–14, 127–46; see also
    Interinstitutional cooperation,
    with business and industry
    in academic consultations,
        130–32
    barriers, 130, 142–44
    benefits, 127–30, 140–42
    in coalition-building, 138
    in faculty visits, 134
    in in-service training, 134–35
    in Pittsburgh, 138–40
    in precollegiate counseling,
        136–37
    in recognition of teaching
        excellence, 137–38

Interinstitutional cooperation (*Cont.*)
    strategies, 144–46
    in teacher education, 135–36
    in taking risks, 18–20, 57–58,
        171–72, 179–91
    in area studies, 189–91
    benefits, 179–91
    in faculty development, 183–84
    within GLCA, 179–91
    in off-campus study programs,
        180–82
    in the problems of untenured
        faculty members, 186–89
    in women's studies, 184–86
International University Consortium
    for Telecommunications, 173
Inter-University Consortium on
    Academic Computing, 175
Iona College, 82
Iroquois Hospital Consortium, 83

Job Training Partnership Act, 117
Johns Hopkins University, 164

Kalamazoo College, 180–81
Kansas City Regional Council on
    Higher Education, 6, 47,
    53–56
Kanter, Rosabeth Moss, *The Change
    Masters,* 171–72
Kellogg Foundation, 53, 174
Kentuckiana Metroversity, 173
Kenyon College, 180–81
Kreplin, Hannah S. and Jane W.
    Bolce, *Interinstitutional
    Cooperation in Higher
    Education,* 195

Lewis, Robert, 194
Library Computer Systems, 67
Lilly Endowment, 183–85
Low, George, 84
Lynton, Ernest A., *The Missing
    Connection Between Business
    and the Universities,* 167, 169

Martin, Dan, 195
Massachusetts Higher Education
    Consortium, 82–83, 94
Massachusetts Institute of
    Technology, 169
McLuhan, Marshall, 171
Mellon Foundation, 190
Michigan, University of, 19, 190
Michigan Intercollegiate Athletic
    Association, 1
Midwest Interlibrary Center, 66
MINITEX, 64–65, 73
Minnesota State University System, 68
Muller, Steven, 164, 166, 168, 170
Murphy, E. Jefferson, 198

National Association of Educational
    Buyers, 95
National Commission on Excellence,
    127
National Higher Education Week, 155
National Library of Medicine, 66, 69
National Technological University,
    174
National Union Catalog, 65
Nebraska, University of, 176
New England Deposit Library, 66
New Hampshire College and
    University Council, 174
New Hampshire Industrial
    Consortium, 10, 104–106, 109
New Rochelle, College of, 82
New Serial Titles, 65
North Carolina, University of, 66
North Central University Center,
    65–66
Northeast Consortium of Colleges
    and Universities in
    Massachusetts, 16, 163, 173–74
Northwestern University, 68

Oak Ridge National Laboratory, 182
Oberlin College, 180–81
OCLC, 67, 73–74

Ohio State University, 68
Ohio Wesleyan University, 180

Papert, Seymour, *Mindstorms,* 169
Patterson, Franklin, *Colleges in
    Consort,* 24
Patterson, Lewis, *Benefits of
    Collegiate Cooperation,* 25
Pennsylvania, University of, 114
Pennsylvania Area Library Network,
    65
Pittsburgh, University of, 69
Pittsburgh College Fair, 139
Pittsburgh Council on Higher
    Education, 12, 127, 138–40
Pomona College, 114
Project Advance, 133
Project for Information Technology
    and Education, 164
Public Service Satellite Consortium,
    173

Quad Cities Graduate Study Center,
    20, 193, 198

Rensselaer Polytechnic Institute, 84
Report on Library Cooperation, 62
Research Libraries Information
    Network, 67
Rhodes College, 114
Robinson, Louis, 167
Rochester Institute of Technology,
    103
Rose, Larry, 194

SDC Information Service, 69
Sioux Falls College, 65
Sizer, Theodore, *Horace's
    Compromise,* 169
Snyder, Gary, 92–93
SOLINET, 68
Southwest Washington Joint Center
    for Education, 10, 102–106, 108

SPHERE, 174
Stanford University, 164
State University of New York, 81–82
Strange, John, 168–69
Syracuse University, 103

TAGER, 173
Tektronics, 102
Teletypewriter Exchange Service, 66
Texas A & M University, 24, 41
Title III, 34, 67
Toronto, University of, 69
Trident Technical College, 117
Tri-State College Library Cooperative,
    70
Tucker, Marc, 164–65

Union List of Serials, 65
United Press International, 69

Vandiver, Frank, 24, 41
Virginia Polytechnic Institute, 68
Virginia Tidewater Consortium, 173
Vonnegut, Kurt, Jr., *Player Piano,* 163

Wabash College, 180, 185
Wadsworth Professional Software,
    Inc., 175
Washington Library Network, 67
Washington State University, 103
Westchester Social Work Education
    Consortium, 39
Western Pennsylvania Buhl Network,
    69
Whitehead, Alfred North, *The Aims of
    Education,* 114
William and Mary, College of, 21
Wisconsin Library Consortium, 64
Wooster, College of 180–81
Worcester Consortium for Higher
    Education, 15, 147, 156
Work/Education Council, 118